Donated by
Ian Thomson

Not for loan

Transnational Capitalism and the Struggle over European Integration

'The scholarship is outstanding. The treatment of the European Roundtable of Industrialists – the major empirical contribution – is rigorous and comprehensive. From a theoretical standpoint, this is a highly sophisticated and path-breaking work.'

Professor Alan Cafruny, *Hamilton College, USA*

'International roundtables of large firms are a new form of interest representation of business and are an important vehicle of class formation at the international level. Van Apeldoorn shows in detail how the European Roundtable of Industrialists developed and how it fits in the present phase in the internationalisation of both politics and the economy. The book is a remarkable achievement that deserves to be widely read.'

Professor Wolfgang Streeck, *Max Planck Institute for the Study of Societies*

'This is a theoretically innovative and empirically sophisticated study of the European Roundtable of Industrialists. Van Apeldoorn demonstrates the contribution of international political economy inspired by neo-Gramscianism to constructivist scholarship and shows in detail how the ERT translated global forces of capitalism into a distinct European political project. Must read!'

Professor Dr Thomas Risse, *Free University of Berlin, Germany*

This book presents an analysis of the transnational social forces in the making of the new socio-economic order that emerged out of the European integration process of the 1980s and 1990s. Arguing that the political economy of European integration must be put within the context of a changing global capitalism, the author examines how European change is linked to global change and how transnational actors – such as the European Roundtable of Industrialists (ERT) – mediate these changes.

Bastiaan van Apeldoorn is a lecturer in International Relations at the Free University, Amsterdam.

Routledge/RIPE Series in Global Political Economy

Series Editors: Otto Holman, Marianne Marchand (*Research Centre for International Political Economy, University of Amsterdam*), Henk Overbeek (*Free University, Amsterdam*) and Marianne Franklin (*University of Amsterdam*)

This series, published in association with the *Review of International Political Economy*, provides a forum for current debates in international political economy. The series aims to cover all the central topics in IPE and to present innovative analyses of emerging topics. The titles in the series seek to transcend a state-centred discourse and focus on three broad themes:

- the nature of the forces driving globalisation forward
- resistance to globalisation
- the transformation of the world order.

The series comprises two strands:

The *RIPE Series in Global Political Economy* aims to address the needs of students and teachers, and the titles will be published in hardback and paperback. Titles include:

Transnational Classes and International Relations
Kees van der Pijl

Gender and Global Restructuring
Sightings, sites and resistances
Edited by Marianne H. Marchand and Anne Sisson Runyan

Global Political Economy
Contemporary theories
Edited by Ronen Palan

Ideologies of Globalization
Contending visions of a new world order
Mark Rupert

The Clash within Civilisations
Coming to terms with cultural conflicts
Dieter Senghaas

Routledge/RIPE Studies in Global Political Economy is a forum for innovative new research intended for a high-level specialist readership, and the titles will generally be available in hardback only. Titles include:

1 Globalization and Governance*
Edited by Aseem Prakash and Jeffrey A. Hart

2 Nation-States and Money
The past, present and future of national currencies
Edited by Emily Gilbert and Eric Helleiner

3 The Global Political Economy of Intellectual Property Rights
The new enclosures?
Christopher May

4 Integrating Central Europe
EU expansion and Poland, Hungary and the Czech Republic
Otto Holman

5 Capitalist Restructuring, Globalisation and the Third Way
Lessons from the Swedish model
J. Magnus Ryner

6 Transnational Capitalism and the Struggle over European Integration
Bastiaan van Apeldoorn

7 World Financial Orders
An historical international political economy
Paul Langley

* Also available in paperback

Transnational Capitalism and the Struggle over European Integration

Bastiaan van Apeldoorn

ROUTLEDGE
Taylor & Francis Group
London and New York

First published 2002
by Routledge
11 New Fetter Lane, London EC4P 4EE

Simultaneously published in the USA and Canada
by Routledge
29 West 35th Street, New York, NY 10001

Routledge is an imprint of the Taylor & Francis Group

Typeset in Baskerville by
M Rules
Printed and bound in Great Britain by
MPG Books Ltd, Bodmin

British Library Cataloguing in Publication Data
A catalogue record for this book is available from the British Library

Library of Congress Cataloging in Publication Data
A catalog record for this book has been requested

ISBN 0–415–25570–8

For my parents, Freek van Apeldoorn and Ciska Thijs

Contents

Tables

Series editors' preface

The process of European integration has experienced a dramatic acceleration over the last two decades. Since the early 1980s, three developments particularly stand out. First, the completion of the internal market was agreed upon through the Commission's White Paper of 1985. This lengthy and complicated process is still not fully realised as recent attempts to unify European financial markets indicate. Second, the Maastricht Treaty of 1991 has resulted in the recent introduction of a European single currency, an unprecedented step towards an Ever Closer Union indeed. Finally, the European Union is on the eve of the most important and far-reaching enlargement in its history. The so-called 'big bang' (the entrance of eight Central and East-European countries along with Malta and Cyprus in 2002–04) will not only have an enormous impact on the economic and socio-political structures of the candidate member states but also on the functioning of the enlarged Union itself. As a result of these three developments, the European Union has fundamentally altered its image of a stagnant and inward-looking entity – so typical for the period of Eurosclerosis between 1973 and 1983 – and is rapidly enhancing its capacity to act as an important player in European and global affairs.

During the same two decades, the world at large has also dramatically changed. On the one hand, the renaissance of political and economic liberalism has manifested itself in successive waves of democratisation in different parts of the world and, on the other, in the process of global neo-liberal restructuring . The European Union is a particularly strong case in point as far as the latter phenomenon is concerned. Under the banner of improving competitiveness as a response to economic globalisation, deregulation, privatisation and flexibilisation have become the key-words in today's integration discourse. But this neo-liberal turn in the process of European integration was by no means an uncontested one. In his *Transnational Capitalism and the Struggle over European Integration*, Bastiaan van Apeldoorn convincingly shows the co-existence of two rival projects in the 1980s. First, a neo-mercantilist concept of European order, first and foremost aimed at creating so-called 'European champions' (of industry) which could face non-European competition, if necessary, by temporarily building a 'fortress Europe'. Second, a neo-liberal project that stressed the need for free-market integration on a world scale and aimed at transforming the 'European social model' into the supposedly more competitive Anglo-Saxon or Neo-American model.

In the first two chapters of this book, Bastiaan van Apeldoorn introduces a novel way of looking at the dynamics of European integration since the early 1980s. In taking a stand against mainstream European integration theory, he develops an alternative approach that he calls 'neo-Gramscian transnationalism'. Van Apeldoorn particularly focuses on the role of big business in the re-launch of European integration, arguing that the two contending conceptions of European integration, initially centred around the completion of the internal market, were very much related to two rival fractions within an emergent transnational bourgeoisie at the European level.

Van Apeldoorn meticulously documents the gradual shift from neo-mercantilism to neo-liberalism in the cupola of transnational business in his analysis of the foundation and development of 'an elite forum of Europe's emergent transnational capitalist class': the European Roundtable of Industrialists (ERT). In the course of the 1990s, the ERT (in terms of its composition and, more importantly, its changing discourse during 1988–91) concentrated its policy and agenda-setting activities almost exclusively on the twin objectives of improving competitiveness and fighting labour market rigidities. Yet, as Van Apeldoorn argues, this supply-side programme for Europe has been constrained by the 'limits of the possible'. The continued importance of manufacturing for the European continental economies, together with the historical and cultural particularities of member states' institutional structures, make it less likely that the European social model will ever be replaced wholesale by those that characterise Anglo-Saxon shareholder capitalism. By partially incorporating the interests of organised labour in a new system of interest mediation, or 'supply-side corporatism', Europe's emergent transnational capitalist class has developed its own variety of capitalism: *embedded neo-liberalism.*

This first book on European integration in the *RIPE Series in Global Political Economy* is essential reading for those interested in the relation between global and European change during the 1980s and 1990s, the role of class agency in the struggle over a future European order and the mediating role of the ERT in formulating a new hegemonic project of Europe's transnational capitalist class.

Otto Holman
Marianne H. Marchand
Henk Overbeek
Marianne Franklin

Acknowledgements

It is a cliché to say of an academic work that it could not have been written without the support of so many people. But, like most clichés, this one too holds a significant truth. Every academic work is always also a social product. Not merely in the sense that the individual author him or herself is a social being (being shaped by society), but also in the sense that the work is always to a greater or lesser extent the outcome of an interaction with other people.

The idea for this book was born back in 1993 when I was a graduate student in political science at the University of Amsterdam. What was then the Department of International Relations of the University of Amsterdam, and in particular the so-called Amsterdam Group of International Political Economy within it, is where my intellectual socialisation started. The people who taught me at this Department have contributed in a major way to the present work. In particular, I want to express my deep gratitude to my Amsterdam teacher Otto Holman. It was his own work on the European Roundtable of Industrialists (ERT) that provided me with the initial inspiration for this study, just as his later enthusiasm, encouragement and critical input have helped me to successfully turn the project into a dissertation at the European University Institute (EUI) in Florence.

The EUI proved in many ways a very congenial environment for doing academic research in the way just described: that is, as always at least indirectly a collective effort. First of all, it was at the EUI that I had the luck to find Colin Crouch as my supervisor. I would like to record my great debt to him here. For me he was the kind of supervisor who was always there when you needed him: patient, interested, encouraging, supportive and with very helpful advice. His enthusiasm for my project, and his encouragement to follow my own path, have been a great source of support.

I also want to thank a number of colleagues and friends at the EUI in particular: Tanja Börzel, Gerold Gerber, Ingmar von Homeyer and Marlene Wind, all for the many stimulating conversations we had about our respective projects; Anja Hänsch, my inspiring and inspired housemate during my years in Florence, and my 'critical' friends Christian Heine, Magnus Ryner, Simona Talani and Maarten van den Berg, the intellectual exchanges with whom have greatly helped to refine my argument during the redrafting stage of what was then my dissertation. Special thanks also goes to Martin Rhodes of the EUI: my collaboration with him on various projects has certainly left its mark on the present work. Marjoleine Hennis, both as an EUI colleague and as a friend, I want to thank for all her support. Marieke de Goede I want to thank for all our inspiring discussions, and Marije Schoonen for her friendship and support during particularly during the last phase of my dissertation project.

I am also grateful to Alan Cafruny, James Caporaso, Stephen Gill, Ankie Hoogvelt, Thomas Risse, Wolfgang Streeck, Geoffrey Underhill and two anonymous referees for useful comments on (parts of) the manuscript. Maria Green Cowles I want to thank for sending me so many of her papers at an early stage of my research. This book also could not have been written without the generous collaboration of the persons interviewed for this research; I am very grateful to them for freely giving me some of their valuable time.

My deepest gratitude is also the most personal one. I want to thank Aline te Kiefte for her support during the final stages of writing this book. Her love proved the best stimulus for finishing the book, and the best antidote to any worries and anxieties that occasionally crept in during the hectic last weeks. Finally, deep gratitude goes to my family, and in particular to my parents, Ciska Thijs and Freek van Apeldoorn, who have always supported me in every way and from whom I have learned so much. It is to them that this book is dedicated.

Bastiaan van Apeldoorn
Eindhoven, September 2001

Introduction

The past two decades have witnessed a significant transformation of the western European political economy. Originating in the 1970s in the context of a world economic crisis, this transformation has involved a fundamental restructuring of state–society relations, and with that, of the social institutions that had embedded the post-war capitalist market economies. This restructuring has been premised on a resurgence of economic liberalism: that is, a resurrection of the ideology and practice of free market economics and private enterprise. In the context of the rise of what is now referred to as neo-liberalism, western European governments have increasingly embarked upon policies of privatisation, deregulation and fiscal austerity, leading to a retrenchment of the public sector in favour of the private forces of the market.

This transformation of western European capitalism is also reflected in the process of European integration as it experienced a renaissance from the mid-1980s with the Single European Act (SEA) and the treaty of Maastricht, paving the way for the completion of the internal market and monetary union respectively. With this 'relaunching', the European integration process has become increasingly biased in favour of deregulation and the free play of market forces, establishing the primacy of negative integration (market liberalisation) over positive integration (providing public goods at a European level). European integration thus has come to be bound up with a restructuring of Europe's socio-economic order. The acceleration of European integration on the one hand, and the rise of neo-liberalism in Europe on the other, have become intertwined inasmuch as the relaunching of Europe went hand in hand with the reconstruction of the post-war order of European capitalism along predominantly neo-liberal lines. This study seeks to contribute to an understanding of the processes underlying this European transformation. It will do so from a (Gramscian) historical materialist perspective that focuses upon the role of *transnational* social forces as engendered by the transnationalisation of capitalist production associated with the global expansion and deepening of capitalism as a social system. In particular, this book conceives of the European integration process as a struggle between transnational social forces. This struggle may express itself ideologically in the form of rival 'projects' for the construction of European order.[1] On the one hand, these projects serve as rallying points around which disparate actors may coalesce into broad transnational coalitions. On the other hand, they are also consciously articulated and propagated by certain elite groups at the apex of (fractions of) transnational social forces. In this study I argue that in this respect a particularly critical role is played by the agency of an emergent transnational capitalist class.

A first argument to be made adopting this perspective is that this European transformation process can only be understood if located in the context of wider global processes of change: the process of European restructuring is crucially shaped by *global* processes of capitalist restructuring. This study, then, deals with the relation between global and European change, between globalisation and European regionalisation. How do structural changes in the global political economy impact upon the European political economy, and how do these latter changes affect the dynamics of European integration? In addressing these questions, I will argue that we cannot limit ourselves to an analysis of the structural forces at work, but that we will have to analyse the interaction between structure and agency. Thus, the 'translation' of 'pressures' emanating from processes of global structural change into European change does not take place in a predetermined fashion but is mediated by the strategic action of key political and social actors who are both constituted by as well as constitutive of those structural changes. Agency matters, but the agency of some actors matters more than that of others. Traditionally, students of international relations (IR) have focused on states as the primary, if not the only, actors, with big states being more powerful than small states. In contrast, this study focuses upon *transnational* actors: that is to say, non-state (private) actors whose identities and practices transcend the boundaries of a single 'national' society. Although transnational relations have existed ever since a system of *international* relations came into being, world politics today is arguably more than ever shaped by the former set of relations. In this study, the growing presence and significance of transnational actors is seen as inextricably bound up with the transnationalisation of global capitalism, and hence is interpreted as a transnationalisation of *social forces* engendered by (the transnationalisation of) the production process.

This transnationalisation of social forces is an uneven process. It is above all capital that transnationalises (or at least some significant parts of capital), with the people who own and/or control this transnationalising capital gaining an increasingly transnational identity and outlook, whereas labour and other social groups remain much more tied to a national perspective.[2] Moreover, to the extent that other societal groups do seek to organise at the transnational level, the fact that they lack the self-reproducing economic base of (transnational) capital puts them at a structural disadvantage in challenging what I will argue to be the latter's growing dominance. This study will thus suggest that it is in particular those social forces bound up with transnational capital that mediate between global and (in this case) European processes of structural change, particularly within the domain of socio-economic governance.

This mediating agency of transnational capital takes place not only through its important role in the global economy but also through more purely political practices of those who represent, own or control transnational businesses. This political agency on the part of transnational capital can take different forms. I will argue that next to the 'traditional' (well recognised as such within the political science literature) political activities of capitalist enterprises, such as lobbying and formal interest representation through (sectoral) associations, we may also distinguish a 'higher' form of political agency that transcends the level of narrow corporate interests. This higher form is oriented towards the articulation of a more 'general capitalist interest', expressing a longer-term and comprehensive view of how the interests of transnational capital, and of private enterprise in general, can be best secured in terms of the general institutional and policy framework in which capital operates. This kind of political agency I will interpret as *class* agency.

Class is here taken as originating in the structure of the social relations of production, in which different groups occupy different positions in relation to the production, reproduction and distribution of wealth. To the extent that individuals within these groups through formal and informal organisations come to construct common interests and a collective identity, they may establish themselves as class actors. Class here is used as a *relational* concept, in which the relation between those who control and supervise the production process (i.e., capitalists) and those who execute the tasks of production (i.e., workers) forms the most basic class division. Crucially, however, the class approach adopted here does not take the capitalist class as a unified social actor but stresses the structural (but not fixed) divisions *within* the capitalist class, pertaining in particular to the functional difference between money (financial) capital and productive (industrial) capital (Van der Pijl 1998: ch. 2) as well as to differences in what we could call the geographical scale of operation of capital, where, even within the elite of large transnational corporations, we find important differences as some firms are more global than others (which may limit their transnational activities only to a single region of the global economy). The process of capitalist class formation is thus conceptualised as one in which the different groups within the capitalist class crystallise into rival class *fractions*.[3] It is furthermore argued that this process of class formation increasingly takes place within a transnational setting, engendering the formation of a transnational capitalist class (Van der Pijl 1984, 1998; Gill 1990) consisting of the world of top executives and owners of the world's largest transnational corporations (TNCs) whose shared experiences and common interest in an open (liberalised) world economy tends to provide them with a common outlook, forming what John Stopford and Susan Strange have called a 'privileged transnational business civilisation' (Stopford and Strange 1991: 37).

It is claimed in this study that within what is increasingly a plurality of transnational actors within global politics (Risse-Kappen (ed.) 1995), rival (but striving for unity) transnational capitalist elites occupy a prominent place, and that the agency of these elites becomes a critical factor in understanding transnational political phenomena inasmuch as they seek to set the agenda and shape policies – as well as the ideological framework of those policies – at both national and international/supranational levels of governance. I will thus argue that the European Union (EU) can be analysed as one arena in which an emergent transnational capitalist class takes the European region as its primary frame of reference and organises itself to influence the (socio-economic) governance of that region. It is thus that this study claims the significance of what I identify as *transnational class agency* in the transformation of the European political economy. At the same time, however, this class agency cannot be understood outside the context of the changing nature of global capitalism. First, as indicated, it is through the processes of globalisation and transnationalisation of capitalism that this transnational class agency is constituted in the first place. Second, these global processes must also be seen as shaping the nature of transnational agency (and this would also apply to other transnational social forces) in terms of its political and ideological content. That is to say, with the changing nature of global capitalism we may also witness a change in the ideological outlook and strategic orientation of capitalist elites.

The argument of this book is informed by an extensive empirical case-study of what I will argue to be a very influential forum of and platform for Europe's emergent transnational capitalist class, the European Roundtable of Industrialists (ERT).[4] The ERT is a group of about 45 leaders of Europe's biggest and most transnational industrial corporations, the members of which transcend their role as business executives by adopting a rather political role: meeting with fellow transnational capitalists to reflect upon and discuss their (often medium to long-term) interests vis-à-vis the state and vis-à-vis other groups (such as labour) in society and, subsequently, to work out a common *political* strategy on the basis of which they then seek to influence European governance.

The world of the members of the ERT is on the one hand the world of the global and globalising market place, and it is this world that to a large extent shapes their identity and interests. On the other hand, the ERT members are also Europeans, whose companies are headquartered in western Europe (mainly the EU), which is often also still their largest market, and whose daily world as heads of these companies is thus also one shaped by the economic, social and political institutions, as well as the prevalent government policies and regulations within this region of the global economy. It is because of the latter that they have an interest in influencing the institutions and policies that make up what we could call the European Union's socio-economic governance regime: that is, all the institutions, policies, regulations, rules and norms (including prevalent ideological norms) that govern the European economic area. As heads of these very large TNCs, the members of the ERT can in fact, I will argue, exercise significant influence on this socio-economic governance regime. It is thus that the ERT can be taken as a case-study to analyse how the agency of transnational elite actors mediates the process by which changes in the global political economy transform the political economy of European integration.

This book will thus present an analysis of the ERT as an actor within what is interpreted as a *transnational struggle over European order*, and hence as *implicated* in the ongoing transformation of global and (embedded within that) European capitalism, shaped by as well as – along with other actors – shaping these processes. In order, then, to elucidate both of these aspects of the mediating agency of Europe's transnational business elite, this study presents a detailed analysis – based on interviews, ERT publications and other primary sources – of the development of the ERT, in particular of the evolution of its overall ideological outlook and the strategic orientation underlying its political agency. This study covers a period of around 15 years, from the foundation of the Roundtable in 1983 to around 1998: that is, the period which starts in the crisis years of the early 1980s, in which the European integration process seemed to be stuck at a historical low-point, then takes us through the later 1980s, which witnessed both a relaunching of the integration process as well as a significant upswing of the European economy, and then into the 1990s, in which – in the aftermath of the Maastricht treaty – both the economic crisis and 'Europessimism' returned, but Europe nevertheless started (what now appears irreversibly) to move towards the goal of monetary union.

Although some recent studies have taken transnational actors such as the ERT seriously and have provided detailed analyses of the ERT's role in the Europe 1992 programme (see above all Cowles 1994, 1995a; see also Fielder 1997), these studies lack a more systematic attention to, and theoretical interpretation of, the *content* of the ideas promoted by the ERT, and hence the ideological power that this forum of transnational capitalists exercises (an exception here is Holman 1992). Understanding this power, I claim, is important not only if we want to improve our understanding of the dynamics of European integration, but also if – from a critical perspective – we want to examine the possibilities for changing the content of that process.

Thus, whereas for instance the detailed study of Maria Green Cowles (1994, 1995a) on ERT's role in the internal market programme focuses on *how* the ERT has successfully set the agenda for this programme, the present study, with reference to the same episode, first of all seeks to answer the question of *why* the European Roundtable sought to promote the internal market, rather than any other project that could promote the relaunching of Europe, as well as *what kind* of internal market it sought to promote. Similarly, with regard to the Maastricht process, and the supranational regime of socio-economic governance that has taken shape since, this study examines not just at which instances the ERT has been able to set the agenda but also *how* and *why* it has sought to shape that agenda in terms of a particular socio-economic content. This book thus seeks to go beyond previous studies of the ERT and other business groups inasmuch as I seek not only to establish that 'the politics of big business matter' (Cowles 1995a), but also to analyse and explain 'the politics' or political strategies of big business. If it can be established that the ideas promoted by an emergent European transnational business elite matter, then it seems pertinent to shift the focus to these ideas themselves, analysing and explaining their origins and development.

This book seeks to contribute to the further development of a growing body of work in which a broad array of neo-Gramscian perspectives within the study of International Relations (IR), and in particular of International Political Economy (IPE), are applied to the *critical* study of European integration (see especially Bieling and Steinhilber (eds) 2000 and Bieler and Morton (eds) 2001; see also Holman 1996). As such, this project touches upon several debates at the core of IR/IPE, as well as within the (sub-)field of European integration studies. In addressing these debates I shall formulate a critique of established approaches and theories, and seek to advance an alternative (historical materialist) approach which I will here call 'neo-Gramscian transnationalism'.

First, as indicated it addresses the question of the relation between global and European change, or (to capture one important aspect of it) between globalisation and (European) regionalisation. This is an issue that thus far has in fact been little studied, although there are recent signs of a beginning of scholarly debate (see Coleman and Underhill (eds) 1998; Rosamond 1999; Wallace 2000). Nevertheless, this question may be interpreted to go back to an already older debate within IR/IPE, the debate on the interaction between *domestic* structure and the international system, and in particular to the arguments developed in what since Peter Gourevitch's seminal article (Gourevitch 1978) is referred to as the *second image reversed* literature (see also, e.g., Katzenstein 1985; Gourevitch 1986), which seeks to integrate the concerns of international relations scholars with those of comparative social scientists by examining how the international or global system shapes domestic politics and structures. In this study, however, this perspective is applied to the study of European integration, or what more broadly could be called the study of European order, thus addressing the question of how changes within the political economy of European integration are related to changes within the global political economy.[5] As suggested before, this link between global and European-level change is not conceptualised in deterministic terms (of one level determining the other) but as established through the agency of opposing social forces engaged in political struggles in which these forces formulate *rival* responses to the changing conditions emanating from the global level.

The emphasis on *contending* responses is crucial here and directly relates to how in this study we will conceptualise the (possible) relation between global and European change. It has in fact been commonly accepted in much of the literature (see Coleman and Underhill (eds) 1998; Sandholtz and Zysman 1989) that the European integration process, and in particular its relaunching in the 1980s (as well as other regionalisms), can be interpreted as an elite response to collectively perceived challenges emanating from a changing global political economy. In order to explain regionalisation in these terms though, it is of critical importance to note that different responses are possible. In very general terms, to the extent that global structural change can be captured with the term 'globalisation', we can conceptually distinguish between on the one hand regionalisation as a defensive response, *resisting* the forces of globalisation (as invoked by the image of 'Fortress Europe'), and, on the other hand, *accommodating* globalisation, even to the extent of amplifying (and one might say institutionalising) its effects. Inasmuch as these different concepts of regionalisation are propagated by different social forces, an analysis of the struggle between these social forces becomes pertinent to explaining regionalisation as an elite response to global change.

Second, this study also addresses different debates within the study of European integration and in particular seeks to advance a new *problématique* within this field, a *problématique* that explicitly focuses upon the *socio-economic* content of the integration process. This socio-economic dimension is to a large extent ignored by established approaches to the process of European integration inasmuch as these are mainly oriented towards explaining the *institutional* outcomes of the integration process, with the debate centring in particular around the question of whether integration is mainly driven by the interests of the member states or by a more autonomous supranational logic in which supranational institutions and actors play a predominant role. Hence, what I will call the question of the 'social purpose' underlying the European order constructed through the integration process remains out of the analytical purview of the established theories. It is thus that I will propose an alternative *problématique* of the study of European integration, that of its underlying social purpose, and argue that such a *problématique* requires us to transcend the state-centrism inherent in conventional IR theory, as well as in the dominant (intergovernmentalist) approach to European integration, and to focus instead on the role of social forces.

Third, by adopting a transnationalist perspective, this study both contributes to a recently revived research agenda within IR on the importance of transnational relations (see, e.g., Risse-Kappen (ed.) 1995), but, from a historical materialist perspective, also offers an alternative to the dominant liberal interpretations of these relations. Moreover, the transnationalism underlying the perspective advanced in this study also presents an alternative to the dominant perspectives within European integration theory that focus rather exclusively on either the supranational or the intergovernmental level of the integration process. As my focus is on the mediating agency of transnational capital, this study also contributes to the (IPE) literature on the role of TNCs as political actors within both global and European politics (see, e.g., Strange 1991, 1996; Stopford and Strange 1991; Eden 1991). Furthermore, in conceptualising and analysing the political agency of transnational capital, I seek to go beyond those studies which tend to interpret this agency solely in terms of lobbying for individual or sectoral corporate interests. In contrast, the analysis presented here stresses the class dimension of the agency of transnational capital. In fact within the perspective adopted for this study, the process of *transnational class formation* is seen as an important context in which we have to understand the European integration process, both its historical development and its current dynamics (upon which this study focuses).

Fourth, this study seeks to contribute to the growing debate on the role of ideas within international relations (see, e.g., Goldstein and Keohane (eds) 1993; Risse-Kappen 1994; Woods 1995; Wendt 1999). It will do so from a Gramscian perspective (see, e.g., Cox 1983, 1986, 1995; Gill 1990; Gill (ed.) 1993), in which it is emphasised that ideas must be located in social practice, and thus linked to the structures in which actors are located and that shape their agency. In analysing the role of ideas, this study will in particular focus on ideology, or sets of ideas that express the world view of particular social groups, and that guide their strategic action, whilst at the same time seeking to articulate and further their interests.

Finally, at the meta-theoretical level, and in a way underlying all of this, we find the so-called structure–agency debate (first introduced into IR discourse by Wendt 1987). What I will call a 'constructivist' approach to the structure–agency problem will here also form a basis for a meta-theoretical critique of established approaches to European integration and for the development of an alternative approach, grounded in a *critical* theory of global politics.

The plan of this book

Chapter 1 presents the theoretical framework of this study. In criticising the established approaches to European integration for failing to adequately address the question of the socio-economic content of the integration process, I will outline an alternative political economy approach based on a perspective here denoted as 'neo-Gramscian transnationalism'. This perspective focuses on the *transnational* dynamics of global (and European) transformation processes as constituted by transnational social, political and ideological power struggles. Chapter 1 will also present the analytical framework that will serve to analyse what is interpreted as the changing class agency of Europe's transnational business elite in the struggle over European order.

Chapter 2 describes and analyses the process of global capitalist restructuring that has taken place since the 1970s – and the concomitant processes of globalisation and transnationalisation – and, within that context, then moves on to an analysis of the crisis of European order as it evolved in the early 1980s, which is here taken as the context in which the transnational struggle over European order evolved. In this historical account we will see how the European integration process first stagnated concomitant with the crisis of European capitalism, and was then relaunched from the mid-1980s onwards. Here, I will argue how within the context of the global and European crises, three contending projects crystallised as rival strategies for the relaunching of Europe. The struggle between these rival projects – identified as neo-liberalism, neo-mercantilism and 'supranational social democracy' – is here interpreted as a struggle over European socio-economic governance that as such has shaped the evolving socio-economic content of the (relaunched) integration process.

The social democratic project sought to re-embed the new European market into a supranational framework of social regulation, and thus to protect and consolidate what is referred to as the 'European social model'. In the neo-mercantilist conception, the project of European integration was first of all conceived as one of creating a big – and partially protected by tariffs and supported by industrial policy – home market for European industry in which (would-be) 'European champions' would be able to successfully confront the non-European competition. The neo-liberal project, on the other hand, emphasised the free market aspects of the internal market, a free market that should also be free for non-European firms, and hence open to and fully integrated into the emerging global economy. The latter two projects will be interpreted as related to two rival perspectives on the part of different groups or 'fractions' within the ranks of the European transnational capitalist class. The difference in ideological outlook and strategic orientation between these rival groups is related to different positions within the globalising economy, in particular their degree of globalisation, as well as to the global 'competitiveness' of different sectors. In line with the analytical framework developed in chapter 1, it is argued that here we may distinguish between a 'globalist' fraction of European transnational capital on the one hand, and a 'Europeanist' fraction on the other, whose rival perspectives are respectively related to the neo-liberal and neo-mercantilist projects.

Chapter 3, then, introduces the ERT as the main case-study of this book. It will be argued that the ERT transcends traditional forms of both lobbying and formal interest representation. Rather, it is interpreted as an elite forum of an emergent European transnational capitalist class. Analysing the evolving strategic orientation of the ERT as a mediating force between global and European change in the next chapters, I seek to show that in this evolution a gradual but fundamental shift has taken place from an orientation that was to a large extent premised on a neo-mercantilist concept of European order to one centred around a neo-liberal vision.

It is this transformation of the ERT's strategic project that is analysed in chapter 4. As the Roundtable was in its first five years – that is, from the early to the late 1980s – dominated by representatives from what I will identify as the Europeanist fraction, its strategic orientation tended towards neo-mercantilism, pursuing a strategy of what I will call protective regionalism as a project for Europe's relaunching. The internal market project was at the heart of this strategy, and it is here that – as others have also shown – the ERT has indeed played a critical agenda-setting role. On the other hand, the new home market did not turn out to be the kind of market – i.e. a relatively protected zone in which 'European champions' could build up their competitiveness vis-à-vis global competition – that a significant part of the ERT membership had envisaged. Rather, it was the neo-liberal interpretation of the internal market that prevailed over its neo-mercantilist rival. In this context, the strategy of protective regionalism failed to establish itself as the dominant capitalist project for the European integration process. Subsequently, then, we have witnessed a gradual transformation of the ERT's strategic project, one that involved a shift away from neo-mercantilism and towards neo-liberalism.

The gradual neo-liberal shift of the strategic orientation of the Roundtable is here interpreted as related to a changing power balance between the Europeanist and the globalist 'fractions' within ERT's membership, in which the latter fraction increasingly came to occupy a leadership position, while at the same time the outlook of the former 'Europeanists' was also transformed by the ongoing globalisation process in which the position of their companies became more global too. Taking these structural changes as enabling rather than determining the formulation of a new common strategy – replacing the concept of protective regionalism – on the part of the ERT executives, I will analyse how it was through a concrete struggle between the rival fractions of European capital that the former opposition between the 'globalist' and 'Europeanist' views was gradually transcended and a new comprehensive orientation articulated. This struggle will be placed within the wider context – in which the social-democratic project also played a role – of a transnational struggle over European order, as the integration process was moving from the SEA to the Maastricht treaty on monetary union and beyond. At the end of the Maastricht process, I argue, we witness the rise of a new concept, denoted as *embedded neo-liberalism*, which can be interpreted both as the outcome between the struggle of our three contending projects and as the emerging *hegemonic project* of Europe's transnational capitalist class. As such it reflects the dominance of the globalist fraction and its by and large neo-liberal world view, but one that, as I will argue, still differs from orthodox neo-liberalism inasmuch as it explicitly acknowledges certain limits to *laissez-faire*. It is with an analysis of the rise of embedded neo-liberalism and how it came to underpin the new European socio-economic order that this book will be concluded.

This project does not pretend to tell a complete story of the transformation of European (socio-economic) order but it does claim – on the basis of its case-study of the ERT – to make three specific contributions to an understanding of this transformation. First, it seeks to advance an interpretation of the ERT as a platform of an emergent European transnational capitalist class. In doing so, the case is made that such a class indeed exists, whereby the ERT is seen as both an organisation through which this transnational capitalist class has taken shape *and* at the same time as a manifestation of that process of transnational class formation. Second, I advance the hypothesis that in the course of its development the strategic and ideological orientation of the ERT underwent a significant shift from what I identify as an almost neo-mercantilist regionalism to a much more neo-liberal globalism, and I seek to explain this shift – combining elements of structure and agency – in terms of a struggle between what I argue to be the main fractions dividing European transnational capital. Third, I seek to demonstrate the influence of the ERT in shaping, at the level of ideas, significant aspects of Europe's emergent socio-economic governance regime. Combining these elements I thus claim – *contra* state-centric explanations – the significance of the agency of an evolving European transnational capitalist class in the transnational struggle over European order. This transnational class agency is significant inasmuch as it constitutes a mediating force between global and European change. We will now turn first to the theoretical perspective underlying this argument.

1 Theoretical perspective

Social forces and the struggle over European order

This chapter presents the theoretical framework of this book. Whilst developing a critique of established approaches to European integration, I outline an alternative approach grounded in a historical materialism that emphasises the role of transnational social forces in the construction of European socio-economic order. I will call this alternative approach 'neo-Gramscian transnationalism', as it builds upon the so-called neo-Gramscian perspective within International Relations (IR) and International Political Economy (IPE), which takes the transnational nature of world politics – as embedded in the social relations of global capitalism – as its point of departure.[1] This then implies a fundamental break with the state-centrism that still dominates IR, not just in the guise of the long-predominant neo-realist theory (Waltz 1979) – which sees world politics as pure inter-*state* politics in which states compete (in a zero-sum game) for wealth and power within an anarchic system of self-help – but also in the form of many contemporary liberal theories, particularly what has been called neo-liberalism (Keohane 1984a, 1989), and recently showing its tenacity in Alexander Wendt's (1999) explicitly state-centric 'social theory of international politics'.

The chapter is organised as follows. The first section proposes to redefine the *problématique* of the study of European integration, away from its traditional rather exclusive focus on the institutional form of the integration process towards one that also addresses the question of its socio-economic content. Then, taking the 'constructivist critique' of conventional IR as a point of departure, the next section develops the meta-theoretical premises of the alternative approach I propose. The third section then outlines the constituent elements of this alternative perspective. The final sections present a critique of established approaches to European integration and seek to apply neo-Gramscian transnationalism to the study of European order.

Redefining the *problématique* of European integration: the social purpose of European order

Conventional integration theory has for too long been focused on the question of sovereignty transfer from the nation-state to an emerging supranational level, whereby the different 'schools' essentially debated the question of to what extent this is happening, and who or what might be driving the process. Such a *problématique* does not allow us to capture what John Ruggie has called the 'generative grammar' or 'structure' (Ruggie 1982: 382) underlying a particular international order, a structure that constitutes the 'social purpose' served by this order:

> Whatever its institutional manifestations, political authority represents a fusion of power with legitimate social purpose. The prevailing interpretation of international authority focuses on power [that is, state power] only; it ignores the dimension of social purpose. The problem with this formulation is that power may predict the *form* of the international order, but not its *content*. (ibid., his emphasis)

The concept of social purpose may be applied to the national level as well as to the international (Ruggie 1982) or *world order* (Cox 1987) level. The starting point for the present study is that it may also be applied to the level of an emergent *European* order. That is to say, we can conceive of the process of European integration as the construction of a regional 'international', and partly 'supranational', order, *serving a particular social purpose*. At the same time, I would suggest that for the study of European integration, *form* and *content* are to a significant extent intertwined. Defining content as social purpose, or the *socio-economic* content of the internationalisation or supranationalisation of political authority, and form as the institutional shape this process takes, it can be argued that form *sets limits to* possible contents and vice versa (cf. Schmitter 1991; Traxler and Schmitter 1995; Hooghe and Marks 1999).

To the extent that social purpose is the outcome of political and social struggles, it may also be changed through such struggles. Within the development of capitalism we may in fact observe an alternation between rival 'social purposes'. Karl Polanyi (1957) argued that in this respect we may distinguish between 'embedded' and 'disembedded' market economies. In the former, the economy is more organised around what Polanyi called the 'principle of social protection' (Polanyi 1957: 132), and the market is embedded in social and political institutions that discipline and constrain the private forces of the market in order to protect 'society', but, often, also particular sections of the capitalist class, against the destructive nature of those forces. In the latter, the economy is more organised around the 'principle of economic liberalism' and the market is disembedded from society: the economic is separated from the political and the market is represented as self-regulating. In Polanyi's view, however, the project of establishing a self-regulating market is in the end a utopia (Polanyi 1957: 3). Historically, the free market has always needed the state for both its emergence and its maintenance. In Polanyi's political economy, the market is not a 'spontaneous order' (as Friedrich Hayek asserted), but rather a social and political construction, hence, in this sense, as is also stressed by the new institutionalism in economic sociology, the economy is always embedded in society (Hollingsworth, Schmitter and Streeck 1994: 3). The separation of the political from the economic and the disembedding of the market which characterises liberal capitalism is therefore an ultimately untenable state of affairs. Hence, Polanyi's notion of the 'double movement' (1957: 132): as the state retreats from its role in providing for social protection, the resulting social disruption will engender a counter-movement in which social forces will organise themselves around the principle of social protection, and the liberal market economy becomes 're-embedded'.

The question of social purpose, or of socio-economic order, has recently also returned to the academic (and indeed political) limelight in the form of the notion of different *forms of capitalism*. Now that capitalism is the only major economic system left, academics and other observers have begun to rediscover the (institutional) diversity of capitalism itself (see, e.g., Hollingsworth, Schmitter and Streeck (eds) 1994; Crouch and Streeck (eds) 1997; Rhodes and Van Apeldoorn 1997; Hall and Soskice (eds) 2001). Moreover, some – in particular Michel Albert (1993) – have suggested that out of this diversity there has arisen a political, ideological and economic contest between rival models of capitalism. In this study I will suggest that this struggle of rival models of capitalism is also manifest at the transnational level, where different social forces pursue rival strategic projects for the construction of what we could identify as an emerging European (supranational) model of capitalism.

Social purpose changes over time. Within the history of the political economy of European integration we may thus also interpret different phases of the process of European integration as bound up with different social purposes. If we want to understand this changing social purpose, we have to examine the social underpinnings of European order. These social underpinnings remain hidden from the established perspectives on European integration precisely because their focus is exclusively on the question of power narrowly defined in terms of political authority of either states or supranational/international public bodies (cf. Ruggie 1982). In order to overcome this narrow focus, we should add a concept of *social* power – in both its material *and* ideological dimensions – that derives not from political authorities, or from the state in a narrow sense, but from the social forces that underpin state power. Traditional IR theory has always abstracted the state from its social base. In contrast, the neo-Gramscian approach adopted here, following Cox, 'consider(s) the state–*society* complex as the basic entity of international relations' (Cox, 1986: 205, my emphasis). This notion of state-society complexes here is broadened inasmuch as the transnationalisation of both state structures and social forces is taken into account.

Before outlining – in conjunction with a critique of established approaches – neo-Gramscian transnationalism as an approach to the study of European order and its underlying social purpose, I should first present the main (meta-)theoretical foundations and outline the central concepts of this alternative approach.

Meta-theoretical considerations: IR theory and the 'constructivist' critique

Neo-Gramscian transnationalism implies a fundamental critique of the ontological and epistemological assumptions underlying orthodox IR/IPE. The way I formulate this critique here is in part inspired by what has been labelled the emerging constructivist perspective within the IR debate.[2] Constructivism as it is understood here explicitly challenges the individualist and rationalistic understanding of social action underlying mainstream IR theory, while at the same time rejecting the structuralist alternative in which there is no room left for human agency. As constructivism seeks to take agency seriously (in fact more seriously than rationalist approaches), it also draws our attention to the role of consciousness and ideas in social practice. It is important, however, to differentiate from the outset the critical constructivism advanced here, which is grounded in historical materialism, from liberal or idealist versions of constructivism (see in particular Wendt 1999).

Beyond individualism

Constructivism seeks to propose a meta-theoretical alternative to the methodological individualism underlying mainstream IR discourse as it developed in the 1980s (Wæver 1994; see also Ashley 1986; Onuf 1989; Wendt 1992, 1999; cf. Keohane 1988). The liberal or later 'neo-liberal' perspective in IR is most explicitly premised on an individualist ontology as it stresses the rationalist logic of utility-maximising individuals, which, under the conditions of a liberal world market, is argued to lead to positive sum outcomes. It can be argued, however, that such an individualism equally underlies Waltzian neo-realism (in spite of Waltz's claim that he is a structuralist), as – premised on assumptions from neo-classical micro-economics – states here are taken as rational actors with given interests competing in a state-system that is likened to a market (see Cox 1986; Ashley 1986; Wendt 1987, 1999; Dessler 1989). In what has been dubbed the 'neo-neo synthesis' of the IR mainstream (Wæver 1994), an orthodoxy only now being challenged by constructivism, world politics, then, is explained on the basis of an 'atomistic' model of social action in which there are only self-maximising individuals (states in neo-realism) and in which the 'the social' (or society) is nothing other than the aggregate of individual actions. In this individualist conception, agency is ontologically prior, which means that agents and their identities and interests are taken as given.

As individualism holds that all properties of social systems can be reduced to the attributes of individual agents, it is thus denied that agents are embedded in social relations that actually shape their interests and identities. As Wendt puts it: 'The consequence of making the individual ontologically primitive . . . is that the social relations in virtue of which that individual is a *particular kind of agent* with particular causal properties must remain forever opaque and untheorised' (Wendt 1987: 343, my emphasis).

In this context, 'constructivists' as well as neo-Gramscians (see in particular Cox 1986, 1995) have drawn our attention to the *intersubjective* making of social reality, at which level we also find the role of ideas. Ideas can neither be simply reduced to interests nor (as in idealism) be reified as existing prior to practice. It is only in human activity that ideas are generated, and here given *structural conditions* (partly of a material nature) in which this activity takes place must also enter into the analysis.

Structure and agency

A constructivist understanding of the relationship between structure and agency is informed by Marx's famous dictum that men make their own history, but not under the circumstance of their own choosing.[3] Such an ontology refuses to make either agency or structure ontologically prior, but instead gives them equal weight (Wendt 1987: 339). It therefore attempts to transcend the dichotomy of voluntaristic individualism on the one hand, and deterministic structuralism on the other, acknowledging that social structures are constructed by real people – and mediated by their consciousness and praxis – but also that the exercise of such 'autonomous' agency is at the same time dependent upon prior social forms. This approach to the structure–agency problem has been articulated by different social theorists, above all by Roy Bhaskar in his 'tranformational model of activity' (Bhaskar 1979), and by Anthony Giddens in his structuration theory (Giddens 1979, 1985). Such a 'structurationist' or 'transformational' ontology, then, starts from the basic premise that structure and agency presuppose each other.

Agency presupposes structure because, as Bhaskar puts it, 'all activity presupposes the prior existence of social forms . . . Speech requires language; making materials; actions conditions; agency resources; activity rules' (Bhaskar 1979: 43). Hence, unequivocally rejecting individualism, the point of departure here is that there is no such thing as a pre-social actor; human agency is always embedded in pre-existing social relations that constitute that agent's identity and interests. In fact, for the individual actor 'social structure is always *already made*' (ibid.: 42, his emphasis). Therefore, although the metaphor of 'making' remains often a useful one, it is in fact, on this view, not correct to say that people create society, rather they *reproduce* or *transform* it (ibid.). At the same time, society 'would not exist unless they did so' (ibid.: 45).The same ontological position is expressed in Giddens' notion of the *duality of structure*, by which he means that 'structured properties of social systems are simultaneously the *medium and outcome of social acts*' (Giddens 1981: 19; see also Giddens 1979: 5, 69). Action always takes place through the medium of some pre-existing social forms; structure must therefore be seen not only as constraining but also as *enabling* action (see, e.g., Giddens 1979: 51, 69–70; 1985: 169–80; see also Bhaskar 1979: 50).

Structure also presupposes agency as it only exists in virtue of intentional human action in which social structures are reproduced or transformed (Bhaskar 1979: 49). Giving pride and place to agency also allows us better to conceptualise historical change as the product of human practice (moving beyond the lack of historicity of IR theory). Moreover, constructivism takes agents as reflexive, knowledgeable and purposeful actors, and hence not as – as for instance in structuralist Marxism – mere 'bearers' of underlying structural forces, or indeed as simple utility-maximisers whose 'rational choice' involves a mere 'automatic computing of expected utilities governed by given preferences' (Hollis and Smith 1991: 409). The position adopted here posits not only that the existence of social structures is dependent upon their instantiation in social action, but also that they 'do not exist independently of the agents' conceptions of what they are doing in their activity' (Bhaskar 1979: 48–49).

Towards a critical theory of global transformation

Constructivism opens up the possibility of new and innovative forms of theorising going beyond the rationalistic mainstream, but it does not constitute a *substantive* theory: it does not tell us how to go about explaining social change. Here I start with the premise that such a theory has to be a *critical* theory and suggest that constructivism (as emerging within IR discourse) has as yet not fully developed its critical potential. My understanding of critical theory follows that of Robert Cox, who opposes it to (positivistic) 'problem-solving theory'. The latter 'takes the world as it finds it, with the prevailing social and power relationships and the institutions into which they are organized, as the given framework of action' (Cox 1986: 208). Taking the existing order as given, indeed treating it completely ahistorically, the 'problem-solving' research programme restricts itself to analyse (and propose solutions to) specific 'operational' problems of the present system. In contrast, critical theory:

> stands apart from the prevailing order of the world and asks how that order came about. Critical theory . . . does not take institutions and social power relations for granted but calls them into question by concerning itself with their origins and how and whether they might be in the process of changing. It is directed towards an appraisal of the very framework of action, or problematic, which problem-solving theory accepts as its parameters. (Cox 1986: 208)

In my view such a critical perspective follows logically from the constructivist position adopted above. First, the notion that the existence of social structures is ultimately dependent upon and indeed constituted by human agency through a process of continuous reproduction *and* transformation of those structures implies the possibility of emancipatory practice. Second, and following from this, constructivism is critical because it historicises the present social structures. Structures are viewed as constructed through the social practice of human actors. They are necessarily *historical* products, and therefore transient and changeable, rather than transhistorical phenomena that would be amenable to the formulation of social scientific laws. Finally, as constructivism treats all forms of intersubjective knowledge as constituent elements of social reality, it sees as an inherent feature of social science that the theories of the social scientist feed back in to the (re-)constitution of the object she studies. As Giddens maintains, if we thus accept that scholarly practice in itself is part of the social world it seeks to explain, critical theory is no longer an *option* but becomes a necessity (Giddens 1985: xxxv). In my view such a 'critical constructivism' underlies the perspective here called neo-Gramscian transnationalism.

Neo-Gramscian transnationalism as a critical theory of global politics goes beyond traditional international relations theory in four interrelated respects. First, it brings society back in as *capitalist* society (and with that brings class analysis back in). Second, it brings ideas back in but avoiding idealism. Third, it brings transnational relations back in, and argues their rise to be bound up in particular with the global expansion of capital. Fourth, it brings the role of human agency back in (rather then merely human *behaviour*). Below, these points will be elaborated as the constituent elements of neo-Gramscian transnationalism, and I will attempt to show how they in fact come together in what is the central focus of this study, the transformative role of transnational class strategy.

Neo-Gramscian transnationalism

The critical constructivism underlying our alternative perspective differs from some other (liberal) forms of constructivism in adopting a historical materialist framework of interpretation. This 'constructivist' historical materialism is inspired by Antonio Gramsci's attempt to reformulate historical materialism away from the economism and 'scientific' structuralism of orthodox Marxism, and to give due place to the role of consciousness, ideology and culture in the reproduction and transformation of social formations, and hence also to the role of collective (class) agency in producing these intersubjective forces.

Historical materialism

Whereas conventional IR theory – particularly in the neo-realist tradition – focuses on state power narrowly conceived as the accumulated material capabilities of the 'state-as-actor', historical materialism seeks to examine the *social* origins of that power. Historical materialism takes as its subject matter the ensemble of social relations in which actors are embedded and claims that at least one set of those social relations is rooted in the economy. Production – taking the form of a social interaction with nature – necessarily forms the material basis of all human life, and therefore of the very existence and reproduction of societies, including their political organisation. As Cox (1987: 1) writes, production is therefore also the necessary material precondition for the exercise of any form of power, including state power. The social origins of power are thus to be at least partly located in the social relations of production. It is in the study of capitalism that an understanding of these social relations of production, and the contradictions and conflicts they entail, becomes indispensable to our analysis. It is within capitalism that, as Giddens argues, the power over 'allocative resources' – that is, power as directly derived from control over the production process – gains primary significance as a medium of social transformation (see Giddens 1981: ch. 5).

It is important to note that our Gramscian historical materialism focuses upon the *relations* of production rather than on the mere *forces* of production (as in technological determinist versions of Marxism). Moreover, these relations are to a large extent dependent upon, and indeed constituted by, ideational structures in the sense of laws, rules, norms and ideas that enable capital to exploit labour. Thus capitalists can only exist in virtue of legally defined and state guaranteed property rights and the acceptance of those rights within society. We should therefore abandon the old Marxist notion of a material base (production) and an ideational superstructure (the state, the law, ideology and culture) inasmuch as the so-called ideational superstructure does not so much reflect a so-called material base, but permeates that base from the very start. Thus Wendt is at least partly right to state that 'relations of production are thoroughly ideational phenomena, namely institutions or rules – which are ultimately shared ideas – that constitute property and exchange relationships' (Wendt 1999: 94). However, there is still an important material dimension to this in three respects: 1) ideas and institutions are produced by human actors who are biological beings with material (even if partially socially mediated) needs that they can only satisfy in interaction with nature (this is of course the classic point of departure for historical materialism), 2) the social construction of these 'ideas' has very real material consequences, and 3) it is at the same time in response to those socially determined material conditions that those ideational structures (which are always already given, as society is already made for the individual) are reproduced and transformed (on this last point see Cox 1995: 34).

With regard to the second point we may note that it very much matters in our society – in terms of well-being and power – who owns and controls economic (income-generating) resources (people without money may starve), and that moreover (with regard to the so-called superstructure) people who do not respect the 'ideational' rules of the capitalist game (by not respecting property rights or managerial authority) meet the very material arm of the law. Our historical materialism, then, is not so much materialist in emphasising the impact of 'material things' as independent from social structures, but more in stressing the centrality of the social relations (which are also constituted by political and ideological practices at the level of civil society and the state) producing and distributing (often very unequally) material resources. It is within capitalism that this production of wealth takes place within a separate economic sphere and on the basis of primarily economic means, hence the centrality of 'the economic' in capitalism.

Within the context of the study of global politics, historical materialism, then, brings not only society back into the analysis, but specifically *capitalist* society. Thus, in contrast to mainstream IR theory, which has always suffered from a lack of any 'concept of social power behind or constitutive of states and their interests' (Ashley 1986: 276), Mark Rupert reminds us that the 'Marxian/Gramscian critique [of orthodox IR/IPE] would take as its point of departure the proposition that international politics as we know it is *historically embedded* in, and *internally related* to, capitalist social relations' (Rupert 1993: 84, his emphasis). Agency in global politics is embedded in the structure of capitalist social relations, and the identity and interests (rather than exogenously given) of any particular actor are thus partly shaped or *structured* by those relations.

In sum, historical materialism takes production relations as a critical element in the structuration of world politics. In line with our meta-theoretical premises, this structuration must be viewed as mediated by the agency of social forces as engendered by the production process. The social organisation of capitalist production gives rise to opposing interests, and hence conflict, between on the one hand those who exercise control over the means of production and thus supervise the production process (capitalists) and, on the other hand, those who actually carry out the tasks of production (workers). Moreover, as will be argued in detail below, within the capitalist class itself we also find conflicting interests and related structural cleavages. Indeed, conflict within the capitalist class is endemic inasmuch as competition is an essential principle of capitalist accumulation. It is only in confrontation with other social groups and classes, and in particular with labour, that capitalists may become conscious of themselves as (members of) a class, and come to act accordingly.

In the historical materialist perspective adopted here, then, the analysis of concrete struggles between capital and labour, but also between different fractions of the capitalist class, is indispensable to an understanding of the relationship between production and power. Emphasising the role of the agency of social forces also brings us, from a Gramscian perspective, to the role of ideas.

The role of ideas: ideology and hegemony

Within a Gramscian perspective, ideas do not float about in an endless universe of meaning, but are seen as produced by human agency in the context of social power relations, and as such are also linked with the strategic action of social (class) actors. Theorising the role of ideas in this way brings us to the concept of ideology. Ideology is here taken – employing a positive rather than a negative definition (see Larrain 1983) – to mean the (political) 'world view' of a particular group or class (fraction).[4] This usage follows Gramsci, for whom ideology in the 'right sense' of the word referred to the world view of a class, i.e., to a *class* ideology expressing a collective consciousness (see Gramsci 1971: 376–77). Thus, against the claim of some post-Marxists that 'there is no logical connection whatsoever between positions in the relations of production and the mentality of the producers' (Laclau and Mouffe 1985: 84–85) – which according to Terry Eagleton (1991: 215) presumably means 'that it is wholly coincidental that all capitalists are not also revolutionary socialists' – the claim is upheld here that the content of any ideological practice is shaped by the social position of the actor who engages in it. Put simply, even though any ideology is never a simple and automatic reflection of material conditions (as ideology is a mediated process), it is very likely to make a difference for your ideological predisposition or world view whether you are the Chief Executive Officer (CEO) of Shell or one of that company's low-skilled employees.[5]

If it is to be a useful tool of analysis in the study of politics, ideology should also be linked to power. We might thus come to a more specific definition of ideology as provided by Eagleton, namely as 'a set of beliefs which coheres and inspires a specific group or class in the pursuit of political interests judged to be desirable' (Eagleton 1991: 44). Ideology defines these interests for the group or class in question but at the same time it seeks to legitimate these interests vis-à-vis other groups and classes. Ideology in a sense relates to the fusion of ideas and power. However, equally important is to link ideological discourse to agency, i.e., to acknowledge that it is dependent upon human practice for its reproduction or transformation. These links are expressed in the Gramscian notion of hegemony.

Hegemony, in its Gramscian meaning, is a form of social leadership or rule based on consent rather than on (mere) coercion, although the latter is always looming in the background (see, e.g., Gramsci 1971: 169–70). As such it refers to an *institutionalisation* of a set of ideas and practices (pertaining to the ideological perspective of the dominant class) constituting a structure of domination.[6] The construction of hegemony involves the building of what Gramsci called a *historic bloc* (see, e.g., Gramsci 1971: 366) or a concrete configuration of social forces whose rule is underpinned by an organic fit between material conditions, ideas and institutionalised practices. The construction of hegemony is a very political process in which:

> previously germinated ideologies become 'party', come into confrontation and conflict, until only one of them, or at least a single combination of them tends to prevail, to gain the upper hand, to propagate itself throughout society – bringing about not only a unison of economic and political aims, but also intellectual and moral unity, posing all questions around which the struggle rages not on a corporate but on a 'universal' plane, and thus creating the hegemony of a social group over a series of subordinate groups. (Gramsci 1971: 181–82)

In connection to hegemony, then, ideology assumes the task of 'unifying' and 'cementing' the 'social bloc' upon which rule by consent rests (ibid.: 328). This involves first of all a process of ideological articulation of diverse and initially opposed ideological elements into a single ideological discourse, which is then the expression of a hegemonic world view inasmuch as it transcends the narrow 'interests' of the leading social group. Here, the *hegemonic* social group is the one 'which has been able to articulate the interests of other social groups to its own by means of ideological struggle' (Mouffe 1979: 181; see also Laclau and Mouffe 1985: 67).

If we view hegemony as the outcome of an articulation of rival ideologies (or ideological elements) into a unifying discourse, this necessarily implies that the original ideological project that sought to establish its own hegemony is transformed in the process through which it achieves this goal. A hegemonic ideology necessarily always transcends any particular class or group-bound view, not only by representing the narrow interests of the dominant class *as the general interest* but by genuinely incorporating opposing interests into its discourse, although in such a manner that they are subordinated to the interests specified by the original class ideology of the hegemonic group.

The stability and endurance of a hegemonic order can never be taken for granted, as it needs to be continuously reproduced (and is therefore also subject to potential transformation). Therefore we should not reify any dominant or hegemonic ideology, but always ask how that ideology came about: that is to say, locate it in the wider politico-ideological struggle out of which it emerged. This is the struggle between opposing social forces in capitalist societies, in particular between capital and labour, but also between different fractions of the capitalist class.

The structuration of capitalism: bringing class back in

Bringing capitalism back in sheds light on the important question of how and why it is that some groups in society have more power to reproduce or transform social structures to their perceived advantage than others (Holman 1993: 13). Capitalist social relations are relations of domination bound up with an unequal distribution of the material capabilities resulting from an unequal control over the means of production. Our focus is thus drawn to how 'the *distribution* of the structural conditions of action' (Bhaskar 1979: 54, his emphasis) specific to capitalism results in structural asymmetries with regard to the exercise of agency. These unequal power relations in capitalist production can be understood in terms of the underlying class structure of capitalist society. Under certain conditions, class structure may generate class *formation*: that is, the moment when class becomes the basis for collective action; a movement from class structure to class agency.

Although the concept of class is still used by sociologists in analysing social stratification (see for a representative recent work, Marshall 1997; cf. Wright 1997: 30), the notion of class as a social actor has almost disappeared from social science discourse, and indeed has been criticised from many different quarters (often on the basis of the argument that we are now *post* something in which class analysis was still relevant, see, e.g., Pakulski and Waters 1996). In contrast, this study, following the pioneering work of Kees van der Pijl (see Van der Pijl 1984, 1998), Stephen Gill (see Gill 1990) and others, seeks to reclaim the centrality of class agency in the study of politics. The class-theoretical premise underlying this agenda is that the class domination by which capitalist societies are characterised cannot be understood from a structuralist perspective that merely focuses on the structural domination of capital over labour (see, e.g., the work of Poulantzas 1973, 1978; cf. Therborn 1978; Miliband 1989; Lindblom 1977), but that the reproduction of this power of capital – and of the capitalist class – has to be explained also in terms of collective human agency within social power struggles taking place on the structural terrain of the accumulation process.

Defining class

Within Marxian class analysis we can, broadly speaking, identify two opposing traditions, one structuralist-determinist, and one historicist. The most notable representative of the structuralist tradition is probably Nicos Poulantzas, who saw classes as a structure that fully determines, and hence is ontological prior to, the practice of individual agents occupying specific class locations (see Poulantzas 1973, 1978). Thus, rather than seeing class position (structure) and class-related practice (agency) as mutually constituting, the latter is seen as mechanically determined by the former. At the other, historicist, end of the spectrum we find for instance the historian E.P. Thompson, for whom 'class happens when some men, as a result of common experiences (inherited or shared), feel and articulate the identity of their interests as between themselves, and as against other men whose interests are different from (and usually opposed to) theirs' (Thompson 1980: 8–9).

To see how and why class happens it is necessary to take a historical perspective as class is a 'historical relationship [always] embodied in real people and in a real context' (ibid.).

Of these two rival conceptualisations of class, Thompson's historicist definition of class as a collective actor making and remaking itself *in* social practice clearly fits better with our 'constructivist' premises on structure and agency. Still, Thompson's historicism can also be criticised for being too much bent towards the agency side, tending to ignore the question of how class as agency relates to (material) structure. Class – as a social subject – is a social construction, but this construction is crucially shaped (but not determined) by the material reality (in the sense of an unequal access to and control over material resources) inherent in the capitalist production process. In fact, I would suggest that it still makes sense to employ the concept of class as referring both to the actual structural position of people as well as to that particular form of agency that *might* be engendered by that position, and that we here call class agency.

In our dual concept of class, then, class refers to *both* structure and agency. It refers on the one hand to the specific distribution of the conditions of action inherent in capitalist production relations and to the social positions emanating from that distribution, and on the other hand, to the agency constituted by those underlying socio-economic structures, or to the practices of the persons occupying the social positions related to those structures. This 'dual' conception of class of course goes back to Marx's distinction between 'class-in-itself' and 'class-for-itself', but it also corresponds to our 'constructivist' perspective on the relation between structure and agency, and in particular to Bhaskar's 'transformational model' in which he conceptualises transformation as taking place through 'position–practice systems' (Bhaskar 1979) that link structure (structure defining the positions) to agency (the practice of the occupants of those positions). Class can thus be viewed as a 'position–practice system' in which positions and practices are mutually constitutive. Practice and position are internally related, but it is only under certain conditions that class *structure* generates class *agency*: that is, that we may call specific practices *class practices*. Here I will only speak of class agency when – even if not unmediated (because it never is) – persons or groups of persons consciously act 'in virtue' of the class position they occupy. In other words, the notion of class *agency* always presupposes a certain degree of class *consciousness* (Van der Pijl 1989b: 241).

Now that we have defined class in the abstract: what are the concrete classes we speak about when we refer to contemporary capitalist society as a class society? Although this study focuses on one class (or class elite) in particular, namely an emergent transnational capitalist class, we do need to define at least that class. In the section below, then, I will conceptualise the structure and agency – and how the two are connected – of the capitalist class.

Structure and agency of the capitalist class

As capitalism is based on the private ownership of the means of production, we find an opposition between the class (always a minority) that owns and controls the means of production, i.e., the capitalist class, and that class of people who only own their labour power, which they are thus 'forced' to sell to the capitalists as a commodity in the 'free' labour market, i.e., the working class. Whether or not one accepts Marx's labour theory of value and the exploitation concept he derived from that, it is clear that the capital–labour relation involves both a form of structural domination arising out of the complete asymmetry in market power (resulting from property relations) between worker and capitalist (Streeck 1992: 41–75), as well as a potential opposition of material interest to the extent that, as Marx put it, wage and profit stand in an inverse relationship (Marx in Marx and Engels 1978: 205).

The internal (as capital and labour and the two related classes presuppose each other), but contradictory and potentially conflictual, relation between capital and labour also determines the historical process of *class formation*, by which we mean the constitution of class as a social actor. This, however, does not mean that we can take the existence of capital and labour as class-conscious social actors as given. A group of people occupying the same position within the socio-economic structure may or may not turn itself into a social actor. Indeed, critics of Marxian class analysis are probably right that in contemporary capitalist societies the working class – due to various developments, such as the rise of the welfare state, the expansion of the public sector and of the service economy, the crisis of Fordism and post-Fordist fragmentation of the labour market, and a concomitant fragmentation of working-class practices (see for instance Lash and Urry 1987) – is no longer constituted as a class in this sense. However, as this study focuses primarily on the capitalist class and its formation and strategy at the transnational level, the problems these empirical trends present for an overall analysis of contemporary class structure do not have to concern us here. As Crompton notes, 'Changes in the class structure have largely taken place in the levels below its topmost reaches' (Crompton 1993: 193).

Now that we have located, in very general terms, the capitalist class within capitalist society, we should come to a further conceptualisation of the process of *capitalist* class formation, moving from structure to agency. First, let us return to the (Marxian) definition of the capitalist class as those who own and control the means of production. This definition seems clear enough, but developments within modern capitalism have rendered the definition problematic (exposing the validity of class analysis in general to various post-industrial, post-capitalist and post-modern critiques) inasmuch as it seems to assume a unity of ownership and control, a unity that was prevalent in Marx's time but much less so in contemporary capitalism. Indeed, Berle and Means (1991), studying the US case, already argued in 1932 that with the rise of the joint-stock company, ownership has been separated from control as the former had come into the hands of an allegedly powerless mass of small shareholders. This argument later developed into the theory of *managerial capitalism*, in which the capitalist class was supposedly replaced by a new class of professional managers free to pursue strategies other than that of profit-maximisation, serving either their own material interests or a more 'public interest' (Burnham 1975; Dahrendorf 1959; Bell 1965).

There are however several theoretical and empirical arguments to marshal against this managerialist theory and to maintain that a) the rise of modern forms of industrial organisation has not led to the dissolution of the capitalist class, and b) that managers of capitalist enterprises have always been by and large part of that class, albeit to historically varying degrees.

First, the managerialist thesis has been subject to a Marxist critique in the form of 'finance capital' (following earlier theories by Lenin and Hilferding). This theory stated that concomitant to the rise of the large industrial corporations we have witnessed the rise of large ('monopoly') banks financing the expansion of those industrial corporations and playing an important role in the control over those corporations. Next to the financial and ownership ties, big banks and industrial corporations were also shown to be linked through personal ties of interlocking directorships (Zeitlin 1974; Fennema 1982). The finance capitalism theory is nowadays outdated inasmuch as banks less and less play the role accorded to them by this theory. On the other hand, we may still identify important links between financial institutions and industry, *inter alia* through interlocks.

Second, the spread of separation of ownership and control as identified by Berle and Means, and typical for the USA and the UK, was never universal (La Porta *et al.* 1998; Scott 1997). In particular in continental Europe, throughout the post-war period large firms continued to be controlled by large block holders owning a controlling minority (or often even a majority) of the shares. This pattern of ownership control still holds to a large extent in continental Europe today with almost 80 per cent of continental European companies among the 100 largest European companies still subject to direct owner control (see Van Apeldoorn 2001). In almost all of these cases, the owners are also represented on the company's board, sometimes even as CEO, so that owners and managers are partly still the same people.

On the other hand, this continental pattern of ownership and control structures is currently, under the pressures of globalisation and the rise of Anglo-Saxon finance, being transformed to such an extent that we may in fact witness a rise of a European shareholder capitalism. In this capitalism, already dominant in the Anglo-Saxon countries, owners increasingly exercise control not individually and directly through the ownership of large blocks, but *indirectly and collectively* through the stock market, i.e. through the buying and selling of stock (exit strategy), where the share price thus functions as a disciplining device vis-à-vis management (Van Apeldoorn 2001; see also OECD 1998; Nestor and Thompson 1999; cf. Rhodes and Van Apeldoorn 1998). Although these developments point to a rather strong convergence on what in the literature is known as the Anglo-Saxon model, we in fact, as I argued elsewhere (Van Apeldoorn 2001), rather see a *hybridisation* inasmuch as some of the old features of European corporate governance systems are still being preserved, in particular the dominance (albeit slightly declining) of large block holders: that is to say, the dispersion of ownership remains limited in continental Europe. But this hybrid model still increasingly tends to a 'shareholder capitalism' inasmuch as the share price, and thus the market mechanism of corporate control, is becoming increasingly central to corporate strategy, and thus weakens the control exercised by traditional block holders, who are also increasingly under the pressures, or maybe the temptations, of the capital market.

As part of this transformation of European corporate governance, the material interests of managers have increasingly been tied to those of mobile shareholders through stock-option programmes and the like, and there is indeed evidence that managers increasingly adopt what we could call the ideology of shareholder value (Van Apeldoorn 2001). In sum, then, in Europe, managers are still bound to the interests of owners inasmuch as their companies are still controlled by large block holders and/or, and increasingly so, are tied to a different kind of ownership interest through the discipline exercised by the capital market and the incorporation of managers into an emerging shareholder capitalism.

This then brings us to the third argument, which concerns the alleged difference in interests between managers and owners. Even if managers are not shareholders themselves, the 'managerialist' assumption not only that managers of modern joint-stock companies are differently motivated than the traditional owner-entrepreneurs, but also that these different motivations would produce different outcomes of behaviour is questionable (see Clegg, Boreham and Dow 1986: 113–15). In fact, empirical studies have suggested that in capitalism the behaviour of managers must be explained in more structural terms (ibid.). Thus, even if motivations of managers may diverge from those of shareholders, the logic of capitalist accumulation may strongly constrain the effects those diverging motivations have. As noted before, to the extent that managers can also generate income from these stock markets (by behaving in ways that these markets reward through stock options), these constraints are reinforced in new ways. Indeed, if we, as Fennema (1982: 32) does, include in the capitalist class all those who obtain a major part of their income from the ownership of capital, almost all of Europe's top managers would only on that account already belong to the capitalist class, rather than to any separate 'managerial class'. Arguing on a similar basis, Wright claims 'that managers should have strong tendencies towards a pro-capitalist orientation, and that these tendencies should increase as one moved towards the top of managerial hierarchies' (Wright 1989: 311). Finally, with regard to this third point, (large) owners and top managers often also share the same perceived interests and ideological outlook, inasmuch as they are socialised through the same elite networks and socio-cultural institutions (Domhoff 1979; Scott 1997).

In sum, and only more so in the present era, we may consider the top managers of large transnational corporations as belonging to the core of the capitalist class. Together with owners (and with varying degrees of autonomy vis-à-vis owners), top managers belong to that class that exercises control over the means of production, in particular what Clegg, Boreham and Dow (1986: 108–09) define as *strategic* control: that is, control over the major decisions that define the 'parameters' within which production takes place, such as decisions regarding (the planning of) investment, mergers and acquisitions, sale of assets, executive recruitment, and the legal structure of the corporation. It is this private control over productive assets that defines the structural basis for capitalist class formation. It is now time, however, to move from structure to agency.

Institutional aspects of capitalist class formation

Organisation is a key factor in the process through which a class establishes itself as an actor. As Lanzalaco argues, in the transformation of class from a class in itself to a class-for-itself, organisation is a key variable inasmuch as it is 'the organization that structures and shapes class, moulding the subjective perceptions it has of its interests, and the way in which they are transformed into collective strategies' (Lanzalaco 1992: 173–74). At the transnational level, the most effective of these organisations are often those more or less informal bodies that are formed and led by an elite of a class (fraction) (see Van der Pijl 1984, 1989a, 1998: ch. 4; Gill 1990). It is these elites who, in organising themselves, also organise and direct the collective action of the wider class, galvanising it into action. An important aspect of this is the formulation by these elite groups of a coherent class strategy – expressing but at the same shaping the interests of the class (fraction) it leads – which can then guide the political behaviour of all class members. Such class leadership is thus involved in the very 'making' of a class-for-itself.

Another organisational mechanism through which the coherence of capitalist class elites is strengthened and maintained is that of so-called interlocking directorships, i.e., the situation whereby an executive or chairperson holds a position at one or more other companies, by acting either as an outside director of the board of directors of an another company, as in the Anglo-Saxon (and partly French) one-tier board system, or as a member of the supervisory board of another company in the Germanic two-tier board system. The corporate elite networks that are formed and maintained through interlocking directorships help to ensure that a relatively small number of persons – persons who may be regarded as leading figures within the capitalist class – exercise control over a large number of companies. Interlocking directorships thus also play a role in the creation of particular capitalist elites that through these networks exercise leadership over the capitalist class as a whole (or at least over particular class fractions). In other words, one important function of interlocking directorships is the creation and maintenance of intra-class hegemony (Clegg, Boreham and Dow 1986: 126; cf. Fennema 1982).

Class fractions, class strategy and the struggle for hegemony

In order to constitute themselves as a class, capitalists somehow have to 'discover' their common interests and construct a shared outlook and identity that transcends the narrow view of their position as individual and competing capitalists. The moment of class agency is thus always a *political* process, in which capitalists transcend the logic of market competition and reach a temporary unity of strategic orientation and purpose, enabling them to articulate (vis-à-vis other social classes or groups, as well as vis-à-vis the state) a 'general capitalist interest'. Any formulation of the general capitalist interest is, however, always formulated from the perspective of what is only a section or 'fraction' of total capital, a fraction that has temporarily achieved a leading position within the capitalist class. As Van der Pijl argues, as a conscious social actor 'the capitalist class at most acts through *class fractions*, groups unified around a common economic and social function in the process of capital accumulation and sharing particular ideological propensities organically related to those functions' (Van der Pijl 1989a: 11). Within this framework, and at the most abstract level, a fundamental distinction (going back to Marx) can be made between two functional forms of capital, those of money capital and productive capital (Van der Pijl 1984, 1998).

Next to this functional differentiation, and at a lower level of abstraction, the process of class formation is also structured by the geographical scale on which capital operates, or what Overbeek and Van der Pijl (1993: 5) call 'the spatial coordinates of capital accumulation'. Capital only operating at a national scale will tend to have a different set of interests from capital which operates on a wider geographical scale: that is, transnationally. Historically, functional and geographical fault lines of class formation tend to overlap, as money capital has never been bound by national borders to the same extent that productive capital has. However, when, as in the current development of global capitalism, sections of industrial capital also become increasingly transnationalised, the spatial dimension becomes more relevant in understanding the structuration of class fractions and concomitant rival class strategies, particularly with regard to differences in identity, interests and outlook *within* productive capital.

Money capital versus productive capital

Historically, by and large the abstract categories of money and productive capital have had their concrete manifestations in capitalist class formation as the fractions of financial and industrial capital. However, this historical identification must be understood historically and cannot be assumed a priori. Thus, although for instance bankers, because of their position in the circulation of capital, may be predisposed to adopt a money capital perspective, in some historical cases they have tended to adopt a perspective closer to that of productive capital because of the specific *institutional* (non-economic) links tying them to industry. Conversely, nowadays, many managers of industry, I would contend (see the above discussion), increasingly adopt a money capital perspective because of the way they are tied to the interests of financial capital operating on globalising capital markets. The ideological outlook of a particular group of capitalists therefore depends on the overall balance within the current capitalist system between money and productive capital understood in functional terms, and on how that balance is constituted institutionally and politically. Nevertheless, there are, as I argue below, in the long run structural limits to which industrial capitalists in particular – as a class fraction not as individuals – can adopt a money capital perspective, as they still in the end need to *produce things*. It is in this sense that the notion of industrial capital as a *potential* class fraction with interests potentially diverging from those of financial capital plays an important part in the argument of this book. What then are the main differences between financial capital as money capital and industrial capital as productive capital?

All the commodities that are produced in the production process are eventually represented in money form. Money capital thus represents capital in its most general and abstract form, as it embodies the total process of capital accumulation (Overbeek and Van der Pijl 1993: 3). In money form, capital is abstracted from the production process, and thus comes to 'express the power of capitalist property *outside of* and *external to* any specific process of commodity production' (Harvey 1982: 284, his emphasis). The money capitalist can abstract from this concrete production process and its material, technical and social requirements, whereas the productive capitalist cannot (Van der Pijl 1995: 94). Therefore, as Van der Pijl writes, money capital not only represents 'the near equivalent of collective capital but also the ultimate "private" moment of the capitalist order' (ibid.). Therefore, in ideal-typical terms, the world view of the money capitalist tends to be organised around what Polanyi called the principle of economic liberalism, 'aiming at the establishment of a self-regulating market, . . . and using largely *laissez-faire* and free trade as its methods' (Polanyi 1957: 132).

The ideological outlook of the productive capitalist, on the other hand, tends to be oriented towards the principle of social protection, 'aiming at the conservation of man and nature as well as productive organization . . ., and using . . . instruments of intervention as its methods' (ibid.). The reason for this different perspective lies in the fact that the fate of industrial capital is more directly tied to the fate of the populations who live in the spaces where industrial capital is located, and of the states that exercise political rule within those spaces.

First, it is directly dependent on labour, whose potential resistance it has to overcome in imposing its discipline. It is in the first instance within the production process that the struggle between capital and labour is waged, and that concessions and social compromises will have to be made. The whole area of labour relations, and with that a host of questions that directly affect the overall socio-economic order, is thus primarily a concern of industrial capital. This also involves the state to the extent that the state is needed to maintain certain compromises that may result from the struggle between capital and labour. In addition to labour acquiescence, industrial capital needs a workforce that is adequately trained. Industrial capital also has a direct interest in maintaining a certain level of living standards: that is, it is also interested in workers as the consumers who constitute their market. Under certain conditions this dependence may again directly involve the state to the extent that it becomes partially responsible for stimulating and maintaining aggregate demand. Furthermore, industrial capital is dependent not only on sufficient demand but also on the ability to continuously make new investments, and to protect existing as well as to conquer new markets to sustain profit-making. In this, industrial capital is not only dependent on a favourable macro-economic framework, but may also – particularly, as I shall argue below, when its operations are concentrated within a single state or a group of states (e.g., the EU) – come to depend upon the state for subsidies and other supporting policies, or even protectionist policies against foreign competition.

In sum, then, we can say that industrial capital is more 'embedded' than financial capital, more embedded within society and its institutions, laws, regulations, etc. Industrial capital here is caught in a contradictory logic. On the one hand, it experiences this 'embeddedness' as a burden from which it seeks to escape. When trade unions get too strong, rising wages undermine profit-making, and state regulations unduly restrict the freedom of enterprise, i.e., when capitalist accumulation is directly under threat, industrial capitalists may start to advocate 'liberal' policies of deregulation. But there will always be limits to the extent to which industrial capitalists will pursue these objectives as, on the other hand, industrial capital is and remains also ultimately dependent upon these various elements of 'embeddedness'. It is thus that for industrial capital there are limits to *laissez-faire*: when these limits are reached, some elements of productive capital, often in a class coalition with elements of the labour movement, may start to rally around some concept based on the principle of social protection.

National versus transnational capital

Money capital is inherently more mobile than productive or fixed capital (Harvey 1982: ch. 9), which is tied to specific locations, with all the ramifications identified above. To the degree that these 'spatial' ties are concentrated within one state, industrial capital also becomes more dependent upon that state, even to the extent that it needs the state to protect it against foreign competition or to subsidise its investments through industrial policy, etc. At the same time, of course, states can also become dependent upon their national industries (for generating the wealth for their populations) and gain an interest in protecting and nurturing their 'national champions'.

As suggested, under certain conditions – depending on the state of the economy, the configuration of social forces, the international context, etc. – the shelter of the nation-state can also become a prison from which industrial capital seeks to escape (cf. Caporaso 1987). Historically, capital has always – with only temporary interruptions – exhibited a drive to internationalise, to conquer new markets for exports as well as new regions to source its inputs. In recent decades this internationalisation process has deepened with the rise of an increasingly *transnational* capitalism. In this transnationalisation process, industrial capital becomes less dependent on a single state and population, and with that its perspective will tend to move away from the principle of social protection and towards that of economic liberalism. A global industrial firm, producing and selling in many different countries, will naturally oppose protectionism and favour a regime of global free trade. It will also not be dependent on any single state for subsidies or other forms of 'interventionist' industrial policy, and will rather oppose these policies as interfering with the 'free market' in which global firms (vis-à-vis domestically based capital) are the stronger players.

We may now summarise our argument as follows. Abstractly, productive capital is more concerned with the principle of social protection than money capital, and national capital is more so than transnational capital. Thus, as *transnational* capital, the ideological outlook of transnational industry as a class fraction will tend to be oriented towards the principle of economic liberalism, but as *productive* capital it will not be able to fully transcend the class perspective bound up with the principle of social protection. What we therefore tend to see is an articulation of elements from both the economic liberalism and the social protection 'world views'. Which principle will be dominant within this articulation will not only (logically) depend on the degree of transnationalisation, and on whether this transnationalisation encompasses the whole global economy or is restricted to one region of that economy, but also on the broader economic, social and political context in which such an articulation takes place.

Class strategy, hegemony and concepts of control

In terms of the formation of a 'collective political consciousness' (including class consciousness), the 'moment of hegemony' is in Gramsci's theorisation that moment 'in which one becomes aware that one's own corporate interests, in their present and their future development, transcend the corporate limits of the purely economic class, and can and must become the interests of other subordinate groups too' (Gramsci 1971: 181). It is in this sense that what we here interpret as class strategy plays a role in the construction of hegemony. This role of class strategy is expressed by the notion of *comprehensive concepts of control* (see, e.g., Van der Pijl 1984, 1998; Overbeek (ed.) 1993). Comprehensive concepts of control are strategic orientations on the part of a class or a class fraction aspiring for hegemony. As such they are integrated political programmes, combining 'mutually compatible strategies in the field of labour relations, socio-economic policy and foreign policy' (Overbeek 1990: 26). Although originating in production relations – reflecting a particular historical configuration of different fractions of the capitalist class and their relations with the subordinate classes – concepts of control must be translated into state policy to become effective. Comprehensive concepts of control are hegemonic projects (Jessop 1983) aimed first at unifying the divergent views, identities and interests of the rival groups or fractions within the capitalist class, and then transcending this class or group-bound view towards a higher and more universal level. A process of ideological articulation of different partial world views into a single discourse is thus a crucial aspect of the construction of a hegemonic concept of control.

Although concepts of control operate at the level of ideas, they are not freely constructed by social actors but are rooted in the structural conditions of capitalism. This is never an unmediated process in which material conditions are simply reflected ideologically. What is proposed here, however, is that there is an 'internal relation' between the structural position and the politico-ideological outlook of any concrete group of capitalists, and that these different outlooks then tend to converge, at a more abstract level, around contending fractional viewpoints.

In formulating and disseminating concepts of control, a key role is played by what Gramsci calls 'organic intellectuals'. The use of the adjective 'organic' here is to denote that intellectuals do not form a completely autonomous social group, but on the contrary, are often 'organically' linked to a specific social class, indeed supporting that class by giving it 'homogeneity and an awareness of its own function not only in the economic but also in the social and political fields' (Gramsci

1971: 5). Defined in this way, organic intellectuals can be scholars, journalists, members of think tanks, government advisers and strategists of political parties, but they can also be far-sighted bankers or industrialists, who take up this critical role in ideology formation themselves. As Gramsci noted:

> If not all entrepreneurs, at least an *élite* amongst them must have the capacity to be an organiser of society in general, including all its complex organisms of services, right up to the state organism, because of the need to create the conditions most favourable to the expansion of their own class; . . . organising the general system of relationships external to business itself. (Gramsci 1971: 5–6)

Transnationalism and transnational class formation

State-centrism as it has dominated IR has two interrelated dimensions. First, it abstracts the state from society, presenting the state as a fully autonomous actor vis-à-vis domestic societal interests, rather than as embedded within society. Second, it takes the state as the primary actor in world politics, presenting a power-political reality to which any transnational actor will simply have to adapt (see Krasner 1995), thus failing to acknowledge that transnational actors may also constitute transnational social relations in which states are embedded and that as such they can be constitutive of state interests. In fact, states and their interests are for neorealism simply 'ontological givens' (Krasner 1995: 257), independent of either domestic or transnational society. Our transnationalist perspective challenges IR orthodoxy on both counts, claiming not only that state and society must be conceived as a relational whole (cf. Cox 1986), but also that as society increasingly overflows national borders this relation can only be understood in a perspective in which we extend our analysis beyond national state–society complexes (Van der Pijl 1998: 3).

Adopting a historical materialist perspective, the rising importance of transnational relations is argued to be first and foremost bound up with a deepening transnationalisation of the capitalist world economy. We should distinguish our approach here from both world-system theory (see, e.g., Wallerstein 1974; Chase-Dunn 1989) and the liberal perspective on transnational relations (Keohane and Nye (eds) 1972; Keohane and Nye 1977; Risse-Kappen (ed.) 1995). With regard to the former, although our approach seeks to analyse the dynamics of the global system (which at present comprises both an inter-state-system *and* a global political economy) as a whole, it rejects the structuralist holism of world-system theory, in which the global system is taken as prior to and determining of the agency of both states and classes, interpreting all relations between the parts of the system and within the parts (i.e., nation-states) as a function of the development of the system as a whole (Holman 1993: 18). In spite of its professed view that classes are crucial 'elements of the world-system' (Wallerstein 1974: 351), it appears in the end that the basic relations in this perspective are not at all social relations (as between classes) but economic–geographical ones in which core areas of the world economy exploit the periphery in what is seen as analogous to class exploitation (Overbeek

1990: 14). Thus, the agency of and struggle between social (class) forces completely disappears from the analysis.

Whereas world-system theory is thus grounded in a structuralist determinism, the liberal perspective on the other hand tends towards a rather individualist conception of transnational relations, in which transnational actors are taken as autonomous entities rather than as embedded in, and indeed constituted by, *transnational structures* (even if at the same time constitutive of those structures). Thus, while for instance in the volume edited by Risse-Kappen (1995), the authors do very usefully focus on *domestic* structures as 'intervening variables' constraining and enabling the agency of transnational actors, and determining their success in influencing state policies (see in particular the editor's introduction, Risse-Kappen 1995), their conception of structures beyond national state–society complexes remains limited to a focus on international institutions (such as international organisations, international regimes, etc.). There is thus no conceptualisation of global and transnational economic structures engendering particular forms of transnational agency. In this liberal perspective the rising significance of transnational relations within contemporary world politics remains unexplained, as are the interests of transnational actors. Going beyond this, the transnationalism advanced here seeks to historicise the emergence of transnational relations, asking how they came about, and examining how transnational actors and their identities and interests are constituted by larger-than-national structures.

As I will argue in more detail in the next chapter, the current capitalist world economy is characterised by a transnational capitalism spanning the whole globe, constituting a new phase in the development of capitalism. It is argued that concomitant with this we witness a transnationalisation of social forces, in particular of those social forces 'whose material interests and key ideas (within a broader political consciousness) are bound up with the progressive transnationalisation and liberalisation of the global political economy' (Gill 1990: 94). In this context we should note the growing *structural* power of transnational capital (see Gill and Law 1993) that we have witnessed over the past decades as liberalisation and the development of facilitating technologies has dramatically improved its cross-border mobility (Frieden 1991). This benefited first of all those firms that were already operating across several states, as transnational capital is inherently more mobile (and thus better able to exploit the greater freedom of capital movement) than its national counterparts (Gill 1990: 113). Moreover, the geographical and economic extension of the free market as inherent in the globalisation process has further enhanced transnational capital's structural power and has led some authors (see, e.g., Gill and Law 1993; cf. Keohane and Milner 1996: 18–19) to hypothesise an erosion of the decision-making autonomy of national states – and of national capital and labour – as national state–society complexes are tendentially subordinated to the exigencies of the world economy of transnational production and global finance (see also Cox 1987: 253ff.).

The structural power of transnational capital has in fact both a material and an ideological dimension. The material dimension refers to the greater exit option –

i.e., its ability to relocate across borders – on the part of transnationally mobile capital (Keohane and Milner 1996: 19). It is important to point out that this growing exit option of capital does not necessarily have to be exercised in order for transnational capital to influence state policies; the very threat of it may be sufficient. The ideological power of transnational capital must be viewed as exercised at a more collective level as class power. That is, we may conceptualise transnational capital as constitutive of a transnational class fraction that from its fractional viewpoint seeks to aspire to represent the 'general capitalist interest'.

Van der Pijl traces the origins of the process of *transnational class formation* and the resulting pattern of international relations back to eighteenth-century Britain when industrial capitalism came into being and was for the first time set on its path of global expansion (see Van der Pijl 1998: chapters 3 and 4). A new phase of expansion set in after the Second World War under the auspices of the *Pax Americana*, in which what Van der Pijl (1984) interprets as a process of *transatlantic* class formation cemented the emerging post-war world order. Recent structural transformations of the global political economy – from the economic crisis of the 1970s onwards – have both deepened and widened these historical transnational relations (Gill 1990; Cox 1987: 357–68). As Cox argues, transnational classes thus formed may be seen as playing a mediating role between production and state power at the global level (ibid.: 357).

To be sure, this process of transnational class formation so far has been restricted to the capitalist class. In contrast to capital, labour only crosses national borders in the form of migrant workers, often feeding into the accumulation strategies of transnational capital, rather than forming a potential counter-weight to it. Indeed, the movement of labour power is tied to that of the worker (labour is only mobile to the extent that workers are), whereas the mobility of capital is not tied to that of the individual capitalist (Caporaso 1996: 44). The enormous material resources of transnational capital can thus be deployed with an ease and speed that works to the structural disadvantage of labour. Moreover, whereas transnational capitalists are relatively few in number, and regularly meet and socialise with each other as a very function of their position as leaders of transnational businesses, workers are many and face a diversity of interests and identities, often tied to national institutions within which organised labour has historically achieved a certain measure of power. In sum, and in addition to its by far superior material power, the sheer organisational capacities of transnational capital by far exceed that of labour (cf. Offe and Wiesenthal 1979).

Hence, it is those people who own and/or control (sections) of transnational capital who form links across national boundaries and thus tendentially constitute themselves as a transnational class (fraction). As was argued at length in the previous section, this process is always a political one of collective consciousness formation, taking place through such organisational channels as corporate interlocks, but also through elite socialisation in all kinds of transnational forums, or what Van der Pijl (1998) identifies as 'planning groups' in which top executives of TNCs and those who have substantial property interests in transnational capital, as well as sometimes key political and opinion leaders (or globalising political elites that transnational capital seeks to co-opt), meet to exchange ideas and if possible forge a common outlook and strategy.

The process of transnational capitalist class formation is, however, still (partially) fragmented along both functional and, albeit in the present context to a decreasing extent, geographical lines. With regard to the latter, it must be emphasised that the process of transnational class formation always takes place within certain settings that may be more or less encompassing in terms of geographical scope (even if always transcending single states). In particular, we may identify (at least in the case of Europe) certain macro-regional patterns of transnational class formation within an overall global pattern of capitalist integration. Now that we have outlined the constituent elements of our neo-Gramscian transnational approach, we should return to the debate on European integration and see how this perspective can be applied to the study of European order.

Neo-Gramscian transnationalism as an approach to the study of European integration

It is now time to substantiate in more detail my claim that the *problématique* of social purpose is not adequately addressed by established approaches to European integration, by presenting a critical review of the different theoretical perspectives on European integration. At the same time, and on the basis of this critique, I will further develop neo-Gramscian transnationalism as an alternative approach. Rather than seeking to formulate a general theory in the positivist tradition, neo-Gramscian transnationalism starts with a different knowledge goal in mind. As *a critical theory of European transformation* it asks the question of how the current European order – which is both a political-institutional as well as a socio-economic order – came about; how this order differs from previous 'European orders' and what the conditions for its future transformation are.

Rival approaches to the study of European integration

Within IR, there are broadly two main theoretical traditions of studying the European Union, one emphasising its intergovernmental character and pointing at the limits to the process of supranational integration, the other taking the opposite view by stressing the supranational dynamics of European integration. The first tradition can be seen as bound up with the (neo-) realist paradigm and concentrates on inter-state bargaining, the outcomes of which are determined by the distribution of relative power among the participating states. This leads to a focus on the most powerful member states, their national agendas and their bargaining behaviour (Cornett and Caporaso 1992: 229). In the 1960s, Stanley Hoffmann was one of the first IR scholars to write about European integration from this perspective (see Hoffmann 1966), but as we shall see, it was only in the early 1990s that 'intergovernmentalism' came to dominate the debate.

The second tradition can be seen as partly related to the pluralist or liberal tradition in which the world is one of *complex interdependence* (Keohane and Nye 1977) created by the beneficial effects of the global market economy, and creating the need for international institutions and regimes to manage this interdependence. Whereas for realism the state is the primary if not the sole actor in international politics, the liberal tradition in principle allows for a conceptualisation of a plurality of state and non-state actors (Keohane and Nye (eds) 1972). The liberal perspective tends to view economic integration as driven by a logic of economic interdependence carried by states but also by non-state actors such as economic interest groups.

The first theory to be discussed below, neo-functionalism, may be regarded as one particular off-shoot of the liberal tradition, but on the other hand has tended to develop, as Andrew Moravcsik (1993a: 474 and *passim*) has noted, into a '*sui generis* theory', explaining (often in a rather ad hoc way) the development of the EU in terms of its own unique, *sui generis* characteristics, rather than in terms of a general theory (of world politics).

Neo-functionalism

At the core of neo-functionalist theory, as first of all developed by Ernst Haas (see, e.g., Haas 1968), is its claim that integration is a self-sustaining process in which it propels itself forward to its assumed federal end goal. Neo-functionalism was thus primarily concerned with institutional form rather than with socio-economic content. To the extent that the emergence of some federal structure was thought to have a specific social purpose, neo-functionalists emphasised technocratic rationality as the benevolent driving force. In fact, it was believed that the gradual evolution of a supranational political community would be in the interest of most societal and political actors and that they would thus come to support this process by 'shift[ting] their loyalties, expectations and political activities toward a new centre' (Haas 1968: 16).

Driving the alleged self-sustaining integration process was, according to the neo-functionalists, a mechanism called 'spillover', referring first of all to a functionalist logic whereby the creation of a common policy in one sector generates the need to transfer policy-making in related sectors to the supranational level as well. Apart from this 'functional' spillover, there is also 'political' spillover, whereby supranational institutions attain ever higher levels of policy making autonomy, resulting in a situation in which the supranational executive sets the political agenda and independently carries the integration process forward, leading the individual member states rather than being led by them. Neo-functionalism also stressed the role of interest groups (especially organised business and trade unions) in this self-expansive integration process. As Leon Lindberg, a student of Haas, stated: 'any analysis of the political process must give a central place to phenomena of group conflict, to the beliefs, attitudes and ideologies of groups participating in the process of policy formation' (Lindberg 1963: 9).

In the neo-functionalist perspective the dynamics of interest group action are, however, very much bound up with the functionalist logic. First of all, European interest groups were seen as coming into existence as a functional response to the requirements of the new supranational system. The new institutions generated by the integration process modify the interests, beliefs and perceptions of national socio-economic actors (Cornett and Caporaso 1992: 239) in such a way that these actors will 'tend to unite beyond their former national confines in an effort to make common policy' (Haas 1968: xxxiii) and in this way constitute an important force in support of further integration. Once formed, European interest groups continue to be subject to the expansive logic of the integration process. Rather than playing an autonomous role, then, they are seen as being instrumental to the self-expansive process of 'spillover'. The fact that both societal actors and national governments often have conflicting interests and ideologies, potentially resulting in diverging strategies for European integration, was not deemed to be important with regard to the dynamics of the integration process. Nor did neo-functionalism pay much attention to the question of power within and between groups, of why some groups are more powerful than others and may thus be more successful in setting the agenda of European integration. As James Caporaso (1998: 9) points out: 'neo-functionalism had no explanation for which groups should succeed, form coalitions, mobilise interests, have access to policy-makers and affect policy'.

Already in 1968, Haas himself acknowledged that his claim that the 'inherent logic of the functional process' could push Europe in no other way than the 'gradual' and 'automatic' expansion of 'supranationality' was no longer tenable (Haas 1968: xxii). When in the 1970s – the era of 'Europessimism' – the European Community (EC) became bogged down in what seemed to be old-fashioned interstate politics, contradicting neo-functionalist predictions, Haas even declared that theorising about regional integration was 'no longer profitable as a distinct and self-conscious intellectual pursuit' (Haas 1975: 1). With 'supranationality' apparently on the wane in EC politics, many scholars re-affirmed the primacy of the nation-state (see Hoffmann 1982; Taylor 1983), and a realist critique stressing the intergovernmentalist dynamics of integration effectively buried neo-functionalism. In the 1980s and 1990s the (realist) intergovernmentalist perspective has in fact developed into the predominant approach to the study of European integration, although, as we shall see, a modified neo-functionalism has also re-emerged.

The 'old debate' with regard to the 'new Europe': intergovernmentalism versus supranationalism

With the relaunching of the European integration process, the study of the EC also returned to the academic limelight and the two theoretical traditions of realism/intergovernmentalism and neo-functionalism staged their comeback in the guise of what Moravcsik has denoted as intergovernmental versus supranational institutionalism (Moravcsik 1991). The former stresses the role played by interstate bargaining (see Moravcsik 1991, 1993a, 1998; Garret 1992) whereas the latter emphasises the agency of supranational institutions (particularly the Commission) supported by various transnational actors (see Sandholtz and Zysman 1989; Sandholtz 1992; see also Tranholm-Mikkelsen 1991; Sandholtz and Stone Sweet (eds) 1998, cf. Keohane and Hoffmann 1991).

In the intergovernmentalist approach – first of all re-formulated by Moravcsik – the evolution of the EU is seen as having proceeded through a series of interstate bargains, which 'reflect the relative power positions', and which tend 'to converge toward the minimum common denominator of large state interests', as states eagerly protect their national sovereignty (Moravcsik 1991: 47). In the intergovernmentalist view, national sovereignty remains paramount even if strong supranational institutions are created, as this is seen not as a 'hollowing out' (Jessop 1992) of the sovereignty of the member states, but, on the contrary, as instrumental to 'their control over domestic affairs, permitting them to attain goals otherwise unachievable' (Moravcsik 1993a: 507).

Not only are transnational actors ignored in the state-centric ontology of intergovernmentalism, but social forces are excluded altogether from the analysis. The state is the central actor, and the state is seen as separate from society. Within this framework, the success of for instance the Single European Act (SEA) – which officially launched the Europe 1992 programme – is explained as the result of an intergovernmental bargain between the three dominant member states (Germany, Britain and France) made possible by a convergence of national preferences of these states (Moravcsik 1991: 48–53: cf. Garret 1992: 540–48). These national preferences are, however, not explained, but taken as given. In line with the realist tradition, state interests are exogenous. As such, this theory has no tools to conceptualise, let alone explain, any social purpose underlying European integration.

In contrast to intergovernmentalism, supranational and transnational actors are given central importance within the rival perspective of 'supranationalism'. Thus, in the account of Sandholtz and Zysman (1989), Europe 1992 is explained in terms of an 'elite bargain' struck in response to structural changes in the world economy, the bargain being initiated by a transnational elite of European big business (ibid.: 116–17) on the one hand, and the supranational Commission on the other. Although Sandholtz and Zysman criticise neo-functionalism (ibid.: 98–100), Moravcsik is right in arguing that their explanation of Europe's relaunch is in fact to a large extent compatible with neo-functionalist theory (Moravcsik 1991: 77). Although down-playing the role of spillover, Sandholtz and Zysman do stress the autonomous and policy-shaping role of the Commission as the supranational executive, interpreting its role as a form of 'policy entrepreneurship' (Sandholtz and Zysman 1989: 114–15).

Moreover, in line with the neo-functionalist theory of interest groups, the role of transnationally organised business is seen as a response not only to the international environment but also to the institutional changes (i.e., the SEA) that were already taking place, leading to a new reality that was perceived as 'irreversible' (ibid.: 116). Although Sandholtz and Zysman tentatively suggest that big business might also have played a role in putting the internal market on the agenda, they interpret its role mainly in terms of supporting pre-existing 'political initiatives' taken primarily by the Commission, which sought to relaunch the European unification process (ibid.: 113–19). After this initiative had been launched by the Commission, subsequent support from business was crucial inasmuch as business leaders lobbied hard to convince national governments of the need to implement the Commission's initiative (ibid.: 117). In this way, the role of Europe's business elite is in fact reduced to that of a 'political interest group [constituted] by community action' (ibid.): that is, serving as a powerful constituency for the Commission. As Haas put it: 'group pressure will spill over into the federal sphere and thereby add to the integrative impulse' (Haas 1968: xxxiii).

A more general problem with supranationalism is that many aspects that this approach apparently deems to be important remain rather untheorised. Thus, for example, there is no explanation of where transnational interests come from and why they would be so powerful. Transnational society is introduced as a concept but there is no *theory* of transnational society. Only the recent volume edited by Sandholtz and Stone Sweet (eds, 1998) can be said to seek to offer a *theory* on a par with intergovernmentalism, and in opposition to it (Stone Sweet and Sandholtz 1998: 3). This theory, although claiming to go beyond the intergovernmentalism versus supranationalism dichotomy, in fact presents an explicit supranationalist account (building on the legacies of Haas and Karl Deutsch) of European integration, of which the three constituent elements are 'the development of transnational society, the role of supranational organizations with meaningful autonomous capacity to pursue integrative agendas, and the focus on European rule-making to solve international policy externalities [i.e., spill-over]' (ibid.: 6). These elements combine to produce an 'inherently expansionary process' (ibid.: 25), in which – through lock-in effects and path-dependence (see also Pierson 1998) – national governments become embedded in 'integration processes, that is, in terms of the development of transnational society and its system of governance' (Stone Sweet and Sandholtz 1998: 25).

The core of this theory is the notion that integration is driven by the rise of cross-border transactions which will 'increase the perceived need for European-level rules, coordination and regulation' (ibid.: 11; see also Stone Sweet and Caporaso 1998). Although in full agreement (contra intergovernmentalism) with this theory's emphasis on the embeddedness in transnational society, the theoretical perspective adopted in this study offers a different and, I would contend, a more *political* conceptualisation of transnational society, focusing on the formation of transnational social forces, rather than on the quantitative phenomenon of cross-border movements as in the transaction approach of Stone Sweet and Sandholtz. The supranationalist theory of European integration remains one of liberal institutionalism in which there are, on the one hand, economic agents conceived in rationalist and individualist terms and, on the other hand, formal institutions (primarily supranational institutions) responding to the needs of those actors but also seen as constituting 'transnational society' (Stone Sweet and Sandholtz 1998: 11). There is moreover hardly any attention to the role played by global forces and processes in the constitution of this thinly conceived transnational society, and the EU thus remains a self-contained entity. From this basis, in my view, this theory cannot really adequately address the *problématique* of social purpose. Although it is stated that the fundamental role played by 'private transactors' accounts for the neoliberal content of the integration process, this is almost understood deterministically and in my view misses the way in which European integration is driven by an open-ended *political* struggle in which different 'private transactors' construct and advance different interests and related projects for European order. As this study intends to show, even within capital there were and are important divisions, and the outcome in terms of shaping the socio-economic content has been a fundamentally political struggle, which moreover has to be located in the context of a *global* restructuring process of capital. In the end, like earlier supranationalist accounts, this theory remains entirely focused on institutional form: 'Our dependent variable remains mode of governance' (ibid.: 5).

Liberal intergovernmentalism

Seeking to go beyond both supranationalism and his own earlier formulation of intergovernmentalism, Moravcsik's *liberal intergovernmentalism* opens the black box of realism's unitary state with the explicit aim to explain 'variation in substantive, as well, as in institutional outcomes' (Moravcsik 1993a: 479). Central to this approach is indeed the role of *state–society relations* in the formation of national preferences (Moravcsik 1993a, 1993b, 1998; see also Moravcsik 1991: 48, 68–74). Moravcsik conceptualises the integration process as proceeding in three stages. First, national preferences are formed at the domestic level by the aggregation of interests formulated by societal actors. In the second stage, the member states of the EU bring their thus formed national preferences to the European bargaining table, and in a third stage a certain choice is made for a particular institutional design: the pooling of sovereignty in international institutions (Moravcsik 1998: 5–10, 23–76). These stages do not interact but are discrete: in particular, a sharp line is drawn between the 'domestic game' where states (or rather national governments) aggregate interests, and the 'international game' where states bargain on the basis of their thus formed preferences (Moravcsik 1993b). Although Moravcsik's explanations of the final two stages are firmly grounded in neo-realist state-centrism – with the critical (independent) variables being respectively 'the relative power of nation-states' (ibid.: 7) and 'efforts by governments to constrain and control one another' (ibid.: 9) – his focus on state–society relations with regard to the first stage (or the 'domestic sources' of national preferences) signifies an important step beyond neo-realist orthodoxy. In his theory, the divergence of interests among societal actors involved in the process of national preference formation may very well lead to a variation in outcomes of European integration with regard to its socio-economic content, depending upon which domestic groups are more successful in setting the agenda in the respective states. Moravcsik has thus sought to transcend the narrow *problématique* of conventional integration theory by bringing (domestic) society and the 'distributional conflicts' of domestic politics (Moravcsik 1993a: 479) back into the analysis.

Underlying Moravcsik's theory, however, is what he calls a liberal theory of state–society relations in which the units of society are 'private individuals and voluntary associations with autonomous interests' (Moravcsik 1993a: 483), the behaviour of which is assumed to be determined by a rational choice logic of utility maximisation. Moreover, in his focus on interest groups, he does not go beyond an analysis of the relative strengths and weaknesses of what he calls 'producer groups', which, he argues, the political system tends to favour over 'consumers, tax-payers, third-country producers and also potential future producers' (Moravcsik 1998: 36). That 'producer interests' are also favoured over those of workers is a point that Moravcsik does not seem particularly interested in, as indeed organised labour is mostly subsumed under the producer category (Moravcsik 1993a: 488). There is no interest in the *balance* of social forces and how this might be changing over time.

Liberal intergovernmentalism is hampered, then, by a rather poor notion of state–society relations, very much modelled on that of neo-classical economics. Society here is not much more than an aggregation of individuals and interest groups engaging in continuous cost–benefit analysis. In the words of two sociologists who have criticised the current 'theoretical retreat from society' found within the social sciences, society in such a conception tends to be reduced towards a mere 'marketplace', i.e., towards the 'instrumental, rational individual, whose choices in myriad exchanges are seen as the primary cause of societal arrangements' (Friedland and Alford 1991: 232). There is no concept here of how historically constructed *social relations* embed these actors and shape their identity and interests. Society is thus emptied of most of its historically produced content. If we want to understand the social purpose underpinning European integration, such an atomistic conception of society is, I would contend, not very helpful.[7] Social purpose is more than an aggregation of individual preferences, but must rather be seen as located (as Ruggie also emphasised) at the macro-structural level, as a structure that, although constituted through human agency, cannot be reduced to it; simply cannot be explained by adding up the actions of 'private individuals and voluntary associations'.

Within a liberal intergovernmentalist framework, a proper understanding of the changing social purpose underlying European order is moreover constrained by the fact that this theory remains very state-centric, to the extent that states remain the only important actors within world and European politics; indeed for Moravcsik (1998: 18) 'European integration can be best explained as a series of rational choices made by national leaders'.[8] Not only are supranational institutions such as the Commission denied significant status as policy-making actors in European integration, but also the theory, as inherent in its conceptualisation of European integration as taking place in discrete stages, does not grant any significance to the role of transnational coalitions in the 'European game'. Transnational society does not really enter into the analysis of national preference formation. Although Moravcsik acknowledges the 'transnational embeddedness' of both governments and domestic groups (1993a: 483), in practice all that is incorporated into the analysis is how 'international constraints' (ibid.) created by economic interdependence (ibid.: 485–86) affect the rational calculations of both societal and governmental actors. Moreover, transnational forces tend to be treated (if at all) as something external to national state–society complexes, whereas by definition they are internal as well. Thus, in Moravcsik's theory an understanding of domestic politics as determining national preferences is 'a precondition to an analysis of the *strategic interaction among states*' (Moravcsik 1993a: 481, my emphasis). In this way, 'social forces' are brought into the analysis but remain locked within national state–civil society configurations. States remain the gatekeepers and the only point of access for private actors seeking to influence European integration.

Beyond the old debate: analysing the European polity

Recently, the study of European integration has moved beyond the seemingly endless debate on whether the process of European integration is essentially controlled by still sovereign nation-states, and thus is largely limited to intergovernmental co-operation, or whether it is driven by a functionalist logic (as expressed in the agency of supranational institutions and transnational actors) moving it beyond the nation-state. This move has been informed by the notion that neo-functionalists at least have been right to the extent that European integration really has fundamentally transformed European politics, and that the EU constitutes a novel polity, the nature and effects of which intergovernmentalism cannot understand. This has subsequently sparked different research strategies: from various attempts to study EU political and policy processes as taking place within a system of *multi-level* governance (a term coined by Marks 1993) to a call to move away from IR theory altogether and subsume the study of the EU rather under the discipline of comparative politics (Hix 1994). These new research agendas in my view signify an important step beyond the 'old debates' in understanding the socio-economic content of the integration process and its underlying politics. Nevertheless, I also argue that the various studies on European *governance* are often rather under-theorised and/or remain within a liberal framework of 'interest group politics'.

Taking the EU as an already existing political system, an increasing number of scholars have begun to explore the 'nature of the beast' (Risse-Kappen 1996), coming to the shared conclusion that we should abandon what is argued to be a false dichotomy of intergovernmentalist and supranationalist ideal-types. Thus, the European integration process must not be regarded as being about the replacement of the national states by a federal 'superstate', but rather as entailing what Philippe Schmitter has called the emergence of 'a novel form of political domination' (Schmitter 1991). As military insecurity is no longer the 'overriding motive/excuse for the exercise of political authority' (ibid.: 12), Schmitter identifies this polity as 'Post-Hobbesian' and emphasises the ambiguity of sovereignty within that system, as he argues that within it:

> there is no single identifiable sovereign – just a multitude of authorities at different levels of aggregation, territorial or functional, with ambiguous or shared compétences at the head of overlapping and diverse organisational hierarchies . . . In all cases it becomes increasingly difficult to differentiate between public and private institutions, the State and Civil Society. (Schmitter 1991: 13)

In a similar vein, Ruggie has noted that whereas in the modern state-system political rule (sovereignty) 'has differentiated its subject collectively into territorially defined, fixed and mutually exclusive enclaves of legitimate dominion' (Ruggie 1993: 151), contemporary transformative processes (induced *inter alia* by globalisation) tend to lead to an 'unbundling of territoriality' (ibid.: 165). Ruggie sees this process as epitomised by the present EU, which could be considered as 'the first truly postmodern political form' (ibid.: 140; see also Anderson and Goodman 1995; Caporaso 1996). Thus, in the EU political rule is no longer tied to fixed and mutually exclusive territories, rather it emerges both above (the supranational level) and below (the empowerment of local and regional government) the existing national systems, without, however, completely dissolving those systems to either of those two new levels of rule.

The latter insight has in the 1990s sparked a whole literature (see especially Marks, Hooghe and Blank 1996; cf. Hix 1998) on what is now called multi-level governance. This literature does not form a coherent research programme, but authors do share the notion that the EU has moved far beyond mere intergovernmental co-operation and that we may study it as a unique system of governance. It is unique because of the interaction between different levels (from regional authorities to the national state to European institutions) which cannot always be conceptualised as a hierarchy but rather overlap and partly conflict with each other. Thus Marks, Hooghe and Blank (1996), for instance, on the one hand (contra neo-functionalism) do not deny the continuing relevance or indeed pre-eminence of states in many respects, but take issue with the core assumption of liberal intergovernmentalism that the state 'monopolizes European policy-making' as supranational institutions also 'have independent influence' (ibid.: 346). Moreover, they argue that as private actors do not just operate in discrete national arenas but also in the supranational arena, 'States no longer serve as the exclusive nexus between domestic and international relations' (ibid.: 372).

Studying European governance, rather than just the process of European integration, implies taking an interest in the role of broader political struggles within the EU, the role of interest groups and processes of public policy making. Although my interest in the changing socio-economic content of the integration project is rather compatible with these concerns, the theoretical question that needs to be answered is how we conceptualise and explain these various political processes. Here, as I suggested, the theoretical underpinnings of most of this governance literature remain rather unspecified. Thus, Hooghe and Marks (1999), for example, similar to my analysis (see also Van Apeldoorn 1996, 1999, 2000; Rhodes and Van Apeldoorn 1997), seek to understand the process of European integration during the 1980s and 1990s in terms of different projects that are formed on both the intergovernmental versus supranational and the traditional left–right axis. There is, however, not much to be found in Hooghe and Marks' analysis in terms of an explanation of the origins of these projects, nor of the evolving political and ideological struggles and the outcome of these struggles (in terms of the emergent social purpose). I contend that the approach presented here does offer the potential of such explanations, and seeks to substantiate this claim in the empirical part of this book.

Most recently, the 'constructivist turn' in IR (Checkel 1998) is now also finding its application to the study of EU governance (Christiansen, Jørgensen and Wiener (eds) 1999), with both theoretically and empirically valuable results. These constructivists equally start from the notion that the EU is already some kind of polity, the study of which thus requires tools beyond those of IR theory narrowly conceived. Their research agenda, however, is much more explicitly oriented to understanding the nature of the broader European project, and in particular its transformative effects on identities and behaviour of states and social actors (Christiansen, Jørgensen and Wiener 1999: 529).[9] It is, however, too early to speak of an emergent constructivist school, as those calling themselves constructivists (within the field of EU studies) cover still a wide diversity of epistemological, as well as to an extent ontological, positions (see Smith 1999, cf. Moravcsik 1999). It is true, however, that as Risse and Wiener (1999: 776) point out, all of these scholars share a commitment to some kind of anti-individualist ontology. In this respect, then, the constructivist approach adopted here is in full agreement. Indeed, I would fully subscribe to Risse and Wiener's position – basing themselves on an argument of Offe and Wiesenthal (1979) – who in their defence of social constructivism state that:

> the shared experience and social structure of a society contribute to whether, and if so how, actors *know* their interests. As Offe and Wiesentahl point out, the rationale of collective actors differs crucially. The difference is, however, not simply based on given interests. Instead, it changes according to experience, i.e. position in relation to other actors and in relation to larger structures. (Risse and Wiener 1999: 780)

The question, however, remains which 'larger structures' we speak about – structures that structure the practices of actors, including discursive practices, and thus the construction of their interests – and about which social relations. Here, I would claim, this chapter has advanced a particular approach, one grounded in (Gramscian) historical materialism, that provides us with an answer to these fundamental theoretical questions (and an answer that differs from the ones given by, for instance, liberal or idealist constructivism, adherents of which we also find among constructivist students of European governance).

Diverging from the above approaches, others, in particular Simon Hix (1994, 1999), have advocated a much more radical departure from (the concerns) IR theory, claiming that the EU could be studied just like any national polity: that is, with the concepts and tools of comparative politics. According to Hix, approaches that are grounded in IR discourse see 'political conflict' within the EU as primarily revolving:

> along a single dimension, where actors (be they nation-states in the Realist approach, or interest groups in the Pluralist approach) either support or oppose further supranational integration. As the 'political' nature of the EC

> develops, however, there is also a conflict over questions of allocation and distribution of resources. On these *socio-economic issues*, political competition is along a fundamentally different dimension. (Hix 1994: 1–2, my emphasis)

Like the other approaches discussed so far, however, Hix's argument remains confined to a rather limited liberal/pluralist conception of state–society relations, which thus in my view cannot account for the underlying social power relations that emanate from the structures of capitalism. Moreover, contrary to Hix's argument, I would argue that, as suggested before, the two dimensions Hix distinguishes are often fundamentally intertwined. The political struggle over the question of how and to what extent European integration should continue (deepening or widening, supranationalism or intergovernmentalism, etc.) is not just a struggle between nation-states caught up in the logic of, on the one hand, wanting to protect their sovereignty and, on the other hand, wanting to profit from the economic and security benefits that integration offers, but is also a struggle between opposing transnational social forces about 'who gets what, how and when', and hence is about socio-economic issues. Indeed inasmuch as these transnational forces also operate through the level of the nation-state, by shaping and reshaping their interests and identities, the two forms of political struggle cannot be really separated.

Even if narrowly defined ('more or less integration'), the European integration process has a clear 'socio-economic dimension'. One could illustrate this by arguing that for instance the minimalist strategy vis-à-vis Europe as pursued by the last British Conservative government in fact amounted to an ideological vision of the EU as a mere free-trade area in which national sovereignty is formally kept intact, but de facto handed over to the global market; a vision of Europe in which transnational capital can reign freely and opposing forces such as labour lack the institutional power to form any effective counterweight. Seen in this light, the choice for a more intergovernmentalist Europe becomes in fact inextricably bound up with issues of social power. Conversely, a strengthening of the supranational dimension of European policy making might favour the building of a 'Social Europe' (as is implied by the example above), but institutional deepening is only a necessary condition and the degree to which a 'Social Europe' is actually realised also depends upon the balance of social (class) forces within Europe. And here too, it is clearly about a *process*, which cannot be really understood if an a-historical and static picture is taken.

Transnational social forces in the struggle over European order

In its constructivist ontology, neo-Gramscian transnationalism differs from both intergovernmentalism and the neo-functionalist tradition. In the latter, the explanation of European integration tends towards determinism as it stresses the self-sustaining logic of functionalist spillover, whereas for instance Moravcsik's liberal intergovernmentalism is premised upon an individualist ontology in which there is no sensitivity to the structural power relations inherent in the social relations of production.

Historical materialism provides us with a different understanding of state–society relations. It brings society back into the analysis as capitalist society, a society that is not just a collection of individuals seeking to aggregate their rational interests but one that is structured *inter alia*, and to a significant degree, by the social relations of production. From this perspective it can be argued that the analysis of the European integration process also has to be grounded in an analysis of capitalism. However, inasmuch as the reproduction of capitalism necessarily presupposes agency, we are thus also led to the role of social forces – and their struggles – within the European integration process. In asking the question of how the current European order came about, neo-Gramscian transnationalism suggests that the answer must be found in the analysis of the social forces that have been involved in its making. As the neo-Gramscian approach adopted here extends our analysis of the dynamics of capitalist society to the realm of ideas and of ideology, it focuses on the strategic action and struggles of social forces as a key constitutive factor. As I have argued above, these social forces struggles increasingly take place within a transnational setting. The neo-Gramscian transnationalist approach, then, conceptualises the EU as a site of struggle for transnational social forces.

Let us examine how our 'transnationalism' contrasts with both intergovernmentalism and supranationalism, and indeed can help us to transcend the false dichotomy between the two (a move prefigured by the governance literature discussed above). The transnational perspective of course contrasts most sharply with the state-centric focus of the dominant intergovernmentalist approach. It goes beyond the attempt of Moravcsik's *liberal intergovernmentalism* to open the black box of realism's unitary state by arguing that as soon as you open the black boxes you will find that many of the so-called domestic social and political forces in fact operate within a transnational setting. This has at least two implications with regard to the understanding of European integration. First, we can no longer treat national states and their interests solely in relation to the supposedly domestic society that they contain, as society now flows across national borders, with national states thus becoming embedded in a structure of transnational social relations. We must thus place the analysis of national preference formation – which is the focus of liberal intergovernmentalism – within a transnational context. Second, however, transnationalisation also makes the notion of the state as the sole, or even primary, actor outside the domestic arena obsolete. Thus within the European integration process, for instance, transnational capital (and its organisations) is in my view an important political actor in its own right. The role of such transnational coalitions remains anathema to intergovernmentalism. In contrast, our transnationalist approach urges us to move *from domestic to transnational politics* in explaining the outcomes of European integration.

Such a focus on the transnational dynamics of the European integration process also moves beyond the supranationalist alternative to intergovernmentalism. Here, transnational society tends to disappear out of sight inasmuch as it is subsumed under the functionalist logic of political spillover. Supranationalism and intergovernmentalism in fact both commit a similar reductionist fallacy by according priority either to the functionalist logic driven by European institutions, or to the power politics of sovereign nation-states, explaining the behaviour of the former largely in terms of the latter, or vice versa. A transnational perspective focusing on the role of transnational social forces transcends the intergovernmentalism versus supranationalism dichotomy by emphasising how, at both levels, transnational actors – and the structural relations they constitute – shape the integration process in fundamental ways, in particular when it comes to defining its socio-economic content. The transnational by definition cuts across all the different levels of policy making in the emerging Euro-polity, and is a constituting force at all these levels. Just as transnationalism does not allow for a neat separation of domestic and international politics, nor does it allow for a clear opposition between intergovernmental and supranational dynamics of European integration.

Although the EU is not a replication of the national state at the supranational level (not even in embryonic form), it does, as emphasised by the multi-level governance literature, represent a political form beyond and above that of the national state. Thus Caporaso has recently suggested that, although not a state in the classic (nation-state) sense, the EU can be usefully analysed as an *international state*, if by state we mean an 'ongoing structure of political authority and governance' (Caporaso 1996: 33). To the extent that the EU, then, represents such an international or transnational state-like structure, we might also ask the question of which configuration of social forces underpins that structure and thus supports and legitimises its rule. Indeed, if with Caporaso (ibid.), borrowing from Cox (1986, 1987) we ask the question of what *form of state* the EU represents, we should analyse state–society relations at the European level and examine which social groups or classes (or class fractions) are dominant, or indeed hegemonic, within European transnational society and how these dominant groups may or may not configure into a historic bloc upon which a hegemonic European order may rest (cf. Cox 1987: 105).

From a historical materialist perspective I would suggest that here we should in particular examine the relation between opposing social (class) forces as emanating from the social relations of production, both the power relations between capital and labour, and the power relations between different fractions of capital. In this study I seek to advance the claim that the growing structural power of transnational capital also manifests itself within the European arena, and that this power also takes the form of political and ideological agency on the part of an emergent European transnational capitalist class. Although, as I will argue in the next section, this transnational capitalist class does not necessarily form a single unified subject, its material and ideological power does contrast starkly with that of organised labour, which remains pertinently weak at the European level (see, e.g., Streeck and Schmitter 1991; Traxler and Schmitter 1995: 206–07; Streeck 1993; cf. Visser and Ebbinghaus 1992). Supranationally, organised labour continues to be hampered by a strong divergence in national economic interests between the different national trade unions, an economic nationalism which is 'reinforced by an institutional nationalism [reflecting] the investments of individuals and organizations in existing, inevitably national institutional structures' (Streeck 1993: 26).

Transnational class strategy and European integration

This study conceptualises the EU as a political arena in which an emergent transnational capitalist class – consisting of the top managers and owners of Europe's largest TNCs – takes the European region as its primary frame of reference and organises itself to influence the (socio-economic) governance of that region. Analysing the European dimension of this process of transnational class formation, Holman and Van der Pijl (1992: 2) speak of a 'European bourgeoisie' consisting of 'an ensemble of concrete bourgeois groups adopting a European frame of reference from which to approach the further unification towards a global pattern'. Within this European capitalist class we may still distinguish different tendencies, linked, as I will argue below, in particular to the degree of transnationalisation and globalisation.

Fractionation of European capital

Refining our earlier analytical framework on class fractions, I outline below what we may regard as three different, but partially overlapping, structural factors that shape the ideological and strategic orientation of different individual capitalist groups within Europe's emerging transnational capitalist class. In chapter 2, and beyond, I will then argue how within the context of the process of European class formation as it evolved in the 1980s, two main rival 'fractions' within an emergent European transnational capitalist elite crystallised around these three factors. The 'fractions' that I will distinguish here are not meant as categories valid for the analysis of capitalism in its historical totality. Rather, they are meant to identify concrete groups within the European bourgeoisie as the process of transnational class formation within the European region evolved in the 1980s.

A first and, I will argue, most critical factor relates to what earlier on was identified as one of the two principal determinations within the process of capitalist class formation, that of the geographical scale of capital. With regard to the latter I distinguish *transnationalisation as globalisation* and *transnationalisation as regionalisation*. Thus, although a firm that has more than 50 per cent of its production located outside the home country but all *within* Europe can rightly be called a transnational company, it does not seem to be justified to call it a *global* company. We might thus distinguish between 'European' TNCs in the sense of firms whose transnationalisation is largely limited to the European region, and truly global TNCs that are active in several regions of the world economy.

A second factor is formed by the sectoral dimension, different sectors having different specific interests. This factor is linked to the first inasmuch as some sectors are clearly more globalised than others. Moreover, sectors differ in their international competitiveness and thus in their vulnerability vis-à-vis global competition. As we shall see in later chapters, some sectors of European industry were highly exposed to the new competition from Japan, a fact which largely accounts for the protectionism of these sectors. However, inasmuch as firms in those sectors also increasingly come to operate on a more global scale, their exposure to import-competition will decrease, and the difference in sectoral outlooks will become less pronounced.

Third, at the 'superstructural' level, we find the institutional context in which capital operates, referring in particular to the relative degree of embeddedness into specific national socio-political structures, including aspects of national (political) culture (cf. Sally 1994). Thus, French big business, for instance, has traditionally been close to the French state and has operated within a context of a national model of capitalism in which protectionism and a state-led industrial strategy were used as instruments to promote so-called national champions (see also chapter 3). In contrast, the British bourgeoisie has always operated in the context of a very internationalised economy in which the state's role vis-à-vis industry was normally one of *laissez-faire*. These different national institutional contexts, then, can be argued to be another factor in shaping the ideological outlook of capitalist elites from these countries, even if these elites are also integrated in a process of transnational class formation. Here, it is important to emphasise that the transnationalisation of capital and the concomitant emergence of a transnational class identity, and hence the transcendence of national lines of cleavage, is indeed a gradual process.

This final factor must be seen not so much as an 'intervening variable' in the process of capitalist class formation, but rather as an integral part of how that process has historically taken shape within the historical trajectories of national state–society complexes. Thus, I would argue, the differences in outlook between for instance French and British capitalists within an emerging transnational capitalist elite can be partly related to the fact that British capital was set on a course of internationalisation, and later globalisation, at a much earlier stage than French capital.[10] As, with the transnationalisation of capital, elements of the national bourgeoisie emancipate themselves from these national contexts (becoming less embedded within any particular national society), these contexts may be hypothesised to gradually lose their significance in shaping the ideological outlook of these transnationalising capitalist elites. To sum up, these different factors are here argued to shape the political and ideological outlook of different groups within the European capitalist class. Inasmuch, however, as the first factor partly conditions the relative weight of the latter two, differences in sectoral and national outlooks are argued to be gradually transcended as the processes of globalisation and transnationalisation progress.

Transnational class agency and European governance

In the emergent *transnational and multi-level* state–society complex of the EU we may, I suggest, start to discern the contours of a transnational power bloc, at the apex of which we find a transnational capitalist class elite allying with the more outward-looking elements of 'EU government', the European Commission in particular. As the case of the ERT will show, parallel to the relaunching of the integration process, the mid-1980s and 1990s witnessed the development of what can be described as a 'partnership' between big business and the Commission.

The strategic alliance between the corporate executives of Europe's leading TNCs and the political executives of the Commission that will transpire from our analysis of the ERT can be seen as indicative of the growing power of transnational capital and is further facilitated both by the position of the Commission within the overall structure of EU governance as well as by the nature of the EU polity in general. With regard to the first point, we may note in the first place the relatively modest size of the EU bureaucracy, which makes it rather dependent on outside 'expert advice' and hence relatively open to those 'outside experts' in order to help it with its policy-initiating role (Mazey and Richardson 1993a: 10). Second, the fact that, although the Commission has the right of initiative (and can thus to an important degree shape the EU agenda), its policy making is dependent upon the decision-making power of the Council of Ministers, which means that it is often crucial for the Commission to enlist the support of powerful social groups. This applies in particular in the case of the development of new grand integration projects that might initially meet the strong resistance of particular member states.

With regard to the second point, the undemocratic nature of the EU polity in general – including its underdeveloped system of political parties and lack of other institutions, strong organised interests for instance, that can generate not just legitimacy but indeed also the demand for legitimacy and (democratic) accountability – makes it easier for the Commission to rely rather exclusively on 'business advice' without needing to legitimate this. Indeed, one could argue that the 'democratic deficit' of the EU on the one hand, and the increasing dominance of social forces bound up with (global) transnational capital and its largely neo-liberal project on the other, are two sides of the same coin, as the former can be seen as reflecting a wider phenomenon that Gill calls the 'new constitutionalism', which:

> is the politico-legal dimension of the wider discourse of disciplinary neo-liberalism [and] seeks to separate economic policies from broad political accountability in order to make governments more responsive to the discipline of market forces and correspondingly less responsive to popular-democratic forces and processes. (Gill 1998: 5)

Although these aspects of the emerging new European order thus facilitate the political role played by transnational capital, this study claims that transnational capital, through the medium of class agency, has at the same time helped to shape this new neo-liberal European order. As argued in the introduction, this role of transnational class agency mediates between global and European change. Thus in particular the deepening of globalisation and the rise of transnational capitalism provide us with an important structural context from within which we have to understand the changing strategic and ideological orientation within Europe's emergent capitalist class, and thus its changing role in the transnational struggle over European order. It is to this changing global context that I will turn in the next chapter, arguing that the changing political economy of European integration is intrinsically bound up with the process of global capitalist restructuring.

2 Global restructuring, transnational capitalism and rival projects for European order

This chapter builds a bridge towards the empirical analysis presented in chapters 3 to 5 by analysing the structural changes that have taken place within the global political economy over the last two decades, and by placing the European political economy within that context. The chapter is divided into two main parts. First, I will deal with some key aspects of the process of global restructuring that unfolded in the wake of the world economic crisis of the 1970s, a process in which context we have to place both the formation and agency of a European transnational capitalist class as well as the ensuing transnational struggle over the relaunching of the European integration.

The second part will present an interpretation of the changing political economy of European integration, setting the scene for chapters 4 and 5. It was within the context of the world economic crisis, and the ensuing global restructuring processes, that the post-war European socio-economic order – the mixed economies and (Keynesian) welfare states of western Europe – also entered into a crisis. With this crisis of European capitalism, in conjunction with the challenges emanating from the changing global environment, the structural conditions were put in place for a restructuring of the European political economy. Different actors, however, formulated different strategies in response to these changing structural conditions and it is hence that we can interpret the restructuring following the crisis of European capitalism as the outcome of a struggle between contending responses. As Gourevitch (1986) argues, there is no objectively best solution to an economic crisis, but always a range of policy options to choose from, and which options are chosen is always an outcome of political struggle.

It is thus that in the wake of the 'European crisis' a struggle ensued over Europe's socio-economic order, a struggle over the future of the mixed economy, of the welfare state, of the post-war institutions of the labour market, of European industry and of its global competitiveness, but also – as, at the elite level, national responses gave way to European responses – a struggle over the future direction and socio-economic content of the European integration process. It is this latter struggle – between what I argue to be three rival projects for European integration: neo-liberalism, neo-mercantilism and 'supranational social democracy' – that forms the broader narrative of this study, and it is in this context that I will place my analysis of the evolving (class) strategy of Europe's emerging transnational capitalist elite.

Global structural change

Two closely interrelated aspects of recent global social change may be identified. The first aspect is the crisis at the world economy (and its supporting social and political structures) unfolding in the 1970s, followed by a (neo-liberal) restructuring process in the 1980s and beyond. The second aspect is that of economic globalisation and the concomitant rise of transnational capital. These aspects are interrelated inasmuch as the world economic crisis provoked capital to look increasingly beyond national borders in order to restore profit levels, whereas at the same time the resulting rise in global competition intensified the perceived need for economic restructuring as well as a restructuring of the socio-economic and political institutions of the post-war capitalist order.

The post-war capitalist order

After a relatively long period of sustained economic growth during the post-war era, the global capitalist system again entered a period of protracted crisis at the beginning of the 1970s. In quite an unprecedented combination of economic ills, output stagnated, inflation soared, and, after decades of almost full employment in most developed capitalist countries, unemployment rose dramatically. Rather than a mere cyclical economic downturn, these phenomena represented a deep structural crisis of global capitalism, or, in Gramscian terms, an 'organic crisis': a crisis of hegemony at the interacting levels of the social relations of production, state–society relations and world order (Cox 1987). As such, it involved a breakdown of the post-war order and concomitant international regime (consisting of common international institutions, rules and norms) of what Ruggie called 'embedded liberalism' (Ruggie 1982).

As Van der Pijl (1984) has argued, the particular socio-economic order or *form of state* (Cox 1987) underpinning this international post-war order was predicated upon a specific concept of control that he labelled 'corporate liberalism', which expresses a notion similar to that of embedded liberalism but explained from the vantage point of class hegemony. Corporate liberalism as a form of class rule synthesises the two ideal-typical orientations of money and (domestic) productive capital respectively, the former premised on the principle of economic liberalism and the latter on the principle of social protection. This synthesis, however, entailed not only an articulation of the interests of these two ideal-typical capital fractions, but also a class compromise between capital and labour as the newly emerging regime of industrial accumulation brought with it a further incorporation of the working class. We can distinguish both a domestic and an international dimension of this 'double compromise'. Both dimensions were closely intertwined through the transnational relations established by American hegemony and the outward expansion of US capital. This internationalisation of US capitalism, then, can also be interpreted in terms of a new outward-looking strategy of the (elite) of the American capitalist class, forging links with its counterpart in Europe (Van der Pijl 1984). Let us now examine these different dimensions in more detail.

The corporate–liberal concept of control originated in the United States with what Van der Pijl calls the 'New Deal synthesis' (see Van der Pijl 1984: chapter 4), which was a response to the mobilisation of social forces calling for social protection (the Polanyian double movement) in the wake of the 1930s depression, and was predicated upon the rise of mass-producing industrial capital in the preceding decades, heralding the so-called Fordist production regime. With the rise of Fordism the balance of hegemonic power within the capitalist class gravitated back towards industrial capital after *haute finance* had dominated the world economy in the preceding era (see Polanyi 1957: 192–200). The interests of the new Fordist industries were articulated with that of 'reformed' international bank capital (Van der Pijl 1984: 93), and it was in this rise of 'finance capital' that the corporate–liberal synthesis found part of its material basis.

At the level of production methods, the Fordist growth model was based on the mass production of standardised goods. At the macro-economic level, Fordist growth was predicated upon the coupling of rising productivity (resulting from the new techniques of mass production) with rising wages, enabling the Fordist workers to buy the new products they were making, hence articulating mass production with mass consumption. At the level of the state, this articulation came to be supported by Keynesian macro-economic (demand) management, which – *inter alia* through rising expenditures for a growing welfare state – kept the Fordist cycle of increasing output going. Increasing state expenditures for a growing welfare state were also part of the state's role in keeping up demand. Moreover, various forms of corporatist co-ordination of wage bargaining ensured that wage rises kept pace with (but did not outpace) productivity growth, in this way helping to match the output of goods with final demand (Lipietz 1982: 35).

Although the class compromise that came to underpin Fordism was also the result of concrete social struggles on the part of organised labour, forcing capital to make significant concessions, Fordism – through higher wages and the new possibilities of mass consumption for a large part of the working population – also provided a material basis for a coalescence of the class interests of industrial capital and the labour it employed. In this context, labour became increasingly unionised and trade unions came to play a legitimate role in the civil societies of all industrialised nations. It is thus that a new historic bloc was forged containing both a coalition of bank capital with the new Fordist industries (with the latter being the dominant fraction), and an alliance of Fordist capital with organised labour. The Fordist model and its concomitant configuration of social forces was 'extrapolated to the international level' (Van der Pijl 1984: 94) when, with the help of the Marshall plan, war-torn European industry was converted to Fordism and successfully integrated into a US-dominated Atlantic economy. In what was very much a project of unfolding American hegemony (Rupert 1995), the thus emerging system of 'Atlantic Fordism' (Holman 1996) fostered the expansion and internationalisation of US capital and thus locked the productivist outlook of Fordist industry into an internationalist perspective.

This international dimension of the embedded liberalism compromise was institutionalised in a multilateral framework that allowed both for a resurgence (after the economic nationalism of the inter-war years) of the internationalisation of capital, *and* for the protection of national welfare states from severe external shocks, allowing national states a certain degree of national autonomy so that the domestic class compromise could be sustained. Thus, the international monetary regime of Brettton Woods served to rein in the freedom of financial capital (Helleiner 1993). The international trade regime that was set up under the General Agreement on Tariffs and Trade (GATT) aimed, on the one hand, at the gradual abolition of barriers to trade, but, on the other hand, also allowed for several exceptions, such as the temporary introduction of quantitative restrictions for countries with 'payment difficulties that resulted from domestic policies to secure full employment' (Ruggie 1982: 397). Liberal internationalism was thus combined with domestic embeddedness.

Global restructuring

The double compromise of embedded liberalism was unravelled as a result of the double process of capitalist crisis and economic globalisation. In fact, it could be argued that embedded liberalism carried to a large extent the seeds of its own destruction. First, the Fordist growth model appeared to have exhausted its potential when at the end of the 1960s productivity growth (the motor of the Fordist growth model) started to decline (Mazier 1982), and Fordist production methods appeared to be increasingly rigid and costly (see Van Tulder and Junne 1988: 2).

Second, the Keynesian welfare state became a victim of its own success inasmuch as the near full employment it helped to produce enhanced the power of organised labour to such an extent that the class balance upon which this state form rested was fundamentally disrupted (Boltho 1982: 24). When productivity growth slowed down, it was the entrenched power of labour that led to a situation in which wages rose faster than productivity, resulting in a sharp fall of profits (Lipietz 1987: 26).

Third, the regime of international free trade and free but stable exchange rates had fostered the internationalisation of capitalist production (Palloix 1977) and a deepening of the economic interdependence of industrialised states. This created the conditions under which, when the economic crisis hit in the 1970s, the forces of globalisation, in response to the unfolding crisis, could be unleashed on an unprecedented scale. As global restructuring thus came to be bound up with globalisation, the domestic–international compromise that had underpinned embedded liberalism was further undermined.

Moreover, when the USA, experiencing its own economic malaise and being bogged down in the Vietnam war, reverted to unilateralism under Nixon, it appeared that the post-war hegemon was no longer willing to sustain the multilateral framework that had thus far contained and regulated the internationalising forces of the world economy. It was in this context of a crisis of American hegemony that the monetary regime of Bretton Woods collapsed under the weight of accumulated Eurodollars, and the return to floating exchange rates heralded a new era of volatility (see Strange 1986) in which national welfare states were no longer offered the protection they had enjoyed under the post-war regime.

Finally, embedded liberalism was also undermined by the very success of the post-war economic growth regime inasmuch as this regime had fostered a further expansion of capitalism to parts of the erstwhile periphery of the capitalist world economy, in the process challenging the economic dominance of the region from which the growth had originally spread (Gourevitch 1986: 182; see also Keohane 1984b: 30–36). Thus, the long post-war economic boom in western Europe and America fuelled the growth and subsequent global expansion of first the Japanese, and later the whole East Asian economy. The resulting intensification of global competition exacerbated the difficulties of the Fordist industries of the capitalist heartland (even if in a later stage the rise of these new – 'emerging' – market economies provided new investment and export opportunities). The challenge of import competition from the former periphery added to the burden of declining productivity growth and rising wage costs, and thus contributed to the further dissolution of the class compromise.

It is thus that through these different but interrelated developments the historic bloc that formed the social underpinning of the post-war order of embedded liberalism disintegrated, generating a crisis of hegemony (Cox 1987: 279–85). The subsequent restructuring process is often interpreted in terms of neo-liberal globalisation. In this study, however, it is emphasised that initially many different conflicting tendencies could be discerned, and that it is only with the benefit of hindsight that we can interpret these restructuring processes of the past decades as constituting the global rise of neo-liberalism. Let me, however, by way of conclusion to this section, make a few general observations with regard to this global restructuring process.

First, at the level of the organisation of production, the crisis of Fordism has produced an international 'restructuring race' centred around competing strategies of accumulation (Ruigrok and Van Tulder 1995), increasingly bringing many transnational firms within global competition with each other (Stopford and Strange 1991; Ohmae 1985). Out of this restructuring process there has yet to emerge a new stable growth model along the lines of post-war Atlantic Fordism. As Ruigrok and Van Tulder (1995) argue, rather than witnessing a new single 'post-Fordist' accumulation regime, the present era of economic and industrial upheaval is still characterised by a plurality of what they call 'rival concepts of restructuring'. Nevertheless, despite this variation and the contradictions of the present situation, some general trends within industrial restructuring can still be observed. These common trends are often captured by the term *flexible accumulation* (see, e.g., Cox 1987: 309–53; Harvey 1989). This has meant a shift towards more flexible production techniques (like 'just-in-time' and 'customised production') originally developed in Japan (see Hoogvelt and Yuasa 1994), but above all, it has come to mean the flexibilisation of labour (as I shall argue in more detail later on).

Second, at the level of state–society relations, we can observe how out of the crisis of hegemony of embedded liberalism, a reconfiguration of social forces has taken place within all Western political economies that has changed the balance of power between different social groups and classes to the detriment of those groups that were hegemonic in the historic bloc of embedded or corporate liberalism.

What is now referred to as the rise of neo-liberalism has been interpreted (by for instance Cox 1987; Gill 1990; Overbeek 1990; Van der Pijl 1998) as a political project to restore capitalist class hegemony by, in its own rhetoric, freeing the market from the shackles of the state (disembedding the market). Thus, politically, the hegemonic project of neo-liberalism can be argued to be about re-establishing the hegemony of capital over labour after, under the previous regime, the growing power of the latter had threatened to undermine capitalist accumulation. At the same time, neo-liberalism represents the ascendance of financial capital (Van der Pijl 1989b; Overbeek and Van der Pijl 1993) after Fordist industrial capital had entered into a crisis. It is thus that with the rise of neo-liberalism we can witness a shift in the power relations between both industrial and financial capital as well as between capital and labour. Let us now analyse how the processes of globalisation and transnationalisation have formed the context in (and partly the medium through) which these shifts have taken shape.

Globalisation and the rise of transnational capital

Globalisation must be viewed as a multidimensional phenomenon (see, e.g., Giddens 1990), of which the emergence of a global economy is just one, albeit maybe the most crucial, aspect. Thus, although the globalisation thesis was initially linked to neo-Marxist writings on the internationalisation and later transnationalisation of capital (Palloix 1977; cf. Madeuf and Michalet 1979), globalisation has now entered the vocabulary of the social sciences at large, and is now also used to denote for instance 'the rise of global cultural flows and "deterritorialized" signs, meanings and identities' (Amin and Thrift 1994: 4).

Although recognising the multidimensional nature of the globalisation process, the focus here is on its political economy dimension (which is, however, multifaceted as well as bound up with other, more cultural, dimensions). This economic 'globalisation thesis' is not uncontested, however. Hirst and Thompson, for instance, argue first of all that the globalisation thesis is ahistorical as it misleadingly suggests that the present degree of international openness and economic interdependence is a historical novelty (Hirst and Thompson 1996: ch. 2; see also Thompson and Krasner 1989; Gordon 1988). Second (and partly following from the first point), Hirst and Thompson claim that the thesis that we witness a shift from an 'international' to a 'globalised economy' (for instance with regard to the transnationalisation of production) remains empirically unsubstantiated, and that, on the contrary, empirical evidence shows that the world economy is still far removed from the ideal-type of a globalised economy (Hirst and Thompson 1996: ch. 4, 8–13; see also Gordon 1988; Ruigrok and Van Tulder 1995).

This critique of the globalisation thesis can, however, be challenged on both theoretical and empirical grounds. With regard to the latter, in this chapter and in chapter 4, I will argue that the most recent data suggest that Hirst and Thompson (and others) may have underestimated the extent to which the globalisation process has deepened in the 1990s, especially within Europe. More fundamentally, however, it can be argued that the focus on statistics of international transactions (such as trade, investment, communication, etc.) tends to miss the *qualitative* dimension of globalisation. Globalisation (even 'mere' economic globalisation) is not just about the increase of cross-border transactions, it is also, and above all, about the transformation of social *practices* as, through economic, social, political and cultural processes, the lives and activities of people across the globe become connected, and social practices in one part of the world come to affect those in other parts.

It is precisely when put in a historical perspective that we see how the present era constitutes a phase of global integration that in some important qualitative aspects goes beyond any of the preceding 'phases' of international 'openness and integration' (cf. Hirst and Thompson 1996: 31–50). The globalisation unleashed by the crisis of the 1970s constitutes a qualitative break in a longer historical process in a number of respects. Of particular significance here is the rise of transnational capital as an increasingly global class fraction to which the autonomy of nation-states is tendentially subordinated. Globalisation must not be seen merely in terms of flows of goods and capital, but also as a process in which social relations themselves become globalised. With respect, then, to the present era of globalisation, it is in particular the deepening of the process of transnational class formation, and the operation of transnational concepts of control which lend a much more organic cohesion to the present global political economy than was the case at the end of the nineteenth-century liberal world order (cf. Gill 1990: 209–11).

Although the internationalisation of capital had in fact been a defining feature of the *Pax Americana*, it was partly in response to the crisis conditions faced by capital in the 1970s that this process both accelerated and deepened, and indeed witnessed a qualitative shift from an internationalisation to increasingly a *transnationalisation* of production (see below). As capital was confronted with declining profitability, declining productivity and stagnating demand, a strategy of geographical expansion (what Harvey (1989: 183) calls the 'spatial fix') was one 'solution' to the accumulation crisis that many large firms came to opt for, investing into new markets where costs are lower and demand is booming. It can be argued that such an internationalisation (or indeed transnationalisation) strategy was, and still is, also a way for capital to partially exit from national regulations – in particular, labour market regulations – that it had come to experience as a burden, and to enhance its bargaining power vis-à-vis labour, and shift the class balance back in favour of capital. As Caporaso argues: 'TNCs, as well as other forms of international capital, were critically important in emancipating capital from its domestic shell, and in providing it with a scope, flexibility and bargaining power far superior to labor's' (Caporaso 1987: 202).

As such, globalisation has also come to be intertwined with the global rise of neo-liberalism, constituting a transnational political and ideological project in response to the crisis of corporate liberalism. Although, as I shall emphasise later in this chapter when discussing the European context, other than neo-liberal responses were also formulated, and although we can only understand neo-liberal hegemony (to the extent that it is established) as the outcome of struggle, the argument here is that the globalisation process as it is presently evolving is bound up with a neo-liberal social purpose.

This neo-liberal globalisation process of course could not take place if it were not for a changing role of the state. Cox argues that as a political counterpart to economic globalisation we witness an 'internationalizing of the state' (Cox 1987: 253), in which 'The state system of the late twentieth century is coming to act more as a support to the opening of the world to global finance and global production, less as a means of defence of the welfare of local populations' (Cox 1992b: 178). Although a sweeping statement, Cox's observation does seem to be supported by the sometimes rather dramatic changes in government policies that have taken place over the past decades in the areas of trade policy, financial regulation, capital controls, foreign investment, etc. Changing government policies thus have to be seen as playing an important enabling role in the globalisation process (Strange 1996). States have also enabled a deepening of the globalisation process through world-wide privatisation (ibid.: 54–57), which has been the result not just of the collapse of the planned economies of the former state-socialist countries, but also of the massive selling off of (especially in the last few years) public enterprises in all western European countries (see Rhodes and Van Apeldoorn 1998: 415–16).

Economic globalisation involves both financial globalisation and the globalisation of production as related to the rise of the transnational corporation. I will now examine these different aspects in some detail, starting with, for the purposes of this study, the most critical production dimension of globalisation.

Globalisation of production

The globalisation of production could in simplifying terms be described as the rise of complex global transnational networks in which corporations source the components of their products around the globe (global sourcing) – placing their investments in those locations where they are offered the highest profitability – and then market and sell these products globally as well (see, e.g., Dunning 1993a, 1993b). It has to be stated from the outset that globalisation of production thus defined must be seen as a tendency rather than as a fully attained state-of-affairs. Not all sectors are equally globalised, and not all big internationally operating firms have achieved the same degree of globalisation (cf. Ruigrok and Van Tulder 1995). Indeed, these differences play an important role in the argument of this book. Nevertheless, I will also argue that these differences have become less pronounced as globalisation has deepened. Hence, the globalisation of production is here viewed as a strong structural trend in the global political economy, with important consequences for the nature and governance of capitalism.

The most important (albeit rough) indicator of the global integration of production is the steep rise of foreign direct investment (FDI) by the world's growing number of transnational corporations (TNCs). The Division on Transnational Corporations and Investment of the United Nations Conference on Trade and Development (UNCTAD) estimates in its 2000 *World Investment Report* that the total stock of global outward FDI amounted in 1999 to a total of US$4,759 billion, up from US$567 billion in 1982, and US$1,716 billion in 1990 (UNCTAD 2000a: 5). These figures indicate that the growth of FDI has not only been enormous but is also of very recent origin, really taking off only in the second half of the 1980s, when (between 1986 and 1990) outward FDI stock grew at an annual rate of 19.8 per cent (UNCTAD 1995: 4). After this steep rise, a brief recession followed in the early 1990s, but growth has picked up again since, with growth rates around 17 per cent again in the years 1998 and 1999 (UNCTAD 2000a: 5). With this strong growth, the ratio of FDI inflows to domestic capital formation has grown from a mere 2 per cent around 1980 to 14 per cent in 1999, while the ratio of world FDI stock to world GDP has increased from 5 to 16 per cent during the same period (UNCTAD 2000a: 1).

The growth of FDI, and its growing importance in the world economy, has been greatly facilitated by national (and supranational, in the case of the EU) governments, which around the world have liberalised their rules on foreign investment, with indeed many of them increasingly actively welcoming and promoting FDI into their countries. According to UNCTAD (2000a: 1), during the period 1991–99, only 6 per cent out of a total of 1,035 regulatory changes (around the world) pertaining to FDI were *not* in the direction of greater liberalisation. States thus increasingly enter into a policy competition to attract or keep foreign investment, seeking to offer the best 'competitive conditions'.

The unprecedented expansion of FDI reflects a very significant qualitative change in the nature of the world economy. Whereas in the post-war era that ended in 1973, the integration of national economies was still primarily driven by international trade, FDI has become the motor force in the last two decades (Hirst and Thompson 1996: 51ff.; UNCTAD 1995, 1993). Thus, the boom in FDI has by far outpaced the still considerable growth in world exports. Between 1983 and 1990, for instance, FDI flows grew at an annual rate of 34 per cent whereas merchandise trade expanded by only 9 per cent (Hirst and Thompson 1996: 55). As Stopford and Strange point out, the relative shift from trade flows to investment flows has a detrimental effect on the relative power of national states to control their economies, as trade flows are easier to interfere with than 'production which is aimed at a *world* market and which does not necessarily take place within [national] frontiers' (Stopford and Strange 1991: 14; see also Strange 1996; cf. Hirst and Thompson 1996: 72–75).

Whereas growth in international trade does, of course, reflect growing economic interdependence, it in itself does not constitute an integration of national economies into a global system, as production can still be largely *nationally* based. The recent explosion in FDI, however, points to a much deeper integration of the world economy. In this respect, the UNCTAD usefully distinguishes different levels or 'stages' of economic integration (UNCTAD 1993). The first stage or '"shallow" form of integration' is that which is formed by international trade (ibid.: 116). The free exchange of goods and services opens up the economy and stimulates 'TNCs to establish cross-border production systems that lead to "deep integration", which is integration at the level of production' (ibid.). Deep integration can be seen as evolving from 'simple' to 'complex' integration (ibid.: 113–17). In the former, international integration of production is still limited as foreign affiliates of TNCs operate with relative autonomy, producing for a single host economy (as in what is called the 'multi-domestic' strategy). In the latter, the affiliates of a TNC are integrated into a complex network that transnationalises the value chain itself, allowing 'a higher degree of functional specialization involving locating specific corporate activities in a number of locations around the world' (UNCTAD 1994: 87). Although these different types of integration strategy co-exist, the latter type of deep and complex integration increasingly predominates. The increasing weight of capital flows relative to trade flows (as not just goods, but production itself is being 'exported') and the concomitant shift of TNCs to complex integration strategies thus marks the advent of a true transnationalisation of capital. Moreover, whereas the process was initially restricted to the expansion of US capital, other regions have followed the US lead (Strange 1996: 50).

The rise of the TNC

Transnational corporations are the 'central organisers' of the transnationalised economic activities described above (UNCTAD 1993: 118). They are the actual decision-making units that determine the volume and direction of the investment flows. It is true that states can in principle regulate this process by erecting barriers that constrain the freedom of TNCs. As we have seen above, however, the fact of the matter is that states have been actively tearing down existing barriers, consistently enhancing the freedom of transnational capital and debilitating their own regulatory capacity. Inasmuch as the TNC internalises through its corporate structure what 'previously had been organised through international exchange' (Pooley 1991: 70; see also Dunning 1993a, 1993b), it is thus a key actor in the globalisation process.

The number of TNCs has been steadily rising over recent decades. According to the UN there are now about 40,000 TNCs in 15 advanced industrialised countries (and a further 23,000 from other countries), up from 7,000 in 1970 (UNCTAD 2000a: 1). Within this large universe of TNCs many firms are rather small, and the control over most international production is very much concentrated in the hands of the big global corporations, with the top 100 TNCs (as ranked by foreign assets) accounting for a third of total global FDI stock and a quarter of total sales by TNCs' foreign affiliates (UNCTAD 1996: 29). Many (but not all) of these global giants have throughout the 1990s become more transnational. Thus the average so-called transnationality index (TI) of the world's top 100 TNCs (ranked by foreign assets) employed by the UNCTAD – expressing the average of the ratios of foreign to total assets, foreign to total sales and foreign to total employment – has gone up from 51 per cent in 1990 to 54 per cent in 1998 (UNCTAD 2000b: 78). This growth of transnationalisation was in fact interrupted in the early 1990s when the transnationality index of many firms dropped (corresponding to the short recession in FDI noted before), but this seems to have been largely due to the global recession of those years. Thus, although we cannot extrapolate from current trends (especially as future economic conditions are uncertain) the overall trend in the 1990s does reveal a deepening of the transnationalisation process. As the data in chapter 4 will show, this applies even more to many of

Europe's large TNCs. At the very least we can conclude that those critics of the 'globalisation thesis' who on the basis of data from 1993 argue that the globalisation process may in fact be reversed in favour of regionalisation (see Ruigrok and Van Tulder 1995; see also Hirst and Thompson 1996: ch. 4) were too quick in drawing their conclusions by not taking the recessionary conditions of the early 1990s into account.[1]

Indicating the present centrality of TNCs in the world economy, we find that the 600 largest industrial TNCs are producing more than a fifth of all of the world's real net output of industrial production (UNCTAD 1988: 34), Furthermore, TNCs employ nearly 20 per cent of non-agricultural workers in the industrialised countries, and indirectly about another 20 per cent (UNCTAD 1994: 90). TNCs also dominate world trade flows, accounting for about three-quarters of world commodity trade in the mid 1980s (Dunning 1993a: 14). An increasingly large part of this trade actually takes place *within* the TNCs themselves, with intra-firm trade now accounting for about one-third of total world trade (Kozul-Wright 1995: 153).

Although TNCs are on the one hand the actors that drive the globalisation process, they are on the other hand also driven by it. As global competition increases, the pressure on companies to further internationalise themselves in response to this also rises. In principle, firms might also choose to retreat into their home region or even their home country. They might opt for what I will call a neo-mercantilist strategy that might involve forms of protectionism at the national or at the macro-regional level. In this strategy, firms try to relieve the pressure from globalisation by keeping out foreign competition from the markets they already dominate (but in which they now feel threatened). However, as we shall argue in chapter 4 and beyond, such a strategy is dependent on governments' willingness to pursue protectionist policies. When the dominant business interests are pro-free trade (because these firms are already more global than regional), the chances of such a protectionist strategy succeeding politically are slim. Hence, in the absence of these (political) conditions, a premium is put on pursuing a globalisation strategy, both to capture new markets and to find lower input costs. Under these conditions, formerly regionally orientated TNCs may also attempt to transform themselves into global players, something which increasingly takes place through mergers and acquisitions (M&A). After the M&A boom at the end of the 1980s and a subsequent slackening in the early 1990s, this phenomenon has again become central to the corporate strategy of many TNCs, with the value of cross-border M&As reaching US$720 billion in 1999, representing a seven-fold increase with respect to 1991 (UNCTAD 2000a: 10).

The rise of global finance

A second feature of the economic globalisation process is the rapid liberalisation and globalisation of finance in the past two decades. As Goodman and Pauly (1993) argue, to an extent the liberalisation of financial markets, and in particular the loosening or even complete abolition of capital controls, followed (rather than preceded) a globalisation of financial markets that was already under way with the development of off-shore markets in the wake of the collapse of Bretton Woods, although these changes in policy regime then subsequently accelerated this process. Whereas in the first post-war decades capital controls had been tight (as an instrument to ensure policy-making autonomy), a liberalisation wave followed in the 1980s as a response both to a rapid growth of global financial markets as well as to the globalisation of production – processes that made it so much easier for firms to evade these controls that governments came to perceive them as less useful and too costly (ibid.: 55).

Financial globalisation has further enhanced the power of transnational capital. As Frieden argues, 'increased financial integration implies an across-the-board, lasting increase in the social and political power of capital' (Frieden 1991: 434; see also Andrews 1994; Keohane and Milner 1996). In a similar vein, Strange has claimed that the rising *structural power* of finance 'has come to be of decisive importance in international economic relations and in the competition of corporate enterprises' (Strange 1988: 30). Signalling another break with the era of embedded liberalism, finance has now once more become a much more autonomous force, ruling according to some as 'an autocrat over the real economy' (Cox 1992a: 29). Hence, and also in the context of the extreme volatility that seems to be a structural feature of global financial markets, we may witness growing tensions 'between financial globalisation . . . and the requirements of production and trade' (Cerny 1994: 226). In this world of 'casino capitalism' (Strange 1986), then, the short-term perspective of finance is argued to replace the long-term perspective of industrial capital that characterised the political economies of countries like Germany and Japan (Albert 1993; cf. Zysman 1983). Indeed, the speed with which financial capital can move across national borders far exceeds that of even globalised industrial capital, which is still tied to specific locations and often faces large sunk costs, impairing its mobility (at least relative to financial capital).

Within the contemporary context, however, we should not exaggerate the divergence of interests between global financial and global industrial capital. First, the liberalisation of financial markets has been accompanied by liberalisation in other areas – such as trade and, as was noted, (foreign direct) investment – directly benefiting global industrial TNCs. Second, although industrial TNCs are still tied to geographical locations, their mobility is enhanced by the often great diversity of their assets (Frieden 1991). A significant part of their assets is in fact often financial as these industrial firms themselves have come to operate in financial markets in order to reduce their risk-exposure to financial volatility. Third, the liberalisation of financial markets has also enhanced the access of industrial TNCs to global capital, an access that they regard as critical to their globalisation strategies. Although, on the one hand, the growing dependence on global capital markets may be taken as reflecting the power of financial capital, on the other hand, as Goodman and Pauly note, the 'wider sources of funding for multinational firms engaged in the process of globalizing their production facilities [have also] enhanced the capability of [these] firms to develop evasion and exit strategies' (Goodman and Pauly 1993: 79), and thus have increased their power vis-à-vis national governments and organised labour.

Nevertheless, *in the longer run*, the as yet only weak tensions between industrial and financial capital, and *within* industry between those increasingly adopting a money capital perspective and those whose outlook is still more premised on the perspective of productive capital, may yet reveal more serious contradictions in the current hegemonic project. I will return to this point in the final chapter.

Globalisation and European regionalisation

As this study deals with (aspects of) the relation between global and European change (and its mediation by transnational social forces), we should now define more precisely how this relation can be conceptualised and, in particular, how we may conceptualise the mediating role of transnational capital – and concomitant transnational class strategies – in this respect.

Within the contemporary global political economy, processes of globalisation are in fact accompanied by different forms of regionalisation, from the EU to NAFTA in the North American region, to Mercosur in Latin America, ASEAN in the south-east Asian region and APEC in the Asian-Pacific region (for a comparative analysis of these various regionalisms, see, e.g., Coleman and Underhill (eds) 1998). This rise of regionalism within the world economy has in the past led some authors to envisage a break-up of the liberal international economy into rivalling politico-economic power-blocs (see, e.g., Gilpin 1987). This, then, raises the question of how to conceptualise the relation between globalisation and regionalisation, and whether these two processes might not constitute a contradictory dynamic. This question has again been put on the agenda in the context of the recent debate on what has been termed *Europeanisation*, in which European integration is made into the independent variable and 'domestic change' into the dependent (Cowles, Caporaso and Risse (eds) 2001). This raises the question of whether some of the observed effects on the dependent variable might not indeed be attributable to globalisation, and of what would be the relationship between these two potential sources of domestic change (see Wallace 2000).

As was argued in the introduction, the answer to this question must be understood in terms of different contending responses on the part of elites mobilising at the regional level. There, a basic distinction was made between regionalisation as resisting globalisation on the one hand, and regionalisation as accommodating and amplifying globalisation on the other. In the latter case, regionalisation is a phenomenon *through* which the present globalisation process takes place, whereas in the former it constitutes a defensive reaction against globalisation (cf. Hettne 1992). Following our stress on the importance of ideas, we may also conceptualise the relationship between globalisation and European integration in terms of different ideological discourses about globalisation, about what it means and how Europe should respond to it. Thus, Rosamond (1999), for instance, from a social constructivist perspective argues that there are in fact within the public policy debate on European governance different discourses on the meaning of globalisation and the relation of Europe to it. Here, it is argued (in contrast to Rosamond, who does not seek to explain these different discourses, or their relative success in hegemonic struggle) that these contending globalisation discourses can be linked to the strategies of concrete social forces that from within their globalisation discourse construct their interests in a certain way with respect to European governance. Furthermore, even if outcomes are ultimately decided in political struggles (and thus in part depend on qualities like political or ideological leadership), I maintain that which discursive response is more likely to become hegemonic also depends on the configuration of social forces, which in part depends on the material resources that these collective actors can command. Here, transnational capital is at a structural advantage vis-à-vis other social groups.

Theorising the relation between globalisation and European regionalisation from this perspective, this study will link these (ideal-typical) contending regionalisation strategies to different transnational social forces within the European arena. In particular, focusing on the mediating agency of an emergent transnational capitalist class, I will link these contending responses to rival class strategies on the part of rival fractions within this European capitalist elite. Here, I will distinguish between that part of European transnational capital that is operating on an increasingly global scale, and that part which operates by and large on a European, regional scale, or is at least still strongly dependent on a European home market. To the extent that these different interests within transnational capital are articulated as rival political strategies, I argue that the former will tend to favour further neo-liberal globalisation, whereas the latter will tend to resist (at least aspects of) global liberalisation.

The European crisis

In western Europe, and in particular within the then European Community (EC), the 1970s and early 1980s became the period of 'Europessimism' as both the integration process (apart from the important start of the European Monetary System (EMS) in 1979) and the post-war Fordist growth engine came rather suddenly to a grinding halt. It was in western Europe that the post-war era had ushered in an unprecedented period of consistent high growth and almost full employment (Boltho 1982; Tsoukalis 1993: 22–34). When this 'golden age' came to an end, the ensuing crisis put this whole post-war model of the mixed economy into question. This, then, was the European dimension of the breakdown of the post-war order of embedded liberalism discussed above. Before analysing the different aspects of this crisis, a brief account will be given of the main elements of the European socio-economic order that had been built up in the post-war era and how this socio-economic order intertwined with the integration process.

The post-war socio-economic order and European integration

Although there was some cross-national variation, with each country to an extent following its own historically conditioned national trajectory, the first decades after 1945 became a period of relative convergence around the 'embedded liberal' or 'corporate liberal' socio-economic order.[2] All European countries – and on a much larger scale than was the case in the USA, for instance – witnessed the rise of the welfare state, resulting in a steady growth of public sector expenditure. Another manifestation of the growth of the mixed economy in western Europe was the growing role of the state – albeit with important national variations (see below) – in the economy, not only through Keynesian macro-economic demand management, but also directly at the micro-economic level through industrial policy, as well as regional and income policies. In several countries, the class compromise underlying the post-war consensus was institutionalised in various corporatist arrangements. Although, as Colin Crouch has argued, corporatism can on the one hand be considered as a capitalist strategy to subordinate labour through non-market means, the fact that capital cannot ensure its domination over labour through the mere discipline of the market is also already a sign of the relative strength of labour and of its capacity to force capital to make concessions that represent real gains for workers, even though they at the same time help to ensure the reproduction of the capitalist system (Crouch 1979: 19). Thus, the incorporation of organised labour into the governance of the post-war European economy gave trade unions a good deal of institutionalised power (albeit still subordinate to that of capital), legitimised in the more corporatist countries by what Katzenstein (1985) has so aptly called the 'ideology of social partnership'.

As we have seen, this 'embeddedness' of Europe's market economies existed alongside an open world economy regulated by the increasingly liberal trade regime of the GATT, allowing for a continuous expansion of the forces of internationalisation. This international order of embedded liberalism was also reflected at the macro-regional level of what was then the European Community (EC). The European integration process in these first decades was on the one hand premised on a regime of trade liberalisation, opening up the national economies of Europe, but, on the other hand, went together with a build-up of the (Keynesian) welfare state. As liberalisation was only restricted to trade (national capital controls remained in place) and this trade liberalisation moreover left non-tariff barriers (NTBs) and all the national regulations with which these were bound up untouched, the different national political economies retained a considerable autonomy. At the same time, as Loukas Tsoukalis argues: 'the welfare state facilitated the progress of internationalisation and European integration by enabling governments to smooth out, and, sometimes, even slow down the necessary adjustment arising from the increased openness of national economies' (Tsoukalis 1993: 31). Thus, international liberalism was combined with national embeddedness. In addition, some Community policies themselves were also clearly more oriented to Polanyi's principle of social protection (e.g., the common agricultural policy).

Moreover, although the Common Market did contribute to the international growth of European business, the Community did not play the same kind of business-supportive role it began to play in the later 1980s and in the 1990s. On the contrary, in the early 1970s, the European Commission began to formulate proposals which were meant to counter-balance the increasing economic internationalisation, and therefore the growing power of TNCs, through some form of transnational regulation. These proposals can be interpreted as constituting what in retrospect appears to have been the first wave in a series of attempts to construct a 'social Europe' (Streeck 1993: 9), and might be seen as reflecting a broader regulatory movement within the global political economy as the crisis of corporate liberalism initially met with a rather reformist response (see Van der Pijl 1993). Following similar initiatives of organisations like the OECD, the regulatory drive of the European Commission culminated in 1980 with the so-called Vredeling Directive on workers' information and consultation rights within European multinationals (see Blainpain *et al.* 1983), which pitched European and international business in a dramatic battle against an alliance between 'essentially the Commission and the European trade union movement' (Van der Pijl 1993: 2; see also Cowles 1994: ch. 3), a battle lost by the latter as the directive was subsequently never carried beyond the drafting stage.

In sum, then, it can be argued that the post-war European integration process was in step with the development of European capitalism as described above. The crisis (or at least slowdown) of the European integration process in the 1970s thus, I suggest, has to be at least partially understood in the context of the crisis of European capitalism. Let us now discuss in more detail the most relevant aspects of this 'European crisis' for our purposes, constituting the context in which the transnational struggle over European integration and European socio-economic order evolved in the 1980s. The first aspect I will examine is the crisis of the post-war 'European model' and the neo-liberal response to this. The second aspect to be discussed is the crisis of European industry as precipitated by a simultaneous decline of productivity, a fall in demand and rising costs in a context of intensifying global competition.

The crisis of embedded liberalism and the neo-liberal ideology of 'Eurosclerosis'

Within the European context, the neo-liberal response to the crisis of European capitalism has to be understood in the context of the crisis of the institutionalised class compromise that had underpinned the post-war European model. The class alliance between 'big capital' and 'big labour' started to unravel when, as noted before, at the end of the 1960s for the first time productivity gains began to decline whereas wages continued to rise – resulting in a falling share of profits within the income distribution (Mazier 1982: 52; Boltho 1982: 24). Workers could successfully resist a decline in their wages because of the strong bargaining position labour had built up during (and due to) the full employment regime. As the Polish economist Michael Kalecki (1990) wrote many years before, from the perspective of the capitalist class the risk inherent in a sustained full employment regime is that it tends to undermine its political and social power vis-à-vis an ever more assertive working class: '[the capitalists'] class instinct [thus] tells them that lasting full employment is unsound from their point of view, and that unemployment is an integral part of the "normal" capitalist system' (Kalecki 1990: 351). The increased bargaining power of organised labour, and the rising wages that were associated with that, were also seen as one of the causes behind the acceleration of inflation (Mazier 1982: 56), hurting in particular the interests of money capital as well as, ultimately, the capitalist class as a whole: money capitalists were losing, quite literally, their money, whereas the high interest rates deterred productive capitalists from making new investments.[3] As again Kalecki wrote in the 1940s, the inflationary pressures created by full employment would lead to a situation in which 'a powerful alliance is likely to be formed between big business and rentier interests, and they would probably find more than one economist to declare that the situation was manifestly unsound' (Kalecki 1990: 355).

Indeed, the crisis of the 1970s was soon met by an intellectual (but at the same time ideological) offensive on the part of neo-classical economists, and other, to use Gramsci's term, 'organic intellectuals' of the ascending neo-liberal forces, against the Keynesian post-war consensus. The unemployment that the Western economies were already facing in the 1970s was in this view not the fault of 'the market', but rather of the systematic inference with that market, leading, in the words of Friedrich von Hayek, one of the leading philosophers of the New Right (writing in the 1970s), to 'a distortion of the system of *relative* prices and wages' which would normally 'establish themselves with free market and stable money' (von Hayek 1991a: 271). In order, then, to restore those markets and stop inflation, the full employment policy had to be abandoned and employment thus had to be deliberately further reduced. Employment could then be subsequently restored by policies aimed at reforming the *structure* of the labour market, as here government regulation and especially trade unions – whose power thus had to be broken – were depriving this market 'of the function of guiding labour to where it can be sold' (von Hayek 1991b: 318). Nevertheless, the goal of *full* employment had to be seen as unattainable and undesirable as there was argued to be a so-called *natural rate of unemployment* below which inflation would be pushed to unacceptable levels. Indeed, the hallmark of the new economic policy orthodoxy (referred to as monetarism) became the complete reversal of post-war macro-economic priorities, from the maintenance of full employment to the maintenance of price stability.

The ideas advocated by right-wing intellectuals like von Hayek, Milton Friedman and others have been argued to be linked to the interests of a transnationalising capitalist class centred in the first instance around global financial capital and intent on breaking the power of organised labour (Overbeek and Van der Pijl 1993; see also Overbeek 1990). This emergent neo-liberal hegemonic project has during the 1980s indeed succeeded in reversing the Keynesian post-war consensus (Armstrong, Glyn and Harisson 1991). In the early 1980s, several European states started to put monetarism into practice, with millions of workers losing their jobs as, in the words of Milton and Rose Friedman, an 'unpleasant side effect' (Friedman and Friedman 1980: 273).

Subsequently, so-called labour market reform, going under the banner of 'flexibility', has come to replace the discredited Keynesian demand management as the principal instrument of employment policy. As will also transpire from later chapters, flexibility has increasingly been defined so as to make labour market reform mainly a deregulation exercise, eroding established workers' rights. Although the concept of flexibility has been given different meanings – having been on the left associated with, for instance, increased worker autonomy (Piore and Sabel 1984) – labour market flexibility has in practice increasingly been defined in terms of external or *numerical* (rather than internal or *functional*) flexibility: that is, enhancing – through the relaxation of hire and fire rules, the promotion of temping, the decentralisation of wage bargaining, etc. – the control of management over the number of people employed, their working hours and their remuneration.[4] Although, and for obvious reasons, most employers (especially those employing post-Fordist production techniques) have in fact an interest in both forms of flexibility, numerical flexibility is what is advocated with regard to the great majority of workers, whereas an investment in functional flexibility is restricted to a small group of core workers, who are then also offered better pay and more job security (see, e.g., Harvey 1989: 150ff). It is thus, as I shall argue later in this study with regard to the European context, above all what we can call the neo-liberal concept of flexibility that has come to underpin the dominant socio-economic policy discourse. Flexibility here is equated with the freedom of capital (in the name of higher profits, or 'shareholder value') to shed 'excess' labour; to differentiate wages (and lower them at the bottom end); to weaken the influence of national trade unions, etc.

In the early 1980s, this neo-liberal programme was in Europe, however, still only in its first stage, a stage of an ideological offensive against the mixed economy that only the Thatcher government had already started to dismantle in earnest. Although, as indicated, by the early 1980s the preoccupation with the fight against inflation had come to dominate government policy in most countries, and (apart from France in 1981) most governments had lost their faith in the traditional Keynesian recipes for economic recovery, a more profound neo-liberal restructuring (in the sense of cutting down the welfare state, deregulating the labour market, etc.) did not start to take place until the 1990s (see chapter 5). Nevertheless, although neo-liberal social forces thus still had to achieve dominance, let alone hegemony, within the European arena, the neo-liberal discourse on the causes of Europe's crisis and alleged decline did significantly influence the intellectual policy climate in Europe, and as such also played its part in paving the way for Europe's renaissance in the mid-1980s.

Here, the rising power of neo-liberal ideology became first of all manifest in the discourse of 'Eurosclerosis', a term first coined in the beginning of the 1980s by Herbert Giersch (Tsoukalis 1993: 1), a German economist who from 1986 to 1988 was president of the Mont Pelerin Society, a think tank founded by Friedrich von Hayek, which from the 1970s became a 'crucial source of neo-liberal propoganda' (Van der Pijl 1998: 129). The concept of Eurosclerosis gained wide political currency in Europe when around 1983 its economy was still (or again) in a recession (with ever rising levels of unemployment) whereas its main competitors were showing signs of renewed economic growth. The neo-liberal 'Eurosclerosis' argument was a straightforward one. The stagflation of the European economy was the result of a number of rigidities – caused in particular by interventionist governments, trade unions acting as Olsonian distributive coalitions, and 'excessive' welfare states draining resources from the private sector – inherent in the mixed economy that had been built up in post-war Europe, and from which its global competitors, above all the USA, did not suffer (Grahl and Teague 1990: 20). The *market-correcting* institutions, then, that had made up the post-war model of European capitalism were seen as hurting competitiveness and impeding the necessary adjustments to the changing global economy.[5] The more free-market-oriented USA was of course the model to emulate here, and indeed, still is within the neo-liberal discourse of today.

Crisis and restructuring of European industry: industrial capital and the challenges of global competition

The world economic crisis also gave rise to a different discourse on Europe's alleged decline and how to reverse it. Whereas the neo-liberal ideology was primarily propagated by social forces bound up with global financial capital and global industrial TNCs, most of continental Europe was still dominated by large firms that were still more European than 'global players'. These former national champions and 'would-be European champions' perceived the forces of globalisation more as a threat to their market shares and competitive position than as an opportunity to force a structural transformation of Europe's 'sclerotic' socio-economic system. The crisis of Atlantic Fordism, in the context of a deepening transnationalisation of production, provoked a global restructuring race that had profound impacts upon European industry (Cox and Watson 1995; Ruigrok and Van Tulder 1995; Steinberg (ed.) 1990). Intensifying the global competition even more, and constituting an additional threat to at least some sectors of European industry (particularly cars and electronics) was the rise of Japan – with the 'Asian Tigers' following in its trail – as an economic and technological superpower, based in particular on its ability to produce equally high-quality products at much lower costs (Dumont 1990).

It was thus from the perspective of the social forces bound up with these sections of European industrial capital that there emerged a different kind of 'Eurosclerosis argument'. Here, the crisis of European industry was above all placed in the context of growing global competition, and the loss of European international competitiveness blamed less on labour market rigidity, trade union power, or the welfare state, and more on the fragmentation of the European market, the (resulting) insufficient economies of scale, and the perceived technology gap vis-à-vis the USA and Japan (see Grahl and Teague 1990: 168–75; Sharp 1990). As a remedy to these deficiencies, a strong European home market was expected to serve as both a stepping-stone to conquer the world market as well as a protective shield against outside competition. It was hence that a strategy of 'Europeanisation' was viewed as the main answer to Europe's economic ills. Although such a strategy is in principle not incompatible with a call for deregulation and flexible labour markets, the difference in emphasis mattered for how the struggle for Europe's relaunching evolved.

The relaunching of Europe

The low-point of Europessimism was probably around 1982 when the European economy was in a dismal state, the EC was still bogged down in the budget conflict between the UK and the other member states, and no new forward steps on the integration road were envisaged. The low-point, however, was also the turning-point as a number of historical events (to be discussed below), born out of underlying structural forces, created the preconditions for an unexpected relaunching of European integration in the mid-1980s. This relaunching was preceded, however, by a phase in which the different member states of the EC chose to follow their own path out of the crisis. It was in the wake of the subsequent failure of these diverging national strategies that the road to a successful restructuring of Europe was then paved.

From national to European responses

In a first phase, then, the member states of the EC, rather than trying to formulate a concerted European-level response to the economic crisis, each went their own way in pursuing a strategy for economic recovery. Countries started to 'experiment' with different policy responses, accentuating the existing differences between the national models of capitalism of the European political economy (see Gourevitch 1986: ch. 5; Tsoukalis 1993: 37; Hollingsworth, Schmitter and Streeck 1994: 11; see also Cox, A. (ed.) 1982). At the same time, the world economic crisis and the capitalist restructuring process to which it led saw 'vastly divergent performances of national economies' (Hollingsworth, Schmitter and Streeck 1994: 11). Whereas Germany successfully managed to hold on to its social market economy, with the economic crisis as yet failing to weaken its neo-corporatist institutions (see Streeck 1984) and its economy performing better than that of several other countries, Britain from 1979 onwards embarked upon a neo-liberal restructuring strategy, which, however, for the moment failed to reverse its long-term industrial decline (see Overbeek 1990). Germany, together with neighbouring 'Rhineland' countries such as the Netherlands, did embark relatively early upon a severe anti-inflation strategy, breaking with the Keynesian orthodoxy, whereas southern European countries like Italy and France continued to pursue expansionary policies that saw inflation soar. Indeed, the latter country became notorious (at least in circles preaching the new monetarist gospel) when in 1981 the newly elected socialist government embarked upon a strategy of Keynesian reflation, nationalisations and mercantilist industrial policies.

The world economic crisis, then, also ended the post-war convergence that had emanated from the unifying 'logic' of American hegemony and Atlantic Fordism. As divergence widened in terms of both economic performance and economic policy, economic 'nationalism' and protectionist tendencies also came to the surface again. As Stanley Hoffmann notes in an essay from 1982: 'the reaction of the public and of the political elites to the partial impotence of the governments, to the constraints of economic interdependence . . . has been to cling to and if possible to re-enforce the nation-state' (Hoffmann 1982: 23). What could be witnessed was a 'nationalisation' of industrial and economic policy by making increasing use of the instrument of NTBs, which indeed by the early 1980s had turned out to be the main obstacle on the road to a real internal market. Industrial policy became centred around the promotion of so-called 'national champions', which were expected to form the core of a revitalised national industry in which new technologies were to be the motor force of renewed economic expansion (see Hayward 1995).

Within a few years, however, these national strategies were to a large extent abandoned in favour of a *European* strategy, laying the basis for a relaunching of the integration process. Whereas Hoffmann (1982: 23) could in 1982 still cite the French socialist experiment as an example of a general trend of re-nationalisation, the subsequent U-turn – conditioned by the severe pressures on the French franc within the EMS and the French desire not to leave that system – made by the French government from Keynesian reflation to an austerity policy that followed the international trend, is now cited by many scholars as the most telling example of the constraints put on the policy making of national governments by the structural forces of the global economy. The French turnaround also implied a much more positive stance vis-à-vis European integration. At the member-state level, France can be seen as the clearest – and probably, given the weight of France in the EC, the most important – example of a shift from an exclusively national to a beginning of a European response to the problems of European economic decline, or as Wolfgang Streeck puts it: 'French nationalism in particular seems to have shaded in the mid-1980s into European supranationalism' (Streeck 1993: 2; see also Schmidt 1996; Moravcsik 1991). Although the determining push towards a concrete programme for a European *relance* was given, as I shall argue in chapter 4, by European big business, these national policy changes did to an important extent clear the way for this relaunching.

As we have seen, the pressure to find an alternative response to the crisis was aggravated because of the intensifying global competition with which European industry was confronted. In a globalising economy the nation-state was no longer capable of nurturing its 'national champions'. Europe, on the other hand, did seem to offer the scale needed to compete with rest of the world. This, then, was the context in which an elite consensus was built around the idea that only a concerted European effort could reverse the continent's perceived relative decline (Sandholtz and Zysman 1989). In this strategy, a relaunching of the European economy was thus wedded to a relaunching of the European integration process. There was, however, no immediate elite consensus on what *kind* of European solution ought to be chosen and hence *how* the integration process should be moved forward. In order to understand the eventual outcome, then, we have to examine the politics that determined why one policy option was eventually preferred to its rivals. This – from a perspective that focuses on the transnational dimension – will in fact be part of our focus in chapters 4 and 5. First, however, we should further identify the different policy options that configured in the debate. It is the notion of rival models of capitalism within Europe, and an ensuing political and ideological struggle in support of one model or another, which provides us with a valuable analytical point of departure in this respect. As suggested in chapter 1, the opposition between competing models of capitalist development is not just reflected in the present institutional diversity of the national political economies of Europe, but is also manifested at the *transnational* level where opposing social forces pursue conflicting strategies along this same dimension of capitalism versus capitalism (cf. Albert 1993; Hodges and Woolcock 1993; Goldstein 1993; Hooghe and Marks 1999; see also Van Apeldoorn 1996; Rhodes and Van Apeldoorn 1997). The struggle over European integration is also a struggle over Europe's socio-economic order, and with that over Europe's (future) model of capitalism.

European restructuring and the political economy of conflicting capitalisms

It was the crisis of embedded liberalism that brought out in the open again the existing differences of Europe's national political economies and opened up new possibilities for change, inasmuch as the dominant socio-economic model bound up with that order was not immediately replaced by a new orthodoxy, and the ensuing state of flux thus allowed for the development of alternative models of capitalism. However, a new, neo-liberal socio-economic paradigm has been developing and has become increasingly dominant. The first countries to follow this path – and thus break with the post-war (Keynesian) consensus – were Britain and the USA. Even though neo-liberalism soon became a pervasive ideological force around the Western world and beyond, other countries, as was pointed out before, did not immediately follow the hyper-liberal example set by Thatcher and Reagan. Indeed, in continental Europe post-war 'corporatist' practices proved to be – at least initially – rather resistant vis-à-vis the pressures of neo-liberal globalisation.

Cox (1993), for instance, has suggested that the world economic crisis and the demise of Fordist mass production and Keynesian demand management have provoked two types of response in Europe, one being the now familiar neo-liberal or hyper-liberal one, the other being more rooted in a state-capitalist and/or corporatist tradition. Although, with the benefit of hindsight, certainly any state-capitalist challenges to neo-liberalism are hard to establish empirically, it could be argued that in the 1980s, and up to the early 1990s, the apparent continuing economic success of 'alternative' types of capitalism – that is, varieties of capitalism that clearly diverged from the neo-classical ideal-type (as prescribed by neo-liberals) – did strengthen the hand of those political and social forces opposing the 'Americanisation' of European society, and imposed at least temporary limits on the rise of neo-liberalism in Europe. The 'institutional economies' of Japan and Germany were both success stories in the 1980s. Within Europe, it was particularly Germany's apparent ability to combine a highly internationally competitive economy with social institutions that put the market under some measure of control (and made for more equitable outcomes) which made the 'prestige [of this model of capitalism] with the left [rise] inexorably in the 1980s' (Crouch and Streeck 1997: 4).

The debate on the varieties of capitalism in Europe also feeds into different discourses on European socio-economic governance, and these discourses *themselves* provide an important key to an understanding of the present transformation processes in Europe. As Crouch notes, to the extent that any European model might be expected to develop in the future 'that model will have to emerge from past and current diversity' (Crouch 1993a: 4). Let us therefore now examine the existing institutional diversity of capitalism in western Europe.

A typology of rival models of capitalism in western Europe

The two competing models of capitalism that are distinguished by Michel Albert (Albert 1993) are the 'neo-American model' (the model of the USA and the UK after the Reagan and Thatcher revolutions) on the one hand, and the 'Rhine model of capitalism' (finding its geographical core in the three Rhine countries: Switzerland, Germany and the Netherlands) on the other. Within the European context, another way of representing these competing capitalisms is to juxtapose what could be called the British model of the *liberal* market economy and the German model of the *social* market economy (Hodges and Woolcock 1993). In a more generic fashion, Soskice (1999) speaks of non-coordinated and co-ordinated market economies respectively. Although within the European integration process the main debate seems to be between those two capitalisms, in order to fully understand the dialectics that have led to the present situation a third model must be distinguished here, which is the 'statist' model, within Europe best represented by France. I will now discuss the main characteristics of these three models of capitalism within Europe.

From a neo-Gramscian perspective, and rejecting state-centric explanations, I argue that the considerable differences between these forms of capitalism are the result of different historical trajectories with regard to the development and organisation of state–society relations. Particularly important in this respect is to examine the configuration of social forces, i.e., the historic bloc, upon which state power rests. In analysing the configuration of social forces (as defining the form of state), and its relation to the state (state–society complexes), we may consider four interrelated dimensions of primary importance: the relative strength of labour vis-à-vis capital, the relationship between industrial and financial capital, the (organisational) relationship between the state and civil society (*inter alia* affecting the extent to which organised labour can influence the management of the economy), and the extent and nature of the insertion of the national economy into the world economy (Hall 1986: 232; Cox 1987: 148), referring to both the position of indigenous capital on world markets – in particular, its degree of internationalisation – as well as to the degree to which the national economy is penetrated by foreign capital.

The British model

The British model of the liberal market economy is not a Thatcherite invention; its historical origins can be traced back to the *Pax Britannica*, or even before. Indeed, Britain can be regarded as the home ground of economic liberalism, dictating a minimum role for the government, relying on the self-regulating market instead. It was England which first saw a full emancipation of its emerging bourgeoisie, establishing a relatively self-regulating civil society that only needed the state to maintain the order necessary for the free market to operate (Van der Pijl 1989a: 30). Throughout its further development, the British state has never fully lost its liberal character. A related enduring trait of its state form is the 'internationalism' that has marked the development of the British political economy and has always been and still is the dominant orientation of the British capitalist class. This British internationalism was thus not a mere ideological legacy of the hegemonic position it enjoyed before, but was very much bound up with the continuing internationalisation (even after the decline of hegemony had set in) of British capital, in particular financial capital (Overbeek 1990: 31, 49–51 and *passim*; Hall 1986: 249). This latter capital fraction soon gained a hegemonic position within the British bourgeoisie, with the City of London continuing to dominate the world financial market long after the decline of British hegemony and continuing to exercise an enormous leverage over the British state (Overbeek 1990; Hall 1986: 58–59; Coates 1989: 22–25). Another structural feature of the British political economy is the archaic nature of its labour relations (Overbeek 1989: 44–45). British trade unions have always been relatively strong at the shop floor level but weak politically as they were unable to organise themselves effectively at the national level (Hall 1986: 44).

There are thus clear historical continuities in the development of the British state. Nevertheless, in the global reaction of productive forces (industry and labour) against what was seen as the destructive power of *laissez-faire* capitalism during the 1930s and 1940s, and the ensuing compromise of embedded liberalism, the liberal British state of the *Pax Britannica* was also transformed. The post-war macroeconomic policy of successive British governments was firmly based on the Keynesian principles of demand management (see Hall 1986: 69–99), involving a substantial expansion of the public sector and the development of the welfare state. On the other hand, however, the structural features characteristic of the post-war 'corporate liberal state' (Van der Pijl 1984) never became as deeply rooted in Britain as in most of continental Europe. Experiments with state-capitalist planning and comprehensive industrial policy as pursued by various Labour governments were never really successful. Attempts to create a solid corporatism in Britain equally failed (Overbeek 1990: 136; Jessop 1991: 139–40). Industrial relations remained anarchic and polarised. Furthermore, the power of the internationally oriented City remained hegemonic throughout, whereas industrial capital continued to suffer from organisational weaknesses. These enduring structural features of the British political economy in fact help to explain why within Europe it was the British government which first adopted a programme of radical neo-liberalism and why indeed, as I will argue in chapter 5, the neo-liberal revolution, when it spread to the continent, could not be cast in the same radical Thatcherite mould. Instead it had to be reformulated and modified as it met with the resistance of pre-existing, historical socio-economic and political and cultural structures prevalent in much of continental western Europe.

The Thatcherite programme successfully restored the continuity with the nineteenth-century liberal British state. The hegemony of financial capital has been furthermore reinvigorated by the global process of financial deregulation and capital liberalisation, something which has helped to make the neglect of British national industry into the hallmark of Thatcherite economic policy (Overbeek 1990), a money-capital bias that the current Labour government at most seems to redress at the rhetorical level. With regard to external economic policy, the present British state is firmly committed to international free trade, and the British economy is fully inserted into the world economy. This is something which in recent years (starting under Thatcher) has been actively facilitated and consciously promoted by the British government, *inter alia* by welcoming FDI on an unprecedented scale, thus leading to a further transnationalisation of the socio-economic base of the British state (Baker 2000).

The German model

The German model of the social market economy (*soziale Marktwirtshaft*) is in many ways no less liberal than its British counterpart. Moreover, the Federal Republic of Germany has always been fully committed to international free trade. These features of Germany's post-war political economy constitute an important break with the earlier 'conservative route' to development which had culminated in the Nazi regime (Spohn and Bodemann 1989). Indeed, the post-war strategy of a firm commitment to the market economy, price stability and international free trade can be seen as partly the result of a reaction to the negative experiences of the 1920s and after (Van der Wurff 1993: 164). Compared to the Anglo-American or neo-liberal model, the German political economy presents two striking features: first, its successful industrial policy as based on the very German conception of *Ordnungspolitik*, and second, the relative strength of the German welfare state, its underlying social consensus, and supporting corporatist institutions. Indeed, it is the corporatist dimension or, more generally, the large role played by formal associations (see Streeck 1992) in Germany's institutionalised economy that provides for an important continuity with institutional traditions originating from far before the Second World War (Crouch 1993b). In the post-war era, this particular model of capitalism developed a strong record of economic performance based on an industry that – employing well-paid but also well-trained workers – became highly competitive in world markets by producing high-quality products in 'mid-tech' sectors such as cars, engineering and chemicals (see Streeck 1997). Let us look in some more detail at the structural features of the German political economy that account for this post-war success of German capitalism.

The German model of capitalism is partly underpinned by an economic philosophy called 'ordo-liberalism' (*Ordoliberalismus*) as espoused by the Freiburg school of economics. Ordo-liberalism has at its core the idea that the free market should be embedded in a regulatory framework, based on an overall social consensus, in which the market forces can operate efficiently. It is the task of the state to provide a stable social and economic environment for sustained capitalist accumulation.

Rather than intervening directly in the economy, the German state plays a much more indirect role by setting the rules in which economic actors are to operate. Streeck thus labels the German state as neither 'laissez-faire' nor 'étatiste', but as an '*enabling state*' (Streeck 1997). What is called *Ordnungspolitik*, then, is not so much premised on discretionary interventionism as is the case with French industrial policy (Hodges and Woolcock 1993: 337), but rather aimed at securing the general conditions for industry to prosper (Van der Wurff 1993: 165).

As noted, the second enduring feature of Germany's post-war political economy is its relatively strong social consensus, expressed in a class compromise, upon which not only the German welfare state is built but much of its economic success also ultimately rests (Albert 1993: 110–17; cf. Streeck 1997: 245). This class compromise – institutionalised at the firm level in the form of the famous (and for neo-liberals notorious) *Mitbestimmung* (employee representation on the supervisory board) – finds its material basis in high wage levels, allowing workers to share in economic growth, which German employers in their turn see as an acceptable price to pay for social harmony and a labour force which is both loyal and highly skilled. It is the relatively strong position (certainly compared to their British and French counterparts) of organised labour vis-à-vis organised capital which helps to account for the particular German synthesis of the free market and the welfare state.

Perhaps the most important structural feature of the configuration of social forces underlying the German state is, however, the close relationship between industrial and financial capital. In the nineteenth century, German banks 'were hardly integrated into the international circuits of money capital' but were instead firmly linked to German industry, on whose development they became directly dependent (Van der Wurff 1993: 167). This symbiosis between industry and banking was consolidated in the post-war German model, in which industrial firms were to an important extent financed by their so-called 'house banks' (*Hausbanken*), which were also among the core shareholders of these firms, thus ensuring – in contrast to the more short-term-oriented Anglo-American model – that bank capital has a large stake in industrial production and has an interest in its long-term development (Albert 1993: 11; Deeg 1999; Zysman 1983). It is this industry-oriented role of German banks which also partly helps to account for the international success of Germany's post-war economy, as well as for the relative resilience of the German model in the face of the challenges emanating from globalisation and the concomitant transnational spread of neo-liberal ideology, at least until the end of the 1980s.

It has been argued that this resilience of the German model has, as global competitive pressures were aggravated by the effects of German re-unification, been broken in the course of the 1990s. According to Streeck (1997), German high-wage capitalism is fatally undermined by globalisation because it erodes the national state capacity needed to organise the public or quasi-public intervention that sustains it, including the associative self-regulation that is undermined by the enhanced exit option of capital. Others are more optimistic about the viability of Rhineland capitalism in the era of neo-liberal globalisation, pointing at factors such as the path-dependency of its institutional development and the continuing (potential) benefits of at least a reformed 'competitive corporatism' (Rhodes 1997), even from the perspective of globalised industry. Although there may be some truth in this last point (cf. my argument on 'embedded neo-liberalism' in chapter 5), some articulation of the German model with particular neo-liberal elements appears to be inevitable, and indeed is already taking place. This is partly driven by the rise of Anglo-Saxon finance in German corporate governance, which tends to sever the traditional ties between banks and industry, and makes owners of German industry adopt a more money-capital perspective (see Van Apeldoorn 2001 for a further elaboration of this argument). Thus what were once *Hausbanken* are trying to turn themselves into leading world players, competing with the likes of Goldman Sachs to share in the huge profits that are to be made in the booming business of investment and corporate banking.

The French model

Whereas the British model is based on a strict, formal separation of the state and the economy, the French model comes rather close to a symbiosis between the two. The historical roots of this model go back to at least the nineteenth century when the bourgeoisie in France, still mainly an agricultural society and lagging way behind England in the industrialisation process, was not yet strong enough to establish hegemony, and it was left to the state, centralised and with a relatively large bureaucracy, to enforce order on a divided society (Cox 1987: 138–40). In ideal-typical terms this model of state-capitalism or *étatisme* is thus characterised by a strong state (in the narrow sense) which is relatively resistant to pressures from private interests located in civil society (Hall 1986: 165). The relative weakness of the intermediate level of civil society meant that the role of the state weighed directly upon the French economy rather than being mediated by strong institutionalised links between state and civil society. The French state has always played a large role in the nation's economic development, but it has been particularly in the post-war period that the French economy has followed a state-led path of development (Hall 1986: 140). This meant that the state played a direct role in steering the French economy and generating industrial growth according to centrally determined priorities. Inconceivable within for instance the British liberal market economy, this role of the French state was seen as completely *legitimate*. Indeed the state, as an institution 'above society', solely capable of perceiving and expressing the general interest, was seen as having a duty to play such a role. The central instrument for the state was the particular form of planning introduced by Jean Monnet, which was not merely indicative but involved a good deal of direct, *dirigiste* intervention (ibid.: 152). In addition to this, France developed a large nationalised sector.

As Hall argues (1986: 166–71), French planning, although not unsuccessful during the first two decades or so, in the longer term paradoxically undermined one of the essential characteristics of French statism, namely the relative insulation of the state vis-à-vis private interests groups. Whereas business was formerly rather dependent and hence subservient to the state, the state increasingly became dependent on the expertise and co-operation of particularly big business. In the 1960s, it was decided that France's industrial structure was too much dominated by small firms and instead needed big conglomerates to compete in an increasingly open world economy. A concentration process followed and the managers of the new 'national champions' (located in what were considered industrial sectors of strategic importance) became the direct partners of the French economic planners in a particular form of government–business alliance. Organised labour was fully excluded from this process, weakened as it was by internal ideological divisions (which is one of the reasons why there never emerged a strong corporatism in France). The symbiosis between big business and the state had also been fostered by the common education and hence socialisation of both elites in the so-called *grandes écoles*. Indeed, what could be witnessed was an increasing penetration between the two, *inter alia* through the famous system of *pantouflage* where senior officials moved to occupy leading positions in French business and to a lesser extent also vice versa (Marceau 1989: 52; Hall, 1986: 168; Birnbaum 1981: 103–11).

Seen from an international perspective, the French *étatiste* model could be described as a form of mercantilism. Protectionist inclinations have therefore never been alien to successive French governments. However, in the post-war order of embedded liberalism, France, as an (albeit not always enthusiastic) member of the Western power bloc led by the USA, was limited in its freedom to follow its own course and was forced to adapt to an increasingly competitive world economy, in which successive rounds of trade talks lowered international tariffs. Moreover, within the Common Market tariffs were abolished in 1968. Direct protectionism, at least at the national level, was only a very limited option. When, as a result of the world economic crisis of the 1970s and the ensuing international restructuring race, the exposure to the pressures of the global economy increased, France had to look for other ways to protect its national industries. In line with the general trend, the focus of French industrial policy shifted from the stimulation of overall expansion to the enhancement of the international competitiveness of targeted industries. This evolved into what was above referred to as a 'national champion strategy' (see Cohen 1995).

When the socialists came to power in 1981, a huge nationalisation programme was initiated and accompanied by a traditional Keynesian reflation of the economy. As noted before, this socialist experiment turned out to be short-lived, however, with the U-turn towards a more neo-liberal austerity policy. This episode can be seen as a first dramatic instance of a longer-term process in which the twin processes of globalisation and Europeanisation transformed the traditional model of state–society relations in France. Thus, Vivien Schmidt (1996) has argued that in particular the deepening process of European integration – further aided by globalisation – has allowed French big business to emancipate itself from its symbiotic relationship with the state and to become a much more autonomous social force with a more European and internationalist outlook. Albert (1993: 230–44) writes that France is increasingly subject to a process of 'Americanisation' affecting the whole fabric of society, its values and the structure of its economy; the income gap is growing, individual achievement as opposed to collective effort is increasingly celebrated, and the stock exchange is growing in importance. Nevertheless, although maybe no longer a distinct model, France still forms a separate case which in the future might again present its own alternative (Boyer 1997).

The transnational struggle over Europe's model of capitalism and rival projects for the relaunching of Europe

It is now time to turn to the transnational dimension of the political economy of conflicting capitalisms, i.e., how this struggle played out in the struggle over European socio-economic order. I argue that what can be viewed as the rival projects of 'neo-liberalism', 'neo-mercantilism' and 'supranational social democracy' struggled over the course of the relaunched integration process, and that it is through this struggle that the socio-economic content of this process has been shaped. We can also view these three rival projects as three alternative *European* (rather than national) responses to the crisis of European capitalism and to the changing global environment, i.e., as different ideological and strategic orientations with respect to the relationship between globalisation and European integration. Furthermore, the three projects can also be linked, in different ways, to the different models of capitalism discussed in the preceding section. At the level of discourse, these models can be argued to function as reference points in ideological struggle and as models to emulate at the European level. Finally, and more abstractly, we can also relate the rival ideological orientations underpinning these contending projects to the opposing principles of economic liberalism and social protection.

As we shall see, all three projects favoured a relaunching of Europe through the completion of the internal market: as such, all three were relatively market oriented. This (particularly on the part of social democracy) in itself already reflected a shift away from previous ideological orientations vis-à-vis the integration process. This pro-market shift is often taken as evidence of the emergence of a 'neo-liberal Europe'. However, the three projects here identified fundamentally differed on the question of *what kind* of single European market it was to be; to what extent it had to be embedded in a strong supranational political framework regulating the market (as in the social-democratic project); and to what extent internal trade liberalisation should be accompanied by increasing external openness as well (as in the neo-liberal project), rather than protecting the new home market by raising external tariffs and through an interventionist industrial policy (as in the neo-mercantilist project).

The supranational social-democratic project

The social-democratic project for Europe's socio-economic order developed within the context of the initial success of the internal market programme and the new 'Europhoria' engendered by it. It was within this context that, in particular within the European Commission, the idea took hold that the internal market ought to be complemented with a 'social dimension' or, more broadly, a project of positive integration ensuring a strong regulatory political framework to embed the new single market. To an extent – that is, in its more minimalist version – this project was not only supported by social-democratic political forces, but also by Christian-democratic political parties and governments (such as that of Germany), hence by a broad spectrum of forces within the European political mainstream. Nevertheless, as a coherent strategy of European integration this project first and foremost developed out of the social-democratic tradition, and was supported by the European trade union movement. At least up to the treaty of Maastricht, the ambitions of this strategy also went beyond the kind of minimal social dimension that others envisaged. As such the project also implied a considerable strengthening of Europe's supranational institutions: that is, a strategy of European state building. Supranational social democracy (as an intellectual programme and as a political strategy) thus saw European federalism as the answer to the dilemmas the European left had (and still has) to confront as it became caught in the logic of globalisation and the perceived 'decline of the nation-state', the traditional power-base of social democracy (see Geyer 1993; cf. Lambert 1991; Marquand 1994). As a concrete political strategy, this project was first and foremost formulated and pursued by Jacques Delors (and the group of intellectuals and Eurocrats surrounding him), who as president of the European Commission displayed the vision and the strategic leadership without which 'supranational social democracy' would probably never have developed into such a concrete political strategy (see Ross 1995).

For Delors, as for many other social democrats, a united Europe offered an opportunity to protect the 'European model of society' (as Delors called it) and its traditions of the mixed economy and high levels of social protection, against the potentially destructive forces of globalisation and neo-liberalism (Ross 1995: 15 and *passim*; Grant 1994: 86–87; Delors 1992). Indeed, the notion of a 'European social model' (as it is also often called) was at the heart of the Delorist vision (Ross 1995: 46), and implied that there was somehow a 'European model of capitalism' different from both *laissez-faire* Anglo-American capitalism and the 'collectivist' Japanese model, combining individual freedom with the virtues of collective action, the competitive market with a system of social solidarity, all in a long-term perspective of sustainable growth and welfare. In the Delorist/social-democratic project, the building of strong European institutions was the only way to preserve this model. Delors had accepted that for relaunching the European integration process, the creation of a competitive home market was a necessary requirement (for both political and economic reasons), but at the same time Delors warned the neo-liberals that 'The Community is not and will not be, a free trade zone. It is up to us to make a *European organized space*' (Delors in Krause 1991), and it was 'For this reason [that] the backbone of Delors' strategy was to promote state-building programs on the back of market-building successes' (Ross 1995: 109).

The European model of capitalism promoted by this project in many ways emulated the German model of the social market economy, as was for example evinced by the Delors Commission's later promotion of the 'social dialogue' between the European employers' and employees' federations. In other respects, inspiration seems to be taken from the French model, particularly in Delors' own favouring of a Commission-led industrial policy, promoting 'Euro-champions' in the face of increasing global competition (see Ross 1993). It is here that we see a partial convergence of Delors's social-democratic with the neo-mercantilist strategy. In defending the 'European social model' against the unregulated forces of global capitalism, the social-democratic project of course appeals to the principle of social protection, and in particular to the protection of the interests of labour, which is seen as losing out in the globalisation process.

The neo-mercantilist project

The neo-mercantilist project developed out of the crisis of European industry within the context of the global capitalist restructuring process and the concomitant challenges of intensifying global competition. As such, neo-mercantilism is oriented towards a defensive regionalisation strategy: that is, the building-up of a strong regional economy – through industrial policy, the promotion of 'European champions' (if necessary protected by European tariff walls), etc. – as a bulwark against the forces of global competition. The neo-mercantilist project is thus underpinned by a perspective tied to the principle of social protection, but specifically from the viewpoint of industrial capital: that is, it is oriented towards safeguarding the interests of productive capital inasmuch as these are seen as threatened by a process of unbridled global liberalisation. This, however, does not exclude certain compromises with labour as well, inasmuch as labour and industrial capital may share a common interest in this respect. The neo-mercantilist project may also be seen as related to (some aspects) of the French model of capitalism, even if it were probably only French (political and economic) elites who explicitly referred to the French model of industrial development as an example for Europe. In the neo-mercantilist conception, regionalisation becomes a defence against globalisation. The internal market project is thus interpreted as the creation of a strong 'home market' that could serve as a launching pad to conquer the world market and at the same time as a protective shield against outside competition. Such a strategy necessarily requires Europe to go far beyond mere negative integration as resources are pooled and new supranational policies are created. This in turn requires strong Community institutions to carry out those policies.

The neo-liberal project

As was argued earlier, the neo-liberal project of Europe – premised upon the principle of economic liberalism – must be seen as arising out of the crisis of Europe's post-war embedded liberal order and the Eurosclerosis discourse that developed in response to it. The neo-liberal project can be seen as related to the (post-1979) British model of capitalism and, in its ideological discourse, as generally appealing to Anglo-Saxon capitalism (that is, including the USA) as the model for Europe. In the neo-liberal conception of European integration, the process should be restricted to negative integration, i.e., market liberalisation and deregulation: more market and less state at all levels of the EU. Hence, the relaunching of the integration process was to be restricted to the implementation of the 1992 project, preventing any state-building projects from taking off. The benefits of the internal market project were seen as principally deriving from the freer market it would create, emphasising its deregulatory effects and the efficiency gains generated by the increase in (cross-border) competition. Rather than creating a protective buffer against global competition, European integration should lead to a further subordination of Europe's socio-economic and industrial space to what are seen as the beneficial forces of globalisation: Europe as an advanced free-trade zone within a free-trading world. As one of its principal advocates succinctly summarised the neo-liberal strategy for Europe's relaunching:

> It should be our aim to make Europe by the year 2000 a model of what free trade and open markets can achieve . . . We have not successfully rolled back the frontiers of the state of Britain only to see them recognised at the European level. (Margaret Thatcher quoted in Krause 1991)

Neo-liberalism and neo-mercantilism as rival European class strategies

Neo-liberalism and neo-mercantilism are here interpreted as ideal-typical strategic orientations on the part of different ideal-typical 'fractions' of European capital (cf. Holman 1992; Van Apeldoorn and Holman 1994). Here we should return to the analytical framework of chapter 1, and in particular to the three structural factors, i.e., the relative degree of globalisation, sectoral position and the remaining national embeddedness of capital, in structuring the process of European transnational class formation. As argued there, the first of these three factors is the most critical, inasmuch as a further globalisation of European capital will also enable a transcendence of the divisions along the other two dimensions. At a somewhat higher level of abstraction, then, we may distinguish between two main rival fractions within the process of European class formation as it evolved in the 1980s. Here, these two rival fractions are denoted respectively as 'globalist' and 'Europeanist'.

The former is made up by the most mobile and most globalised fractions of transnational capital, i.e., global financial institutions as well as industrial 'global players', or, following Holman (1992; see also Frieden 1991), 'export-competing firms producing for the world market'. This latter category has shown a growing dominance within post-war Germany, the productive superiority of German capital having 'preordained a world market strategy' (Holman and Van der Pijl 1992: 9). Given the historically strong internationalisation of British capital, this fraction of European industrial capital also dominates British capitalism, while global financial capital has of course its stronghold in the City of London. With regard to the sectoral dimension (and confining ourselves to industrial capital), it is in particular the oil, chemical (see Martinelli (ed.) 1991) and food sectors that at least since the 1980s have shown both a relatively high degree of globalisation and a high degree of global competitiveness, whereas the European electronics and car industries were in the 1980s still much less globalised.[6] These sectors, moreover, have also never particularly suffered from the growing competition of Japanese TNCs, as Japanese industry has remained relatively weak in these sectors.

The 'Europeanist' fraction, on the other hand, is constituted by large industrial enterprises that, although operating on a transnational scale, nevertheless primarily serve the European market, competing against often cheaper imports from outside Europe, i.e., what we could also call 'import-competing producers for the European market' (Holman 1992). This section of European industrial capital is predominantly (but by no means exclusively) located in the southern European countries, in particular France and Italy, where many former 'national champions', or at least firms that used to be heavily dependent upon the domestic market, in the 1980s pursued an internationalisation strategy that was primarily oriented towards the European market, making this market into their home market. With respect to the sectoral dimension, we may identify in particular the car (see Dankbaar 1994) and electronics (see Cawson 1994) sectors, which at least up to the end of the 1980s showed relatively low levels of globalisation, and were particularly exposed to rising global competition, especially import-competition from Japan.

The basic structural division identified here is thus between, on the one hand, that group within the European capitalist class whose interests and identity are bound up with *global* transnational capital, and who are therefore wary of any claims about a specific *European* (capitalist) interest, and, on the other hand, those capitalists who, partly because of their relative dependence upon the European market, precisely do posit such a regionalist interest. On the basis of my case-study of the ERT, I will argue that the Europeanist fraction has mainly identified with the neo-mercantilist project, whereas the ideological perspective of the globalist fraction of European capital has been (and still is) bound up with the neo-liberal project. Within the globalist fraction, we should, however, still distinguish between its industrial and financial sections. As I have argued in chapter 1, as the latter can never fully disengage itself from the requirements of the production process, there are structural limits to the extent to which its ideological perspective can fully move away from the principle of social protection and towards the principle of economic liberalism.

In this study I argue (see chapters 4 and 5) that the struggle between the globalist and Europeanist fractions of Europe's emergent transnational capitalist class, and its related opposition between neo-liberalism and neo-mercantilism, constituted in many ways the central axis around which the ideological struggles within the transnational capitalist elite revolved. It was thus through this struggle that part of the transnational struggle over European order transpired, with the social-democratic project in the background as a potential counter-point as well as a possible point of convergence. Before presenting this analysis, however, we should first further introduce the ERT as an elite forum of (sections of) Europe's transnational capitalist class, and hence as one forum through which part of the struggle between the two rival fractions of European capital has taken place.

3 The European Roundtable

An elite forum of Europe's emergent transnational capitalist class

> I would consider the Roundtable to be more than a lobby group as it helps to shape policies. The Roundtable's relationship with Brussels is one of strong co-operation. It is a dialogue which often begins at a very early stage in the development of policies and directives.
>
> Wisse Dekker, chairman of the ERT, 1988–92 (Dekker 1990: 18)

> The ERT is not a lobby, but rather a group of European citizens who express their opinions on the best ways to make Europe and European companies competitive on a world-wide basis to politicians, governments, the Commission, and other institutions.
>
> Jérôme Monod, chairman of the ERT, 1992–96 (Monod in ERT 1994a: 1)

> The ERT is partially a lobby, but not for the interests of individual sectors, but for the competitiveness of Europe. As this is a fundamental concern, which the European public authorities share with us, we are also a privileged partner in the dialogue about these concerns.
>
> Helmut Maucher, chairman of the ERT, 1996–2000[1]

In this chapter the main protagonist of this study, the European Roundtable of Industrialists (ERT), is further introduced by outlining its characteristics, objectives and institutional development. I will also examine in some detail the composition of the ERT's membership on the basis of the analytical framework proposed in chapter 1. The main argument of this chapter will be that the ERT as a business forum is unique both in representing large sections of European capital at the highest level, and in transcending the conventional forms of corporate lobbying in the EU, influencing the EU public policy debate in a more comprehensive way by operating at the level of ideas and ideology formation. I will argue that the Roundtable synthesises and organises ideas into a coherent political strategy that, while effectively representing the perceived material interests of European big business, ideologically transcends those interests as well by appealing to a wider set of interests and identities. It is thus the purpose of this chapter to show that we can interpret the role of the ERT in the terms developed by our theoretical framework: that is, in terms of a transnational class strategy.

The formation of the ERT

The background against which the ERT was formed was that of the crisis of European order as analysed in the preceding chapter. When integration was at a low-point in the early 1980s and growing global competition threatened the position of large sections of European industry, leading members of Europe's business community such as Pehr Gyllenhammar of Volvo, Umberto Agnelli of Fiat and Wisse Dekker of Philips, began to perceive the need for a European-level political initiative to recover from this European decline. In their view, what Europe first of all needed was a move to the 'European scale in industrial and market development', which, as we shall see in chapter 4, above all meant the creation of a unified European home market. Such an initiative was not forthcoming from Europe's politicians, who still seemed to be trapped in the dominant 'Europessimism' mood. Europe's industrialists thus realised that it was up to themselves to launch such a new political initiative (see Cowles 1994: 210–11), and, moreover, that they could not do this through the established European business associations, in particular the Union of Industrial and Employers Confederations of Europe (UNICE) – the 'official voice' of European industry – which was at that time considered to be rather ineffective (see below).

The two most important men behind the formation of the ERT were Pehr Gyllenhammar, the then chief executive officer (CEO) of Volvo, and Viscount Etienne Davignon, at the time one of the vice-presidents of the European Commission and charged with industrial affairs.[2] In the year leading up to the Roundtable's foundation, Gyllenhammar – an industrial heavyweight, whose leadership qualities and international (political) influence were widely recognised both within Europe and across the Atlantic (Green 1993: 9) – had on several occasions publicly called upon his fellow transnational businessmen to, within a framework of European co-operation, 'play an active and important role in the formulation of the industrial strategies for future growth' (Gyllenhammar 1982). This was part of his campaign for what he later called a new 'Marshall Plan for Europe'.[3] Although Gyllenhammar was from a country that was at that time not a member of the EC, one might argue that it was precisely the fact that Sweden was not part of the Community that activated a concern within Swedish industry (particularly that part oriented to the EC market) that it might be excluded from the European developments. Gyllenhammar's company Volvo also had relatively high market shares in several EC member states and was also keen to secure these shares for the future.[4]

Gyllenhammar's ideas appeared to coincide with those of industrial affairs Commissioner Davignon as the two men met several times in 1982 to discuss the possibility of setting up a cross-sectoral forum in which business leaders could work out a common strategy to promote the interests of transnational European industry (Cowles 1995a: 504). Viscount Davignon was not only seen as one of the few effective members of the weak Thorn Commission, he was also considered to be one of its more pro-business-oriented members (see Cowles 1994: 141–47).

As Cowles argues (Cowles 1994: 141) in her study of the politics of European big business, Davignon's tenure as Industry Commissioner (from 1977 to 1984) marked a significant shift in EC industrial policy inasmuch as before (when European capital was still more nationally oriented), the Commission had not been very concerned with the views of industrialists, an attitude of indifference that, as noted in chapter 2, in some cases turned more explicitly adversarial. According to Davignon himself, when he entered the stage, he was surprised about the Commission's attitude vis-à-vis European business, which, in his view, put too much emphasis on mere technical/juridical aspects, not knowing how to deal with the problems of European industry and how to involve the industrial leaders themselves in looking for solutions, whereas industry for its part was uncertain about what it could expect from the Commission.[5]

After his successful management of the restructuring process of Europe's steel sector (see Swann 1983: 175ff), Davignon moved on with establishing a dialogue with Europe's leading electronics companies around the theme of information technology and the possible role of the Commission in supporting its development. This dialogue formed the basis for what later was to become Europe's first big, Commission-sponsored, programme on technological co-operation, namely ESPRIT (see Sandholtz 1992). It formed the beginning not only of a whole series of programmes on European technological co-operation, but also of a much more permanent dialogue between the Commission and an elite group of European multinationals. As such, the 'Telematics' initiative can be interpreted as to 'prefigure the 1992 movement and display the same configuration of political actors' (Sandholtz and Zysman 1989: 114).

The role of Davignon in taking European industry on board in the integration process reached a high-point when in 1983 the ERT was created. After successful experiences in dialoguing with business CEOs of specific sectors, Davignon had come to the conclusion it would be useful to create a more permanent group that could represent the bulk of large-scale European industry and with which the Commission could engage in a permanent dialogue.[6] In developing this idea together with the Volvo CEO, Davignon too consciously bypassed UNICE, which he did not find an effective interlocutor for his purposes since this was more a traditional lobby club than a partner with which a dialogue could be developed.[7] Davignon, together with his colleague, the French Commissioner (and former Commission president) Ortoli, was also present during the largest part of the first 'conference' of the ERT in April 1983. Nevertheless, Gyllenhammar was the charismatic figure who dominated the ERT in its first years (Green 1993: 13).[8]

When the first meeting of what was then called the Roundtable of European Industrialists was held on 6–7 April 1983 in Paris, the group consisted of 17 members. All were chairmen or CEOs of European multinational companies, from a range of different sectors and from both EC and non-EC countries. A list of these founding members is given table 3.1.

As we have seen, the formation of the ERT took place in the context of a close interaction between prominent European business leaders on the one hand, and Commissioner Davignon on the other. From the very beginning, then, the Roundtable had the highest-level access to the Commission and was perceived to

Table 3.1 Original members of the ERT, April 1983

Name	*Company*	*Country*	*Sector*
Umberto Agnelli	Fiat	Italy	motor vehicles
Peter Baxendell	Shell	UK	oil
Carlo De Benedetti	Olivetti	Italy	electronics
Wisse Dekker	Philips	Netherlands	electronics
Kenneth Durham	Unilever	UK	agro-alimentary
Roger Faroux	St Gobain	France	building materials
Pehr Gyllenhammar	Volvo	Sweden	motor vehicles
Bernard Hanon	Renault	France	motor vehicles
John Harvey-Jones	ICI	UK	chemicals
Olivier Lecerf	Lafarge Coppée	France	building materials
Helmut Maucher	Nestlé	Switzerland	agro-alimentary
Hans Merkle	Bosch	Germany	motor vehicles (components)
Curt Nicolin	ASEA	Sweden	engineering
Louis von Plata	Ciba-Geigy	Switzerland	chemicals (pharmaceuticals)
Antoine Riboud	BSN	France	foods
Wolfgang Seelig	Siemens	Germany	electronics
Dieter Spethmann	Thyssen	Germany	steel

Sources: Cowles (1994: 215) and own research.

be a legitimate player by Europe's policy-makers. The way in which the ERT was formed thus laid the foundations for the development of an enduring 'partnership' between the Roundtable and the Commission. Let us now examine the different institutional features of this new elite organisation of European big business.

The structure of the ERT

When the ERT was founded in 1983 its principal aim as perceived by its founders was, in the words of its later chairman Wisse Dekker: 'to revitalise European industry and make it competitive again, and to speed up the process of unification of the European market' (Dekker 1990: 17). The latter objective (unification of the market) can be seen as a means to achieving the former. Promoting European integration is therefore not a goal in itself, but the by-product of what the ERT sees as its primary task, strengthening European industry in the face of growing competitive pressures from Japan and the USA. From the very beginning, the ERT has been convinced of the fact that for a relaunching of European industry a relaunching of the European project itself was a necessary condition: 'the emphasis of the group's work is on *developing ideas* and taking initiatives to promote the European scale in industrial and market development – strengthening European industry's competitiveness . . . by promoting competition and co-operation on a European scale' (ERT 1985: 2, my emphasis).

It is important to note that, as we shall see in the next chapter, for the Roundtable capitalists the project of relaunching European integration was to go beyond market integration. The most urgent need was for the creation of a unified European home market, to serve as a springboard for the world market. But what was also needed, forming the second aspect of the ERT's initial project, was a strengthening of 'European government' and a deepening of the Community's institutional structure. This strengthened government could then play a supportive role by stimulating and partly funding technological co-operation, by helping to develop trans-European infrastructure networks, and, at times, by providing some selective forms of protectionism. In chapters 4 and 5, we will, however, see how this strategy was abandoned in favour of a more explicit (albeit still 'embedded') neo-liberal project, in which the primary task of European governments is defined as promoting the competitiveness of European industry first and foremost through deregulation, the promotion of labour market flexibility, etc. It is thus a central argument of this book that the ideological and strategic orientation of the Roundtable has shifted over time.

Institutional development and leadership

When the ERT was formed in 1983, it was no more than a very informal club of businessmen engaged in a dialogue with the Commission about the future of European industry. In these first years, the Roundtable was really in its 'experimental phase',[9] lacking any fixed procedures, and being run by part-time staff from the Paris office of Volvo. In 1988, Dekker of Philips took over from Gyllenhammar to become the Roundtable's second chairman. Before the founding of the ERT, Dekker had already started to play a pioneering role in pursuing what one observer has called a 'Europeanizing mission' (Krause 1991: 71), which made him one of the more visible crusaders for a unified market (see also, e.g., Krause 1992; Colchester and Buchan 1990: 27).

Under Dekker's new leadership, the ERT underwent the very same year an institutional transformation of great significance, marking the year 1988, in the words of a senior ERT official, as a 'watershed' in the development of the organisation.[10] First, as a testimony to the growing contacts between the ERT and the Commission, and the Roundtable's desire to develop these links further, the secretariat moved to Brussels. Second, with this move the ERT also became a formal organisation – registered as an 'Association International avec un But Philantropique, Scientifique, et Pédagogique' under Belgian law – and was, moreover, from now on fully equipped with a professional full-time staff. The Roundtable hired Keith Richardson, a former journalist who had later worked for BAT (Cowles 1994: 252), for the new position of secretary-general; a job that he held until the end of 1997, providing the organisation with a great deal of continuity that would otherwise be hard to maintain with a private club that has a relatively high turnover in membership. The secretariat is now run by Wim Philippa, a Dutchman who previously worked for Heineken.

Third, constituting the most important institutional change, 1988 saw the 'merger' with another Roundtable of European business leaders, the *Groupe des Présidents des Grandes Entreprises Européennes*. The *Groupe des Présidents* (GdP) had been founded in 1967 as a low-key discussion group of prominent industrialists from all EEC countries, and was regarded by the ERT as more of a 'dining club' than a platform seeking to influence public policy.[11] The merger however was important because of the resulting major expansion of the ERT's membership. Over the years the membership had already grown from the original 17 to 29 in the year before the merger. Now, the incoming members from the GdP (there was of course considerable overlap in memberships) brought the total up to 40 (Cowles 1994: 253). More significantly, as will be discussed in the next chapter, the merger brought with it a change in the composition of membership inasmuch as it shifted the weight from what could be called (potential) 'European champions' with a more regionalist orientation to 'global players' such as Unilever and Shell, whose CEOs had a more 'globalist' (neo-liberal) orientation.

Finally, and partly as a result of the merger with the GdP, from the end of the 1980s onwards, the ERT becomes more conscious of its role as a pro-active shaper of policies. As a former senior official of the ERT reflects on this redefinition of the ERT's role in the wake of the merger with the GdP:

> I think it [the merger with the GdP] also led us to define more clearly our role, because the *Groupe des Présidents* discussed important issues, policy issues, but much more like a dining club, a good dining club [but] with the merger we sort of really thought: well let's define what the ERT should do, and we defined it really like an input into policy making, providing an input into those policies that are important to industry at European level. So it is *not* a dining club, we are there actually to influence what happens in the real world. Although of course we are also a dining club, and members can learn from talking to one another, and they value that, it's terribly important, but it's not the object, the object is to produce some output in terms of influence on policy making.[12]

The merger thus also led the Roundtable to become even more clearly focused on influencing the European policy process. Moreover, in the Dekker years, the ERT's influence over EC policies was increasingly exercised through the development of personal relationships (on the part of Dekker and other prominent ERT members) with key European policy-makers, in particular with the then Commission president Delors.[13] His successor, the Frenchman Jérôme Monod – the then CEO of utilities company Lyonnaise des Eaux-Dumez, as well as, like so many French businessmen, a former politician active in the Gaullist RPR, and a close ally of current President Chirac[14] – successfully raised the profile of the ERT even further, in particular vis-à-vis national government leaders.

In 1996, the ERT chose Helmut Maucher, then one of the few remaining 'founding fathers', as its fourth chairman. Maucher was the chairman of the food giant Nestlé headquartered in Switzerland, but is of German nationality. In the many years that he led Nestlé, Maucher earned himself a reputation as a very successful manager, who turned around the fortunes of his company and turned it into a world leader in the global food business.[15] In 2000 Maucher was succeeded by the Dutchman Morris Tabaksblat, who was formerly CEO of Europe's other global food giant, Unilever, and now heads the Anglo-Dutch publishing house Reed Elsevier. The two current vice-chairmen are Gerhard Cromme, former CEO of Krupp and now chairman of the supervisory board of ThyssenKrupp, and Carlo De Benedetti, formerly of Olivetti and now heading his private industrial investment company, the Cofide-Cir Group. De Benedetti is in fact the only remaining founding father of the current ERT roster, and was one of the leading personalities in the ERT's early Europeanisation drive. Gerhard Cromme is one of Germany's most high-profile managers, especially since the failed hostile take-over bid of Krupp (engineered by Cromme) for its rival steel giant Thyssen in 1997 (after the bid failed, the companies later decided to merge peacefully). In his, according to the *Financial Times*, 'extremely Anglo-Saxon take-over bid',[16] Cromme gained himself a reputation – in the financial press but also among the public at large – as an 'aggressive' and 'ruthless' cost-cutter, who in his drive for rationalisation sometimes (as in the case with the take-over bid) opts for 'confrontation' rather than 'consensus', antagonising Germany's labour unions as well as its politicians in the process.[17]

Under the four former chairmen, the ERT has thus developed from an informal but already influential group of businessmen into an established, but still private and independent organisation, recognised as such by both the Brussels bureaucracy and members states' national governments.

Structure and membership criteria: 'a club of bosses'[18]

At present the ERT has around 45 members, meaning that its membership has not grown much beyond its 1988 expansion. In fact, as the ERT believes that the relative smallness of its organisation is one of its principal strengths, a ceiling has been set of a maximum of 50 members.[19] The membership of the ERT is personal, i.e., it is not companies that are members of the ERT but individuals leading companies – in practice always *men* (the ERT has not so far had any female members). The Roundtable is therefore not a conference of transnational corporations meeting to discuss possible forms of co-operation or common strategies, but a group of individual businessmen who, although they are heads of certain TNCs, do not necessarily represent those companies within the Roundtable discussions. Membership is by invitation only. That is to say, members are recruited by way of co-optation, in which personal relationships within a wider network of elite interaction play a predominant role. The selection of new members is informed by the following set of (informal) criteria.[20]

A first criterion is that the company from which the prospective members are drawn must be a European-based (industrial) TNC, preferably private. The prospective members should 'represent' their company at the highest level, that of chairman or chief executive officer (CEO). The company itself should also be independent and not a subsidiary. This is, incidentally, also one major reason why the European heads of companies that are headquartered in the USA ('European companies of American parentage') are refused membership of the Roundtable. Many of them have in fact at several times sought to join the ERT but their requests have consistently been turned down.[21] A senior official of the Roundtable explains the rationale behind this refusal thus:

> We insist that it is multinational companies headquartered in Europe, for the simple reason . . . that we insist that it is the chief decision maker who is the member, for the simple reason that eventually these great men, when they have decided something around the table, have to go home and *put their mouth and their money to the policies*. It cannot be that we have somebody agreeing around the table and then going back to the American [parent] company, it wouldn't work . . . It would probably destroy it from the inside.[22]

Indeed, it is the way in which Roundtable members can combine 'mouth' (ideas or discursive power) with 'money' (the structural economic power of the TNCs that they lead) that explains much of the unique political influence they can exercise, as will be discussed below.

Other criteria for membership are that the spread between sectors as well as between countries should be more or less even. Maybe the most important informal criterion is that the prospective member not only shares the (official) objectives of the Roundtable but can make a credible commitment that he will contribute to the achievement of those objectives. As the membership is personal, the choice is also made on the basis of personal characteristics, where 'personality, opinions [of the person], capabilities and vision, all play a role'.[23] Of course, of particular importance here is the compatibility of the political views of the prospective members with those of the current. It is thus that membership, and who is considered to be worthy of it and who's not, becomes an important (although with regard to the latter, unfortunately hard to access) indicator for shifts in the ERT's strategic orientation. On the basis of these and other criteria, membership has been refused to interested candidates on several occasions. Regular attendance at ERT meetings is expected from all members. If members consistently fail to attend without good reason, they are asked to withdraw from the organisation.[24]

Organisational structure

The leadership of the Roundtable is in the hands of a so-called Steering Committee. The Steering Committee presently consists of eight members, including a chairman and two vice chairmen, who are elected or re-elected every two years. The ERT organises a plenary session twice a year, as a general rule in the member state holding the EU presidency. The primary function of the plenary sessions is to have an exchange of ideas about the course the ERT should take; the policies and themes it should focus upon, etc. The plenary session is the ultimate decision-making body that not only sets the policy direction for the organisation, but also gives final approval to reports, to the admittance of new members, etc. The Steering Committee meets in between the plenary sessions, to have a more inner-group discussion about the ERT's course, discussing draft reports and coordinating planned activities.

Each ERT member chooses his own associate – usually a senior manager of the same company – to prepare most of the ERT work that the member is involved in. It is at this level of the associates' 'network' that most of the actual (practical) work – such as preparing meetings and drafting reports or statements – of the ERT is done.[25] The ERT's secretariat runs the day-to-day organisation of the Roundtable activities and moreover takes care of communicating these externally. Many of the more frequent activities of the Roundtable are undertaken by the different working groups into which the ERT has been divided since 1987. These working groups play a vital role in the ERT's internal policy-making process. As a senior ERT official put it, they are the 'laboratories that produce what the ERT people have to say [although] the final result is always the endorsement by ERT members'.[26] There are currently eight working groups, each chaired by a leading ERT member (on: accounting standards; competitiveness; enlargement; environment; foreign economic relations; industrial relations and social policy; pension reform; and taxation).[27]

Composition of membership

The ERT is Europe's only transnational, cross-sectoral pressure group that primarily 'represents' (non-financial) big business. Table 3.2 presents a list of the ERT members as of May 1999.[28] From this list, we find that 36 members' companies out of 45 appear on the *Financial Times* Europe 500 (which ranks Europe's companies by market capitalisation), of which 20 are among the top 100.[29] On a global level, *Fortune's* Global 500, which ranks companies by total sales, lists 27 companies of ERT members.[30] Moreover, 20 companies of ERT members can be found on the UNCTAD top 100 of TNCs ranked by foreign assets, and of those, seven are among the first ten European companies on the list (UNCTAD 2000b: 72–75, see also table 3.3 below). Finally, the Roundtable companies have a combined turnover of more than 950 billion euro and together employ more than four million people world-wide.[31]

We are thus dealing here with a group of persons leading Europe's largest non-financial capitalist enterprises. In addition to these statistics, the names of the members themselves give an indication of the very elite character of the ERT. In fact, most ERT members are among the most prominent and influential (industrial) business leaders of their respective countries. Two examples will suffice here (next to the ones already mentioned and those that we will encounter later on). Thus, from Sweden, we find Percy Barnevik who as CEO of ABB quickly rose to stardom in the global business community – portrayed as the most global of all global managers – and who now heads Investor, the holding company which is the main investment vehicle of the Wallenberg empire, which controls most of Swedish industry.[32] Among the Italians (for a long time the two Agnelli brothers (of Fiat) had been among the most prominent Italian members), we find Marco Tronchetti Provera, chairman and major shareholder of the very global (with a degree of globalisation especially striking in the Italian context) tyre-maker Pirelli, whose views on Italian and European politics are regularly reported on by the Italian media, and whom the *Financial Times* tipped as the 'new prince' of Italian industry to step into the shoes of Giovanni Agnelli.[33] Among the ERT membership, then, we find many of the 'stars' of Europe's corporate elite, those successful transnational

Table 3.2 Members of the ERT and their companies, May 1999

Name	*Company*	*Country*	*Sector*	*Ownership (%)**
Americo AMORIM	Amorim Group	Portugal	cork products	Amorim family
Percy BARNEVIK	Investor AB	Sweden	holding company	Wallenberg family (41.0)
Jean-Louis BEFFA	Saint-Gobain	France	building materials	Vivendi (9.3); BNP (5.3)
Peter BONFIELD	BT	UK	telecoms	no major shareholders
Cor BOONSTRA	Philips	Netherlands	electronics	no major shareholders
Anthony BURGMANS	Unilever	Neth./UK (N.)	agro-alimentary	no major shareholders
Bertrand COLLOMB	Lafarge	France	building materials	no major shareholders
François CORNÉLIS	Petrofina	Belgium	oil	A. Frère and P. Desmarais (39.9)
Alfonso CORTINA	Repsol	Spain	oil	Spanish banks (17.1)
Gerhard CROMME	ThyssenKrupp	Germany	mech. engin.	Krupp Foundation (16.8)
Dimitris DASKALOPOULOS	Delta Dairy	Greece	agro-alimentary	–
Etienne DAVIGNON	Société Générale de Belgique	Belgium	conglomerate	Suez Lyonnaise d. Eaux (100.0)
Carlo DE BENEDETTI	Cofide-Cir Group	Italy	holding company	De Benedetti (family)
Thierry DESMAREST	Total	France	oil	COGEMA (9.3)
Jean-René FOURTOU	Rhône-Pouelenc	France	chemicals (pharma)	core shareholders (SG, AGF, Fiat, BNP, Credit Suisse: 8.4)
Paulo FRESCO	Fiat	Italy	motor vehicles	Agnelli family (30.1)
José Antonio GARRIDO	Iberdrola	Spain	utilities	Spanish banks (14.8); Chase Manhattan Bank (10.2)
Fritz GERBER	Roche	Switzerland	chemicals (pharma)	Founding families (50.0)
Ulrich HARTMANN	Veba	Germany	conglomerate	Allianz (11.5)
Daniel JANSSEN	Solvay	Belgium	chemicals	Solvay family (54.0)
Alain JOLY	Air Liquide	France	chemicals	no major shareholders
Jak KAHMI	Profilo Group	Turkey	electronics	–
David LEES	GKN	UK	engineering	no major shareholders
André LEYSEN	Gevaert	Belgium	holding company	Almanij (majority)
Flemming LINDELØV	Carlsberg	Denmark	agro-alimentary	Carlsberg Foundation (51.0)
Helmut MAUCHER	Nestlé	Switz. (Ger.)	agro-alimentary	no major shareholders
Charles MILLER-SMITH	ICI	UK	chemicals	Capital group (6.9)
Jérôme MONOD	Suez Lyonnaise des Eaux	France	utilities	A. Frère and P. Desmarais (12.6)
Mark MOODY-STEWART	Shell	Neth./UK (UK)	oil	no major shareholders
Egil MYKLEBUST	Norsk Hydro	Norway	oil	Norwegian State (51.0)
Jorma ØLLILA	Nokia	Finland	electronics	no major shareholders
Lars RAMQVIST	Ericsson	Sweden	electronics	Wallenberg family (38.8)
Frank RIBOUD	Danone	France	agro-alimentary	M. David Weil (8.6); Agnelli family (6.4)

Table 3.2 Continued

Name	*Company*	*Country*	*Sector*	*Ownership (%)**
Nigel RUDD	Pilkington	UK	building materials	no major shareholders
Richard SCHENZ	OMV	Austria	oil and gas	Austrian State (ÖIAG: 35.0)
Manfred SCHNEIDER	Bayer	Germany	chemicals (pharma)	Allianz (5.0)
Jürgen SCHREMPP	Daimler-Benz	Germany	motor vehicles	Deutsche Bank (22.0)
Louis SCHWEITZER	Renault	France	motor vehicles	French State (44.2)
George SIMPSON	Gen. Electric Company	UK	electronics	no major shareholders
Michael SMURFIT	Jefferson Smurfit	Ireland	forestry and paper	Bank of Ireland (14.0); Michael Smurfit (6.5)
Peter SUTHERLAND	BP Amoco	UK (Irish)	oil	no major shareholders
Morris TABAKSBLAT	Reed Elsevier	Neth./UK (Ne.)	publishing	no major shareholders
Marco TRONCHETTI PROVERA	Pirelli	Italy	rubber products	Marco Tronchetti Provera and family, Pirelli Family (40.5)
Cees VAN LEDE	Akzo-Nobel	Neth.	chemicals	no major shareholders
Heinrich VON PIERER	Siemens	Germany	electronics	no major shareholders
Mark WÖSSNER	Bertelsmann	Germany	publishing (media)	Reinhard Mohn (90.0)**

Sources: Names of members and companies: ERT website (http://www.ert.be/pc/enc_frame.htm, accessed 10 May 1999). Country, sector, and ownership: personal research. Information on ownership is taken from 1999 company annual reports and company-provided (1999) data from the internet.

Notes: If the nationality of the member differs from that of his company, the former is given in parentheses.

– = information on major shareholders not available.

* Of all the major shareholders, I have identified the so-called 'ultimate owners': that is, those people who stand at a sometimes long chain of control (thus for instance the Wallenberg family does not directly own 38.8% of Ericsson but controls these voting rights through the ownership stakes of a number of family controlled foundations in Investor, which in turn controls Ericsson). The percentages – when known – given in parentheses thus refer to voting rights controlled rather than to shares owned.

** Of which 20.5 directly owned by the family, the rest controlled through a foundation.

capitalists who are well respected and influential – and perceived as real leaders (also in a political sense) – both at home and abroad. As Gardner notes in his study of lobbying within the Community: 'The names and positions of the individuals who make up the ERT offer a clue to why this small, ultra-elite organisation wields such extraordinary clout in the EC [forming] the single most powerful business group in Europe' (Gardner 1991: 48).

Let us now briefly examine the structure of ownership of the companies of the ERT members. All companies except Norsk Hydro are more than 50 per cent (and in most cases fully) privately (in the sense of non-state) owned, with most companies publicly trading their shares on the stock exchange. The only two other companies with still significant state ownership are the Austrian oil company OMV and Renault, which is one of the last few remaining large French firms that has not been fully privatised again after the earlier (re-)nationalisations of the 1980s. We can furthermore note that family ownership is still extensive among the large firms present in the ERT, confirming the general picture in continental Europe (Van Apeldoorn 2001), with 13 cases of families or individuals controlling large stakes. It is also important to note that in several cases (Amorim, De Benedetti, Smurfit and Tronchetti Provera), ERT members themselves have large (minority) interests in the ownership of the company they manage (most ERT members in fact have – in terms of income that they may generate – considerable shareholdings in their companies, but these holdings are usually not large enough to be reported as minority interests). In cases where the managers (ERT members) and the controlling owners are different people (as in the case of Fiat and the Wallenberg-controlled companies), we may assume that the CEOs maintain close personal links with the controlling family members, and that although occupying different functions within the capitalist class (see Scott 1997), they all share the same basic ideological commitments (i.e., they are part of a class-conscious capitalist elite).

I will now examine the national composition of the ERT's membership, before looking at sectoral 'representation' and the degree of transnationalisation attained by the companies of ERT members, thus approximating the three factors identified in chapter 1 as underlying the most important lines of cleavage (in terms of ideological and strategic outlook) *within* the elite of Europe's transnational capitalist class.

National composition

In terms of country representation, we see that all EU member states are represented except Luxembourg. The other three countries represented are Switzerland, Norway (both part of the European Free Trade Association) and Turkey. The balance the Roundtable strives to maintain does not imply that all nationalities are equally 'represented'. To an extent, the inequality reflects the unequal size of the different countries. So, in 1999, 'the big three' of Germany, the UK and France together accounted for nearly half of the members. On the other hand, whereas there are only three members from Italy and only two from Spain, there are four each from two much smaller countries, Belgium and the Netherlands. It appears, then, that the balance is clearly weighted in favour of the most developed part of western Europe. What this imbalance boils down to is basically a north–south divide, which is not surprising since the largest and most internationalised European companies are to be found within the northern countries. Indeed, one may wonder to what extent the members of the southern European companies are yet fully incorporated into Europe's transnational business elite. Here, one probably has to distinguish between a group of core members and an outer peripheral group of 'backbenchers'.[34] With a view to the prospective eastern enlargement of the EU, we may also note the glaring absence of any members from central and eastern Europe – clearly these countries as yet do not have large enough indigenous TNCs.

Let us now examine the national composition of the Roundtable in more detail by looking at the membership from the three big countries: France, the UK and Germany. As these countries tend to dominate the intergovernmental policy-making process within the EU, it is also members from these countries on which the Roundtable primarily has to rely to influence intergovernmental decision making. Moreover, I would suggest that it is with these countries that the nationality factor weighs most heavily, or at least is most easily identifiable. That is to say, it is here that we can most clearly see how nationality is one factor – through socialisation within the countries' economic, political and social-cultural institutions – in shaping the ideological outlook and political views of the respective members. I thus maintain that, just as we can identify a German, French and British model in western Europe's institutional diversity of capitalism, we can also distinguish German, French and British perspectives within Europe's emergent transnational capitalist class (and hence also within the ERT).

THE FRENCH

The French were from the start well represented within the ERT, both in numbers and in terms of influence. Among the original 17 members, there were four Frenchmen. Wisse Dekker recalled that in these first years the French were very active within the Roundtable.[35] Maria Cowles' detailed research has also shown that in 1983 'nowhere were the links between the ERT and government leaders closer than in France' (Cowles 1994: 226) and that this 'French connection' made an important contribution to the ERT's early success. The relatively dominant role of the French in these early years can partly be explained by the relative weak transnationalisation of the French members' companies, both inside and outside the European region.[36] When the ERT was founded, the companies of the French members were still very much dependent on the French home market (see, e.g., Savary 1993), and they needed the ERT and the *relance* of Europe in order to further internationalise their corporate activity and to be able to compete on the world market. The first step in this process was the creation of a new, bigger home market, being the Community's proposed internal market. The dominant role of the French can furthermore be linked to the role of the French government, and especially Mitterrand himself, in sponsoring pan-European technological co-operation (see Sharp 1990; Sandholtz 1992).

In terms of ideological orientation, the link between world view and nationality is maybe nowhere more apparent than in the case of the French. In other words, the French ERT members, or at least their companies, must be seen as relatively strongly embedded into the socio-political structures of their home country. The specific features of the French model of 'statist' capitalism as identified in the previous chapter, such as its centralist mode of government, the proverbial *dirigisme* and mercantilism of French economic policy and the close links between the political elite and French big business are all factors that need to be taken into account here.

In 1999, the ERT counts eight French members, still the largest group, but their weight within the Roundtable seems – notwithstanding the chairmanship of Monod until 1996 – to have been in relative decline since the early years when they more than any other national group shaped the Roundtable's outlook. The other side of the coin of the relative decline of the French is the rise of the British and the Germans, in both quantitative and qualitative terms. At the same time it must be noted that the French members of today are of a different kind than those of the 1980s. As we shall see in the next chapter, French business has in the course of the 1990s become much more globalised, with French business elites gaining a much more globalist outlook.

THE BRITISH

When the Roundtable was founded, three British industrialists, of Unilever, ICI and Shell, initially joined the new club. But they all left the (still very informal) organisation only a few months after the first meeting in April 1983 (Cowles 1994: 218), leaving the Roundtable temporarily without any British members until in 1984–85 several new members were recruited, among whom were three new British. We will return to this episode in the next chapter, but a plausible hypothesis is that the three British industrialists – all leading global companies – did not feel at home in a group of businessmen that was evidently 'Europeanist' in its orientation. The initial British non-participation in the Roundtable is all the more striking as British industry since the 1970s had been in the forefront of gradually changing the face of European interest representation by introducing 'Anglo-Saxon style' lobbying into the European policy-making process, with many British multinationals being among the first to open their own political offices in Brussels (see Cowles 1994: 133–38). It therefore does not seem to be likely that it was a lack of interest in Europe that withheld British capitalists from (continued) involvement in the Roundtable.

Over the years more British capitalists joined the ERT, British nationals numbering six in 1999 (plus one Irishman, Peter Sutherland, heading the British company BP). The last few years have seen several new additions. Moreover, (some) British members have started to play an active role within the ERT. For instance, Sir David Simon of BP (who joined the ERT only in 1993 and left the organisation when he joined the new Labour government) became one of the ERT's vice-chairmen, and was in fact the first British member to join the Steering Committee. As the Roundtable has become more globalist (and neo-liberal) in its outlook, and has lost its earlier penchant for 'Europrotectionism' and a French-style European industrial policy, it has become more acceptable for the internationalist-oriented British.

THE GERMANS

Over the years, German members have started to participate much more actively in the Roundtable than before, when their attitude was one of indifference at best.[37] The relative invisibility of the German ERT members may be seen as symptomatic of the disinterested attitude German industry at that time expressed vis-à-vis the integration process, and in particular the supranational policy-making dimension of it.

Cowles argues that German big business was slow to learn the 'European game' and did not become a player in the Brussels policy-making process until the late 1980s (Cowles 1995b: 2). Several reasons for this can be identified. First, we have to understand this in the context of the rather unique structure of interest representation in the German national political economy, with its large role of formal associations.[38] In this corporatist structure there is hardly room for other (Anglo-Saxon style) independent business lobbies. German business leaders were simply not used to involving themselves in 'politics' but left this to the officials of the associations that represented them.[39] Thus, German industrial leaders were under considerable institutional and concomitant cultural constraints emanating from the 'German model'.[40]

Second, the relative non-participation of Germany's industrialists in forums like the ERT was also related to the structural position of German transnational capital in the European and world economies. German big business already benefited from a very large and strong home market so that initially it did not perceive the need for a European internal market to the same degree as for instance the Dutch and Belgian TNCs. The German home market also served as a base for an offensive and successful export-oriented world market strategy. But in the context of the success of a group like the ERT, and as with the SEA the national veto was abolished – thus making the national route upon which German business had previously relied (Cowles 1995b: 5) much less reliable – the German attitude slowly began to change and German companies, and their leaders, emerged as important actors in EU politics (ibid.: 16–25), inside and outside the ERT.

Sectoral composition and degree of transnationalisation

Examining the sectoral 'representation' within the ERT, we see that it has indeed become a truly cross-sectoral group with 'representations' from most of the important industrial sectors. There are five to seven members from companies within each of four basic sectors: agro-alimentary; chemicals (incl. pharmaceuticals); oil; and electronics. With almost all European oil companies present, this sector appears to be relatively over-represented. In contrast, the ERT of the 1990s shows a rather low presence of companies from the service industries and from what is now referred to as the 'new economy' or information and communication technology (ICT) sector. Thus, on the May 1999 roster, only British Telecom and 'new media' company (formerly a traditional publisher) Bertelsmann can be seen as falling within the non-manufaturing ICT sector (although the fortunes of Nokia and Ericsson as *manufacturers* of mobile phones are closely linked to this sector). However, and apart from the fact that Europe does not yet have many large firms in this sector, the ERT does increasingly seem to make an effort to redress this imbalance, as in 2001 we find two more telecom firms (Telecom Italia and Deutsche Telekom), as well as German software giant SAP.[41] The ERT is thus

Table 3.3 ERT companies among the top 100 TNCs ranked by foreign assets (1998 data)

*Ranking by**		*Company*	*Assets ($ billion)*		*Sales ($ billion)*		*Employment*		*Transnationality*
FA	*TI*		*Foreign*	*Total*	*Foreign*	*Total*	*Foreign* (*number of employees*)	*Total*	*index*[a] (*%*)
3	45	Shell[b]	67.0	110.0	50.0	94.0	61,000	102,000	58.0
8	21	BP Amoco	40.5	54.9	48.6	68.3	78,950	98,900	74.9
9	59	Daimler-Chrysler	26.7	159.7	135.4	154.6	208,502	441,502	50.4
10	3	Nestlé	35.6	41.1	51.2	52.0	225,665	231,881	94.2
12	7	Unilever	32.9	35.8	39.4	44.9	240,845	265,103	90.1
13	63	Suez Lyonnaise des Eaux	n.a.	84.6	12.9	34.8	126,500	201,000	45.6
19	52	Siemens	n.a.	66.8	45.7	66.0	222,000	416,000	53.6
21	34	Renault	23.6	43.2	25.4	38.8	92,854	138,321	61.8
26	33	Bayer	21.4	34.3	21.9	31.1	80,900	145,100	62.8
27	13	Roche	21.2	40.6	16.7	17.0	57,142	66,707	78.7
31	26	Rhone-Poulenc	n.a.	28.4	12.0	14.7	31,421	65,180	69.1
32	27	TotalFina	n.a.	27.0	20.8	28.6	35,100	57,166	69.0
33	14	Philips	19.0	32.8	32.1	33.9	189,210	233,686	77.8
50	82	Fiat[b]	14.2	76.1	19.4	51.0	87,861	220,549	32.1
65	88	Veba	n.a.	52.2	1.7	49.0	39,220	116,774	28.2
72	29	Danone	10.3	17.6	8.8	14.4	58,602	78,945	64.6
77	16	Akzo Nobel	10.1	14.0	11.6	14.6	67,800	85,900	76.8
80	37	Ericsson	9.6	20.7	17.8	22.8	56,668	103,667	60.4
86	15	Air Liquide	n.a.	10.6	5.1	6.8	20,306	28,600	77.0
96	39	ICI	7.2	14.9	10.9	15.1	n.a.	59,100	60.2

Table 3.3 Continued

Sources: *World Investment Report 2000* (UNCTAD 2000b: 72–75), based on the UNCTAD/Erasmus University Database.

Notes:
* FA = Foreign assets, fourth column.
  TI = Transnationality index, last column.

Three current ERT companies (Saint-Gobain, Lafarge, and Solvay) have departed from the list with respect to 1997, all of these have very high TI indices (58.7, 71.3, and 92.3 respectively, UNCTAD 2000: 77).

a This transnationality index is calculated as the average of foreign assets to total assets, of foreign sales to total sales, and of foreign employment to total employment.

b Foreign assets, sales, and employment are outside Europe.

n.a. means either not available or that the data on foreign assets are suppressed (by the UN) to avoid disclosure. In the case of non-availability, they are estimated on the basis of the ratio of foreign to total employment, foreign to total sales, and similar ratios.

becoming less of a club of predominantly manufacturing industry, although it is still a club of industrialists in the sense of excluding financial firms.

Nevertheless, it must be pointed out that not all – and probably not even a majority – of the ERT's members should be exclusively categorised as industrial capitalists. First, some ERT members wear more than one hat: that is, they are not only at the head of an industrial corporation but are also active as financial capitalists. One example is that of Carlo De Benedetti, who next to leading Olivetti for many years has also always been an important Italian financier (with a large private capital), investing not only in industry but also on financial markets. Another is Fritz Gerber, since 1978 head of Swiss chemicals giant La Roche, but also until recently head of Switzerland's second largest insurance company Zürich.[42] Maybe the most striking example is Peter Sutherland who recently joined the ERT as chairman of BP, but who is also a partner of Goldman Sachs – Wall Street's privately owned top investment bank – and chairman of its 'European arm', Goldman Sachs International. Second, many ERT members – although full-time industrialists in their daily occupation – are linked to the financial world through interlocking directorships, i.e., they sit on the boards or advisory committees of banks, insurance companies, or other financial institutions, within their own country but also in other countries (see table 3.4 for some examples). Third, some ERT companies, although industrial firms, in fact make a substantial part of their profits within the financial sector. Thus, all large TNCs nowadays have a so-called foreign exchange or FOREX department through which they trade in the global money market to insure themselves against currency fluctuation risks. In sum, the industrial capital 'represented' by the Roundtable is therefore far from completely separated from financial capital. Indeed, some of the ERT members – through their directorships at financial institutions, or (as in the case of Sutherland) through their double position as head of both a financial and an industrial firm, or because a part of their company is in fact active in the financial sector – should be regarded not as industrialists proper but as *finance capitalists*.

The final factor to examine is that of the degree of transnationalisation. In table 3.3, the absolute and relative transnationality rankings of ERT companies (from 1998) among the world's top 100 TNCs are presented. All companies except Suez Lyonnaise des Eaux, Fiat and Veba (whereby the data for Fiat only refer to activities *outside* Europe) show a transnationality index of over 50 per cent, with several being among the most transnationalised firms of the world. What does not show up in this table, however, and is particularly relevant for the argument to be developed in the remainder of this study, is the *geographical* pattern of the transnationalisation of Roundtable companies, distinguishing in particular between Europe and the rest of the world. Such an analysis will be presented in the next chapter.

Theoretical interpretation of the ERT: an elite forum of Europe's emergent transnational capitalist class

Having outlined the major organisational and structural features of the ERT, I shall now interpret the structure of the ERT more theoretically by arguing that it is neither a lobby group nor an association, but rather a private forum for Europe's transnational capitalist class. To place this interpretation into context we should first briefly discuss some of the recent scholarly debates on the rising phenomenon of transnational lobbying and interest representation within the EU.

The 1980s witnessed a spectacular growth in the number of so-called European interest groups (Greenwood, Grote and Ronit 1992: 1; Mazey and Richardson 1993a: 5–7), and is now estimated by the Commission to total about 3,000, including over 500 European and international federations (Greenwood 1997: 3). Argued to be partly a response to the SEA and the resulting rise in importance of Brussels as a centre of policy making and of the Commission as a supranational policy-making body (Mazey and Richardson 1993a: 6; Greenwood, Grote and Ronit 1992: 24), this emergence of Euro-lobbying and transnational interest representation has sparked a growing literature. Much of this literature shares the assumption that the EU, although not a state, can be seen as having 'state-like properties' and in this sense can be analysed as one would the national state in its interactions with interest groups (Greenwood, Grote and Ronit 1992: 17–20; see also Hix 1994).

Much of the debate, then, concentrates on the question of how to characterise the nature of the relationships between the EU and the European interest groups. Here, the two opposing models are corporatism (or neo-corporatism) on the one hand, and pluralism on the other. In a seminal article, Streeck and Schmitter put forward the argument that given the sheer number and diversity of interest groups at the European level, i.e., 'the profound absence of hierarchy and monopoly among a wide variety of players of different but uncertain status' (Streeck and Schmitter 1991: 159), and moreover given the absence of any class balance between capital and labour (ibid.: 146), the coming about of a 'Eurocorporatism' seems most unlikely. They instead argue that the present European policy process represents a form of transnational 'pluralism' (cf. Mazey and Richardson 1993a, 1993b). Streeck and Schmitter use the term pluralism merely to indicate the plurality of actors and the lack of institutionalist links (as in corporatism) between these actors and 'government' within the Euro-polity. A large part of the literature on the growing phenomenon of lobbying in the EU tends to interpret European (interest) politics, however, also in a more narrow pluralist sense, following the old pluralism of American political science for which society consisted of a collection of interest groups competing for influence over the legislature, and in which no group was in any sense privileged.

Whether referring to such an uncritical pluralism or to the more descriptive pluralism of Streeck and Schmitter, the thesis that the emerging EU polity reveals a pluralist pattern of interest intermediation has been contested – on the basis of extensive case-studies of government–industry relations at the European level – by a number of authors. Cawson, for example, has argued that the 'case of the consumer electronics sector suggests a trend towards a form of micro-corporatism where policy is determined and implemented through bargained agreements between the EC and major firms' (Cawson 1992: 117). This *micro*-corporatism (on the distinctions between micro-, meso- and macro-corporatism, see Cawson 1986) is however a different kind of corporatism from what Streeck and Schmitter refer to when they identify the absence of a class balance as one of the impediments to the emergence of Eurocorporatism, i.e., tripartite institutionalised bargaining at the EU level. The pluralism versus corporatism debate thus seems to be misguided in as much as different kinds of corporatism are not clearly distinguished.

Many of the 500 or more Euro-organisations represent specific business interests. The overwhelming majority of these are sectoral or trade associations. According to Lanzalaco, there at least 20 sector-unspecific peak associations of business, and within the industry sector, we find the following six: UNICE; Eurochambres; the European Centre of Public Enterprises (CEEP); the European Community Services Group; the EC Committee of the American Chamber of Commerce (Amcham); and the ERT (Lanzalaco 1992: 180). In the argument of this book, the ERT takes up a unique place within this group, and indeed within the whole 'system of business interest representation' (ibid.).

The Roundtable must first of all be distinguished from the kind of 'functional' interest groups to which early integration theorists accorded such an important role. As we have seen in chapter 1, in neo-functionalist theory, the formation of supranational interest organisations, itself seen as the product of the functionalist logic of the integration process, was expected to form a motor force in the further development of a supranational community. These neo-functionalist expectations with regard to the formation and role of interest groups were, however, not borne out by subsequent events. Although supranational interest groups were called into existence, with UNICE for instance being already founded in 1958, most of these organisations remained largely ineffective and in any case certainly did not develop into the pillars of a kind of tripartite supranational corporatist structure, forming the effective socio-economic basis for the newly born European polity (cf. Streeck and Schmitter 1991): 'Euro-groups, far from being dynamic agents of integration, have tended to be rather ineffective bodies unable to engage in constructive dialogue with the Commission' (McLaughlin, Jordan and Maloney 1993: 192).

UNICE was no exception in this respect. Until at least the early and mid-1980s – that is, until after the ERT was founded – UNICE, although formally the most important business group at the European level, was regarded 'with little respect from political and business leaders alike' (Green 1993: 14). In recent years, however, UNICE has undergone a reform process that has made it a much more effective body. Significantly, a critical role here was played by the European Enterprise Group, an informal structure consisting of European-affairs directors from a number of European TNCs (Cowles 1994: ch. 4), among which were several ERT companies. The result has been that, whereas in the early 1980s the top executives of Europe's largest firms regarded this peak association as slow, bureaucratic, and not at all capable of defending their interests (the frustration with it, as argued before, partly motivated the foundation of the ERT), they now view it as a lobby force that, although being fundamentally different from the pro-active ERT, still plays a very useful complementary role. Since 1990 large TNCs are directly represented in UNICE through the Advisory and Support Group while the chairs of its committees are also drawn from these ranks (Greenwood 1997: 109). Indeed, in the 1990s, several prominent ERT members have also served within UNICE. The transformation of UNICE may in fact be seen as an important manifestation of a general process whereby the efforts of TNCs are transforming Brussels-based business interest groups, including key sectoral organisations, 'from Eurogroups comprised of national federations to organizations increasingly led by large firms' (Cowles 1995b: 18). Moreover, also as individual actors, large firms have increasingly become key players in European politics (Grant, Martinelli and Paterson 1989; McLaughlin, Jordan and Maloney 1993).

Maybe the most telling development in this context has been the recent emergence of a number of less formal business groups modelled on the light structure of the ERT, with CEOs themselves being directly involved and exercising leadership based on their experience and prestige gained as members of a global power elite. The most prominent among these have been largely initiatives of ERT members. Examples are the Association for Monetary Union in Europe (AMUE, see chapter 4) and the Transatlantic Business Dialogue (TABD, see below). The most recent addition to the growing number of Roundtable-inspired forums is the European Roundtable of Financial Services, consisting of the chairmen and CEOs of initially 12 European financial institutions (among which are AEGON, Allianz, AXA and Deutsche Bank) and headed by the first chairman of the ERT, Pehr Gyllenhammar.[43] Business groups have thus increasingly centred their organisation and activities around large transnational firms and their CEOs, who have thus gained a leadership position in what is increasingly less a system of associational governance – that is, the representation of interests through (several layers of) formal organisations – and more a system of elite governance dominated by an emergent European transnational capitalist class, whose power must be linked to the rising structural power of transnational capital as bound up with the ongoing globalisation process.

These developments, however, were largely taking off only in the 1990s, partly inspired by the success of, and sometimes initiated by, the ERT. In the 1980s, where UNICE failed, the ERT did succeed in articulating the interests of large sections of European transnational capital, as well as in, as we have seen, establishing a *rapprochement* between (big) business and the Commission. This fact, however, does not warrant a neo-functionalist interpretation of the role played by the ERT. First, rather than being driven by the dynamic of the European integration process, the Roundtable was formed with the objective of reviving this dynamic after it had been moribund for so many years. It is in this sense that the Roundtable's role goes far beyond that of a mere constituency for the Commission (cf. Sandholtz and Zysman 1989; see chapter 1). Second, neo-functionalist interest group theory is ill-equipped for an analysis of the ERT inasmuch as the ERT represents a transnational pressure group that differs fundamentally from the 'Euro-groups' of integration theory, and plays accordingly a fundamentally different role. Below I suggest that the class-theoretical perspective developed in chapter 1 in fact allows us to make more sense of this role than any theoretical framework that centres around the corporatism versus pluralism dichotomy. It has to be pointed out in advance though that this interpretation is based on how the ERT has developed over the course of its existence. Its role as a vanguard of Europe's transnational capitalist class was a role that it itself had to develop, that it had to construct within the process of elite socialisation and the arbitration of rival ideological perspectives present within its ranks. At the same time, we can say that it has been in part through this process, and hence through the evolution of the ERT and its articulation of a collective ideological and strategic orientation, that the process of transnational class formation has further taken shape.

The ERT: neither an association nor a lobby group

The agency of the ERT, then, falls neither under the logic of pluralist lobbying nor under that of corporatist interest intermediation. Thus whereas for instance UNICE, as a peak association, has a public and formal – one might say 'corporatist' – role to play vis-à-vis the Commission and as a 'social partner' in the dialogue with the European Trade Union Confederation (ETUC), the ERT is not an interest association at all. In contrast to corporatist organisations, the ERT has no members either to represent or to discipline (into acceptance of the 'general interest'). Rather, the ERT *is* its members. As ERT vice-chairman, Gerhard Cromme, who formerly also had a leading position within UNICE, puts it:

> The European Roundtable is a forum in which European business leaders meet . . . we are not an association, we are not an interest group . . . and we also do not engage in lobbying in that sense but leave that to the relevant institutions . . . UNICE is an association of interest representation whereas ERT is not [but is] a private gathering of people who discuss themes and then try to arrive at a common opinion.[44]

As many ERT members and associates emphasise, these organisational characteristics of the ERT – a private and relatively small club of heads of Europe's largest corporations – give it a number of advantages over formal associations.[45] First, compared to big cross-sectoral associations representing several 'constituencies', the Roundtable has – lacking any formal responsibility to represent the whole or indeed even a particular part of European industry – less diverging interests to balance, and can act with relative speed and flexibility.[46] As a private group consisting exclusively of heads of TNCs and operating through a process of informal consensus formation, the ERT can more easily reach a consensus that is more than the lowest common denominator.[47] Moreover, unlike UNICE, which as the official voice of business has to respond to the details of all proposed EU regulation, the ERT is free to 'set the political highlights' according to its preferences.[48] This freedom, or 'selectivity', is in fact an important justification for having an organisation like the ERT next to UNICE in the first place.[49] Within the ERT it is the CEOs themselves who have the power to communicate what they would like to be put on the European agenda. As André Leysen, former ERT vice-chairman and formerly vice-chairman of UNICE, points out:

> [when it comes to] selling two or three points in a simple manner, a business leader can do a better job than someone who is mandated by hundreds of organisations and sub-organisations, which is to say that he is in a 'corset', whereas we just take the freedom to express our opinions.[50]

Second, and following the former point, the fact that the members themselves *are* the Roundtable, *and* that these members control Europe's biggest companies, gives the ERT a power that cannot be matched by any interest group in which that power is mediated through a bureaucracy of representation. It is thus that according to former ERT vice-chairman Leysen, the Roundtable 'tends to be taken more seriously': precisely 'because it is the big industrial leaders [themselves] who go and talk with the Commissioners, [the ERT] has a more direct access'.[51] The ERT thus has a privileged political access directly deriving from the power positions of its individual members, as is also underlined by the following quote from Peter Sutherland, now ERT member, but also a prominent former Commissioner (for competition) under the first Delors Presidency:

> I think that the importance of the ERT is not merely in the fact that it co-ordinates and creates a cohesive approach amongst major industries in Europe but because the persons who are members of it have to be at the highest level of companies and virtually all of them have unimpeded access to government leaders because of the position of their companies . . . That is exactly what makes it different [from other organisations]. The fact that it is at head of company level, and only the biggest companies in each country of the European Union are members of it. So, by definition each member of the ERT has access at the highest level to government.[52]

The political power of the ERT is thus directly related to the structural power of transnational capital. As a senior official of the ERT explains:

> When you have five business leaders of, let us assume, Nestlé, Daimler-Benz, Lyonnaise des Eaux, BP, and [let us add] a Spanish [company] to that as well, in the [same] room, then you have a different political weight than when just – between quotation marks – an official of an interest association speaks, who, although [formally] having behind him the whole of [European] industry, cannot actually speak for 2000, 20,000, or 200,000 jobs.[53]

Third, the ERT's elite character allows it to play a more strategic role, one that transcends lobbying or interest representation in a more restricted sense. The ERT does more than defending relatively clear-cut (narrow) corporate interests. In their role as leaders of Europe's corporate elite, ERT members come to the table with a wider vision, in which they seek to express what they think is good not so much for their company, or for their sector (for these they have other channels), but for European business in general. These general business interests are also formulated from within a relatively long-term and forward-looking perspective oriented towards the shaping of Europe's socio-economic order.[54] As former ERT vice-chairman David Simon explains, precisely because it brings together around '45 bosses who run businesses, they [the ERT members] will tend to take a more strategic view than an association . . . because after all that's what they're responsible for, they're responsible for direction and strategy. [The ERT thus] tries to concentrate on strategy and direction for the economy at large.'[55]

It is the Roundtable's longer-term and more strategic orientation – as enabled by the elite character of the organisation – that is here taken as an expression of the 'general' capitalist class interest as formulated from the vantage point of transnational (industrial) capital. This class interest is, I would contend, one that transcends the corporatist level inasmuch as it is tendentially articulated at the level of hegemony. It is true that the ERT does not *represent* the European capitalist class as a whole; indeed, as we have seen, it is in fact not at all an organisation of interest *representation*. The argument made here, however, is that precisely *because* the ERT is not a formal interest association, but rather a relatively informal elite club of Europe's most prominent business leaders, it can formulate and propagate a concept of the general (capitalist) interest, which, as was argued in chapter 1, is always formulated from the vantage point of a particular class *fraction*. The general capitalist class interest is in fact something that has to be *constructed* through an organisation like the ERT, where leading capitalists come together to reflect upon what their common interests might be – vis-à-vis labour and vis-à-vis the state – and how they can articulate them into a coherent and comprehensive strategy that can then be represented as serving the general public interest.

The ERT is a forum in which transnational capitalists can meet, socialise, but above all discuss their different viewpoints. These viewpoints can be related to the different sectors represented within the ERT, to the different nationalities with their concomitant ideological propensities, and, crucially, to the different degrees of transnationalisation: above all, to the different degrees to which this transnationalisation has taken place on a global rather than a merely regional scale. It is by seeking to articulate these rival *fractional* viewpoints into a cohesive common strategy that the members of the Roundtable fulfil a critical role in the European process of transnational class formation.

The ERT as a network of transnational business leaders must be seen as operating in a broader context of more encompassing transnational elite networks in which transnational ties are established and consolidated. As argued in chapter 1, interlocking directorships are one organisational mechanism through which this networking also operates, and through which the transnational capitalist class is lent more cohesion. As is shown in table 3.4, such a network of interlocking directorships can also be found within the ranks of the ERT. The table presents a list of (outside) directorships of ERT members at other current ERT companies for the year 1999. As it was not possible to find data on outside directorships for all members or members' companies, the actual network of interlocks is probably more extensive than this table indicates. Moreover, as we are primarily interested in the personal links between ERT members, the table only looks at interlocks between

ERT *members*, rather than between ERT companies (i.e., ERT companies linked through interlocks by other than ERT members). The latter analysis would have made for a much more extensive network indeed (see Nollert 2000 for an analysis of these structural company links).

In total, I found 29 'directorships' (see explanatory note below table) held by ERT members at other ERT companies. About half (16) of the total number of directorships are held at companies of a different nationality than that of the member's own company. It is of course these *transnational* interlocks that can be taken as one more indicator of the degree to which Europe's business elite is also a transnational elite. This network of interlocks must be seen as further facilitating the contacts and exchange of views among ERT members, and thus as contributing to the overall cohesiveness of the group. To the extent that data on this could be found, some significant directorships of ERT members at non-ERT companies have been listed in the third column of the table. Several of these interlocks consist of links between ERT members and companies within the financial sector. Among the Roundtable members listed in table 3.4 we find 12 such finance capitalists. Several ERT members also hold directorships at American financial or industrial corporations. These include members who are not listed in the table (such as Percy Barnevik who is director at General Motors) because they do not hold any directorships at other Roundtable companies. Of course, these transatlantic interlocks can be taken as a measure of the degree of integration of ERT members in a wider pattern of global class formation (see below). Several of the members listed hold three or more directorships at other companies, both ERT and non-ERT. Here we find current ERT vice-chairman Cromme (ThyssenKrupp) and former vice-chairman Leysen (Geveart) topping the list, each with nine directorships at other major companies.[56] Cromme is also the 'big linker' (Fennema 1982) within the ERT network itself, with four directorships at other ERT companies, followed by Davignon who holds three. Other well-connected members (within the ERT and globally) are Sutherland (BP) through his directorship at three companies from the Wallenberg empire and his chairmanship of Goldman Sachs International and current ERT chairman Tabaksblat, who holds positions at Renault-Nissan and Veba (now EON) and is also for instance an adviser to a major US investment bank.

The ERT and global capitalist elite networks

The process of transnational class formation within the European arena cannot be understood outside the context of wider *global* processes of class formation. As we have seen in chapter 1, an earlier study by Van der Pijl has identified a process of Atlantic class formation for the post-war era, a process that to a large extent structured the early European integration process (Van der Pijl 1984). With regard to the present era, in the wake of the crisis of corporate liberalism, the process of transnational – and increasingly global, or at least trilateral: that is, integrating capitalist elites from North America, Europe and Japan (Gill 1990) – class formation has deepened, with the capitalist class reaching new levels of global integration. My

Table 3.4 Interlocking directorships of ERT members in 1999

ERT members	*Directorships of ERT companies (DECs)*	*Other directorships*	*Total DECs*	*Transnational DECs*
Jean-Louis Beffa (Saint-Gobain)	Petrofina	Vivendi; *BNP Paribas*	1	1
Bertrand Collomb (Lafarge)	Unilever	Elf Aquitaine, *Allianz*	1	1
Gerhard Cromme (ThyssenKrupp)	ABB; Bertelsmann; Suez Lyonnaise des Eaux; Veba	*Allianz*; RAG; Ruhrgas; Volkswagen; Thomson	4	2
Etienne Davignon (SGB)	Petrofina (vice-chairman); Solvay; Suez Lyonnaise des Eaux	BASF; Arbed; *Fortis*	3	1
Thiery Desmarest (Total)	Air Liquide		1	
Fritz Gerber (Roche)	Nestlé (vice-chairman)		1	0
Alain Joly (Air Liquide)	Lafarge	*Banque Indosuez*	1	0
André Leysen (Geveart)	Bayer; Veba	Agfa-Geveart (chairman); BMW; Deutsche Telekom; SHV Holdings; Philipp Holzmann; Schenker	2	2
Helmut Maucher (Nestlé)	Bayer	*Allianz* (advisory council); *Credit Suisse*; Loreal; *Morgan Bank* (US, Int. Council); *Zürich*; Deutsche Bahn AG	1	1
Jérôme Monod (Suez Lyonnaise d. Eaux)	Total	Gen. Water Works Corporation (US/vice-chairman); *NatWest* (Int. Adv. Cttee)	1	0
Franck Riboud (Danone)	Fiat, Renault		2	1
Manfred Schneider (Bayer)	Daimler-Benz	*Allianz*; Metro, RWE	1	0
George Simpson (GEC)	Nestlé; ICI		2	1
Peter Sutherland (BP)	Investor; ABB; Ericsson	*Goldman Sachs International* (chairman)	2	2
Louis Schweitzer (Renault)	Philips	*Credit Nat.*; *BNP Paribas*	1	1

Table 3.4 Continued

ERT members	*Directorships of ERT companies (DECs)*	*Other directorships*	*Total DECs*	*Transnational DECs*
Morris Tabaksblat (Reed Elsevier)	Veba; Renault Nissan (advisory board)	*Aegon*; TNT Post; *Salomon Smith Barney* (US, advisory board)	2	2
Heinrich von Pierer (Siemens)	Bayer	Volkswagen	1	0
Mark Wössner (Bertelsmann)	Daimler-Benz		1	0
		TOTAL	29	16

Sources: Company annual reports.

Note: The 'directorships' include both outside directors in Anglo-Saxon or French-style one-tier boards and members of supervisory boards in the Germanic two-tier system of management. In some cases, ERT members hold even 'higher positions' at other companies (such as that of vice-chairman or chairman). If this is the case, the name of the position is given in parentheses. Among the list of 'other directorships' those at financial institutions are given in italics.

argument is that the degree to which Europe's emergent transnational capitalist class is integrated into a 'global' pattern (here broadly defined to include any pattern encompassing two or more of the current regions of the global political economy) of class formation logically in part depends upon the extent to which European transnational capital is in fact 'global', i.e., operating on a global rather than a merely regional scale. Of course, even in the absence of any 'indigenous' global, or even transnational, European capital, links might still be forged between European capitalists and their counterparts in other regions of the world (for instance the USA), but this kind of 'integration' might be better identified with the term 'incorporation', as such a process is likely to be one in which European capital occupies a subordinate, 'dependency', position vis-à-vis the more global capital from non-European countries. Arguably this was the case during the first decades of the post-war period in which US capital was the driving force of internationalisation (Poulantzas 1978: 38ff.), and before the rise of European TNCs in the 1970s and beyond, in which the European capitalist class thus also emancipated itself vis-à-vis American capital (Van der Pijl 1984: ch. 9).

What I have identified as the globalist fraction of European capital will be more part of emerging global patterns of capitalist integration than the Europeanist fraction. This implies that inasmuch as the former fraction gains dominance within Europe's transnational business elite, the members of this elite can be expected increasingly to be part of global elite networks as well. In recent years, the ERT has progressively strengthened its ties with business groups in other regions. Thus, some of the global links of the ERT as described below have to a significant extent only been forged in the most recent years, and can thus be taken as reflecting (and at the same time partly constituting) what I will later argue to be the ERT's shift towards neo-liberal globalism, and a continuing deepening of transnational class formation on a global scale.

ERT members and their companies are now well integrated into the current global capitalist elite networks. At the centre of these networks we find the World Economic Forum (WEF), founded in 1971 and best known for its annual meetings in Davos (and the protests from the anti-globalisation movement it has drawn in recent years). The membership of the WEF, called by Van der Pijl (1998: 132) 'the most comprehensive transnational planning body operative today', is made up of the '1000 foremost global enterprises',[57] although its meetings are also attended by political leaders, leading journalists, academics and other leaders from global civil society. Among the governing bodies of the WEF, we find many prominent ERT members. Thus Percy Barnevik, Helmut Maucher, Heinrich von Pierer and Peter Sutherland are members of the highest governing institution, the Foundation Board which is responsible for 'establishing and guiding the long-term direction and objectives of the Forum', whereas the Forum Council, responsible for implementation of the strategic plan, counts another three ERT members.[58] Apart from the annual meetings, the WEF also organises many regional meetings, such as the European Economic Summit, the most recent of which was held in July 2001 debating issues such as EU enlargement, consolidation of financial markets, pension reform, corporate governance, European security, environmental policy and

European monetary policy.[59] The WEF thus provides a crucial institutional link between the leaders of Europe's capitalist elite as first and foremost organised within the ERT and representatives of capitalist elites in the other major regions of the world.

A similar, but nowadays probably less prominent, role is played by the Trilateral Commission (see Gill 1990), a private planning forum drawing its membership from the three Triad regions and dominated by transnational business executives, but also counting politicians, journalists and even trade union leaders among its members. The current European chairman of the Trilateral Commission is Peter Sutherland, who thus, serving also on the WEF's Foundation Board, and being chairman of the now Anglo-American oil company BP Amoco, and of the European arm of a Wall Street investment bank, must be considered as one of the ERT's most globally connected members. Finally, at the global level, we may mention the International Chamber of Commerce, the world's *formal* business organisation, of which Helmut Maucher, confirming also his centrality within the global capitalist elite networks of the 1990s, served as president at the end of the 1990s, whereas currently ERT member Jean-René Fourtou (Rhône-Poulenc, now Aventis) serves as vice-president.[60]

Let us now look in some more detail at the links between the European capitalist elite and those of the USA and Japan. With regard to transatlantic relations, many of the ERT members and associates interviewed for this study stressed the good relations with their American counterparts. Thus, the ERT maintains good contacts with Amcham, the organisation in which American-based TNCs operating in Europe are represented. Outside the European context, and thus moving on to Atlantic business relations proper, we find that the relations between the ERT and American business groups have deepened in recent years, and have become partly institutionalised into such initiatives as the Transatlantic Policy Network, which brings both businessmen and policy-makers from both sides of the Atlantic together in a policy-oriented discussion forum, and, more recently, the aforementioned Transatlantic Business Dialogue (TABD). The latter organisation brings together CEOs of leading TNCs from both sides of the Atlantic, mainly to discuss Atlantic trade relations with a view to promoting – on the basis of the principle of mutual recognition – further liberalisation (see Cowles 2001; Balanyá *et al.* 2000: 97–108; Stern 1997). Since its first meeting in November 1995 in Seville, Spain, transatlantic business summits have been held annually. Although the TABD is in fact a private forum, it is actively supported by both the US government and the European Commission, and has been credited with advancing transatlantic trade liberalisation over several difficult issues (Cowles 2001). The ERT is not itself a participant in the TABD, but ERT members were actively involved in the process from the start and, indeed, from the European side, the TABD was partly a Roundtable initiative, with the TABD serving as an important channel through which the ERT maintains its transatlantic links.[61]

What initiatives like the TABD show is that the process of Atlantic class formation has only deepened in recent decades, now premised on a neo-liberal rather than a corporate–liberal concept of control. The end of the 1960s had marked not only the disintegration of the corporate–liberal historic bloc, but also a temporary crisis in Atlantic relations (Van der Pijl 1984: ch. 9) in which the European political and capitalist elites sought to 'emancipate' themselves from a declining US hegemony. This was the time that French intellectual Servan-Schreiber (1967) wrote about 'the American challenge', i.e., the dominance of US multinationals over the European economy, which had to be met by developing Europe's own base of internationally competitive firms. For a part of European elites (particularly in France) at that time, then, being a 'good European' implied taking a critical attitude vis-à-vis the USA. With regard to the issue of transatlantic relations, European elites were in fact often split along the lines of Europeanism versus 'Atlanticism'. Traces of this opposition could still be found within the European capitalist class in the 1980s. However, in the context of above all a continuing globalisation process intensifying the links between American and European capital, these differences have now largely been transcended. As Davignon – who is also a member of the Trilateral Commission – noted, co-operation with the Americans is no longer a contentious issue; there is no longer a need for compromise in that area.[62]

The ERT's links with the business community of the third part of the Triad, i.e., Japan, are still much weaker. In the 1980s one reason behind this might have been the fact that for many ERT members, Japan constituted a great threat to their businesses, and competition from Japanese rivals was seen as 'unfair' because of alleged dumping practices and the protectionism of the Japanese home market (see the next chapter). This perception of a 'yellow danger' has very much waned in more recent years. Nevertheless, the ERT's relations with Japanese business organisations remain underdeveloped. Part of the reason lies in the fact that the economic ties of European business with Japan are still weak compared to the links with American capital; Atlantic capitalist integration goes considerably deeper than Euro-Japanese integration.[63] Moreover, Euro-Japanese transnational class formation, and *ipso facto* close links between the ERT and Japanese business groups, seems to be impaired by cultural barriers (cf. Gill 1990: ch. 9).[64] On the other hand, recent deals between European and Japanese firms (such as between Renault and Nissan) may suggest that when the pressures for consolidation (as resulting from globalisation) in a particular industry are high enough, then these cultural obstacles may yet be removed, at least at the level of inter-firm co-operation. Nevertheless, at the moment we should consider the process of transatlantic class formation as still being at the core of global capitalist integration.

The political agency of the ERT

In analysing the strategic role of the ERT as identified above, we may analytically distinguish three 'levels'. The first level is the least strategic one and concerns what is normally labelled *lobbying*, and is hence an activity that the ERT only marginally engages in. However, it does sometimes lobby with regard to specific issues or projects where members feel this may be necessary (for instance, where they feel that UNICE's efforts are insufficient). In addition, the ERT also lobbies for the implementation of important projects, which it has often successfully brought on to the political agenda in the first place. Important examples are the internal market programme, and Trans-European infrastructure Networks (TENs). The second level, which following Cowles (1994, 1995a) I call *agenda setting*, does not necessarily involve ideas that the Roundtable itself has 'invented'; rather it involves ideas that are reformulated and presented in such a way (and within an overall 'vision') that policy-makers and politicians pick up on them and carry them forward. The most important example here is once more the internal market (see also the next chapter).

A third level, related to but at the same time 'transcending' the agenda-setting level as understood here, may be best described as the level of *discourse production*, or the level of *ideological* power. It is important here to note that the term 'discourse production' does not mean that a discourse is constructed *de novo*; rather existing (ideological) discourses are transformed through the re-articulation of their elements, changing the meaning of those elements. More concretely, a new discourse may emerge when a particular concept, to which a particular meaning is attributed, is used and 'pushed for' over and over again, and within a particular context. With regard to the ERT, the best example (analysed in chapter 5) is the concept of competitiveness. Of course, the distinction between these three (inter-related) levels is an analytical one and empirically the lines between them will be blurred. Nevertheless, the distinction is useful precisely because it is the last two levels of agenda setting and discourse production that mark out the distinctiveness of the ERT. Although in a way these three levels seem to represent different levels (in increasing order) of abstraction, all three levels involve very concrete forms of agency.

The ERT communicates its ideas in different ways. It regularly publishes reports either on specific themes or of a more comprehensive nature, and frequently sends letters and communiqués to individual politicians or to collective bodies such as the European Council. But as the ERT's former secretary-general, Richardson, points out: 'the most influential mode of all is perhaps still face-to-face communication' between the CEOs of the ERT and Europe's leading politicians and policy-makers (Richardson 1989). Let us now look at how the ERT operates at the different 'levels' of European governance: national, intergovernmental and supranational.

At the national level, the ERT primarily operates through its individual members, whose elite positions within their respective national societies should enable them to disseminate ERT ideas very effectively at this level. At the intergovernmental level, the ERT has (in contrast to UNICE, due to its more 'constitutional' role as European social partner) no direct and formal access to the European Council or to the Council of Ministers,[65] but it does for instance, in conjunction with its plenary session, meet with one or more prominent members (often the head of government or state) of the government then taking over the Council presidency for the next six months.

This transnational elite interaction between business and political leaders is probably the strongest between the ERT and the Commission: that is, at the supranational level.[66] As noted before, it is here – arguably a strong indication of the

Commission's centrality as an agenda-setter in European policy making – that a true partnership has developed, centring around a transnational network that ties together the elite of European business with key policy-makers and politicians, and thus blurring the lines between state and civil society within Europe's emergent polity. It is here that the ERT's access is most institutionalised, although not formalised, and its influence – at least as a collective actor – is probably most direct. The Roundtable – or at least a delegation (often the Steering Committee) – generally meets the Commission president about twice a year in a rather formal way.[67] In addition, the ERT or individual ERT members often have more ad hoc meetings with different Commissioners. That these meetings are also considered to be very useful on the part of the Commission is for instance confirmed by Peter Sutherland, who recalled that in his time as Commissioner for Competition he had had numerous meetings with the Roundtable to discuss both competition matters as well as more general affairs.[68]

As suggested in chapter 1, the powerful positions that the ERT members occupy within their own countries can also be used as a resource for the Commission (at least to the extent that the Commission and the ERT have reached a consensus with regard to certain issues) in its dealings with the Council and individual member states. In this respect, the ERT's access at the supranational level, i.e., to the Commission, is partly a function of the ERT's privileged access to national governments, as this can make the support of the ERT for a particular Community policy a powerful lever against unwilling member states. As one adviser to Delors' cabinet put it: 'when necessary, they [the ERT members] can ring up their own prime ministers and make their case' (Bruno Liebhaberg quoted in Merrit 1986). Similarly, the general or strategic level at which the ERT operates also makes it an effective interlocutor for the Commission.[69]

As was indicated before, much of this elite interaction between the corporate executives of the ERT and the political executives of the European Commission, as well as those of national governments, is supported by personal relationships. In this context it is also worth noting that the Roundtable has had a total of three former Commissioners among its membership, most notably Davignon from 1986 onwards, and more recently Peter Sutherland.[70] At the national level, former ERT vice-chairman David Simon made the reverse step – that is, from business (and membership of the ERT) to government – by becoming a minister for Trade and Competitiveness in Europe in the newly elected UK Labour government of 1997, making him, in the words of one senior ERT associate, 'a very useful contact'.[71] In sum, what we see developing around the ERT is a transnational elite network that ties together the elite of European business with key policy-makers and politicians at both the national and supranational levels of the European polity.

Now that the structure and agency of the ERT have been analysed and interpreted in this chapter, we will turn in the final chapters of this book to an analysis of the ERT's *changing* strategic project within the context of a transnational struggle over European order.

4 The Roundtable's changing strategic project and the transnational struggle over European order

In chapter 2, I identified three rival projects within the struggle over European order. In this chapter I interpret the relaunching of the integration process from the internal market programme to the Maastricht treaty on European Union (concluded in December 1991) in terms of a struggle between these three contending projects. The struggle between the two most important of these projects – those of neo-liberalism and neo-mercantilism – was partly manifested within the ranks of the European Roundtable, which at the same time also played a critical role in shaping this struggle. My analysis of the changing strategic (class) agency of the ERT will therefore be at the heart of this chapter and the concluding one, and can be taken as a case-study of this transnational struggle over European order. I argue that within this struggle we have witnessed within the ERT, and within Europe's emerging transnational capitalist class more widely, a gradual shift from a more neo-mercantilist towards a more neo-liberal orientation, although some elements of the neo-mercantilist world view (and its roots in the interests of industrial capital) were in a modified version incorporated into what became an increasingly hegemonic neo-liberal discourse. The third project, that of supranational social democracy, and the underlying socio-economic structures of continental Europe, also necessitated some accommodation on the part of neo-liberal social forces, but was never able to realise its ambitions. In the end, I argue, the outcome of these struggles was one in which a new comprehensive concept of control was articulated, one that I will denote with the term 'embedded neo-liberalism'. Embedded neo-liberalism will be interpreted in the next and final chapter as the emerging hegemonic project of the European capitalist class, and argued to underpin the current socio-economic European order. It is in this chapter that I will analyse the struggle that preceded and enabled the rise of this hegemonic concept.

This chapter is divided into three main parts. The first part will examine the ERT's strategic project in the context of the first phase of Europe's relaunching, that of the internal market programme, as well as examining the role of the initiating role of the ERT with regard to this programme. I argue that the internal market was supported by both neo-liberal and neo-mercantilist forces, i.e., that there were rival interpretations of this project, and that although the latter initially appeared to be rather dominant in setting the agenda, their neo-mercantilist project in the end failed to materialise. This failure of the neo-mercantilist version of the internal market coincided with a gradual shift in the ERT's strategic orientation away from neo-mercantilism.

The second part seeks to examine the *structural* changes that have enabled this transformation of the ERT's strategic project. I claim that these structural changes must be understood within the context of a changing global political economy, and in particular within the context of the rise of transnational capitalism and of the process of neo-liberal globalisation. As the process of globalisation deepened, forces supporting a more liberal European order became more powerful. As such the neo-mercantilist project faced a political opposition that was hard to overcome and as the content of the internal market programme became increasingly neo-liberal, also in terms of its openness vis-à-vis the world economy, those sections of European capital that favoured industrial policy and protectionism had to adapt to these new political realties. 'Fortress Europe' was no longer an option, and globalisation became an increasingly dominant strategy. The latter in fact transpires from an analysis of the ERT's changing composition of membership, showing a changing power balance between the Europeanist and the globalist fractions in favour of the latter. As the ERT's membership became more globalised, indicative of a wider trend of globalisation in European industry, those adhering to a more neo-liberal conception of European integration also became ideologically more dominant. The rise to hegemony of what I call embedded neo-liberalism within Europe, however, was in the end only possible through concrete political and ideological struggles both inside and outside the ERT.

Thus moving from structure and agency, these struggles (continuing from the first part) will be our focus in the third part. Here, I will analyse the changing strategic project of the ERT as the relaunching of Europe moved into its second phase: that is, moving from the internal market to monetary union. In terms of the class strategy of the Roundtable, this period (from about 1988 to about 1992) in many ways constituted a transition phase, in which the ERT's orientation shifted to neo-liberalism only gradually, and not without fierce internal battles. Analysing the ERT's discourse in this period, we can find strong elements both of a neo-mercantilist discourse still enduring in some areas, in particular industrial policy, and of a rising neo-liberal discourse, above all in the area of labour market and social policies. With regard to this latter area, the Europeanist and globalist fractions within the ERT's ranks were increasingly united in their opposition to the 'Social Europe' agenda that in the years leading up to Maastricht was promoted by social-democratic forces. In the end, I argue, Maastricht represented a kind of compromise between the three rival projects, a compromise in which the neo-liberal ideology was clearly dominant though, and that as such prefigured the emerging synthesis of embedded neo-liberalism.

Neo-mercantilism versus neo-liberalism in the relaunching of Europe

As noted in chapter 2, in the neo-mercantilist project of European integration, the internal market programme was about creating a European home market as a bulwark against global competition:

> According to the mercantilist view, a strong home market, allowing for the early achievement of economies of scale, and securing a solid profits base, is the key to success in international competition. 'Non-Europe', national rivalries and the fragmentation of Community market, have, in this view, deprived European companies of a key element in competitive success, which the 1992 programme will correct. (Grahl and Teague 1990: 172)

Although neo-liberals also saw the internal market as enhancing competitiveness, they believed this because of the market liberalisation resulting from deregulation rather than, as in the neo-mercantilist view, because it would favour European companies over their US and Japanese competitors. In terms of the solution they offered, the fundamental incompatibility between the neo-liberal and the neo-mercantilist projects concerned the fact that the latter implied going beyond the mere free movement of goods, services and capital, towards a supportive supranational political framework for the pursuit of interventionist and protectionist policies. Thus, although, as we shall see with the case of the ERT, the neo-mercantilist orientation at least partly shared neo-liberal ideas on the necessity of labour market flexibility, welfare state reform, etc., it did not share the neo-liberal commitment to global *laissez-faire*. As Pearce and Sutton argued, it was a debate between 'Europrotectionists' on the one hand and 'liberals' on the other: both groups shared the goal of lowering trade barriers *within* Europe, but were at loggerheads about the question of whether to raise them *externally* (Pearce and Sutton 1986: 4–5 and *passim*). In the latter (neo-mercantilist) strategy, such an external trade protection would be complemented with a European industrial policy centred around 'strategic sectors'.

French versus British projections

At the member-state level, the neo-mercantilism versus neo-liberalism debate was manifest in the rival conceptions for the relaunching of European integration of in particular the French and British governments respectively. Whereas, as we saw, the declared aim of the latter was 'to make Europe by the year 2000 a model of what free trade and open markets can achieve' (Margaret Thatcher, in Krause 1991), the former promoted the industrial and technological *relance* of Europe through EC-sponsored technology programmes and other industrial policy initiatives, all aimed at harnessing European industry in their battle for the world market. As early as September 1983, the French government presented a 'Memorandum on a Common Industrial and Research Area' to the European Council (French

Memorandum 1983; see also Pearce and Sutton 1986; Tsoukalis 1993: 300; Cowles 1994).

In the 1983 memorandum, the French government expressed its concern over the alleged 'technological gap' of European industry vis-à-vis its global competitors, and argued that the fragmentation of Europe's industrial area was the main cause of Europe's industrial decline. Rather than containing any concrete proposals for finally removing many of Europe's NTBs, the memorandum focused on ideas like new co-operation programmes in the field of high-tech research; the encouragement of alliances between European firms (creating European champions); and the launching of European infrastructure projects. Moreover, the document explicitly called for a mercantilist commercial and trade policy premised on the notion that the European industrial area should not 'merge entirely and without limitations into the world industrial area [as] the trade practices of our major competitors are [also] not conducive to this' (French Memorandum 1983: 4). Thus, whereas in the past the EEC had rightly supported declining industries, 'a significant, if temporary, increase in customs duties must be possible' for 'certain sectors of the future' (ibid.). Moreover, 'community product' legislation should prevent products assembled in so-called 'screwdriver' plants (that is, containing 'too many' foreign components) from freely circulating within the Community (ibid.). The language of the document was clearly set in a defensive tone: Europe should organise against the threats of Japanese and US competition, otherwise it will lose its autonomy. Only the 'mastery of the major scientific and technological changes [can] safeguard Europe's independence' (ibid.).

Europeanism versus globalism: fractional struggle within the ERT

The rivalry between the neo-liberal and the neo-mercantilist concepts of a relaunching of European integration was also manifest within the ranks of the Roundtable, in turn reflecting, I would suggest, what constituted the central axis of intra-capitalist struggle in the Europe of the 1980s. In order to analyse this struggle let us first – along the dimensions discussed in chapter 1 – identify more concretely the different fractions among the original Roundtable capitalists and how these fractional viewpoints crystallised into the ideological struggle between neo-mercantilist and neo-liberal orientations as potential concepts of control of the European capitalist class.

In table 4.1, an analysis is given of the relative degrees of 'regionalisation' versus 'globalisation' for the 17 original ERT companies. Although as accounting practices differ between companies (and as some data for some companies were unavailable) we should be cautious in making cross-company comparisons, we may safely interpret some of the larger differences as indicators of different degrees of regionalisation and of globalisation. I have thus (for the companies for which sufficient data were available) constructed a 'regionalisation index' showing the extent of concentration on the European market outside the home country and a 'globalisation index' expressing the degree of transnationalisation outside Europe.

The data collected do show a considerable divergence. On the globalisation index, the scores range from a mere 7.5 per cent for French food company BSN (now Danone) to 60.3 per cent for Anglo-Dutch oil giant Shell. Other companies that score high on this index are Nestlé, Unilever, Lafarge Coppée, Philips and ICI. In order to be able to interpret the composition of membership in terms of our analytical framework, we should, however, also look at the relative degree of regionalisation as opposed to globalisation, as well as to the sectoral (globally competitive versus less globally competitive sectors) and national dimensions (e.g., the more mercantilist orientation of the French political economy versus the more liberal orientation of the British model of capitalism).

Thus, although Philips shows a relatively high degree of globalisation, its regionalisation degree is even higher, indicating a relatively great dependence on the European market, whereas for instance ICI shows the inverse pattern with most of its foreign activities located outside Europe. Philips, moreover, operates within the vulnerable electronics sector, for which the threat of Japanese competition was perceived to be particularly great. ICI is both a British company and within the internationally competitive chemicals sector. It is thus that we can give a structural explanation of why Philips' Wisse Dekker was the one Roundtable member who most consistently pleaded for a neo-mercantilist strategy, whereas the ICI chairman left the organisation shortly after its founding, out of disagreement with its 'Europeanist' orientation.

As I will argue below, the Roundtable was in its first five years dominated by what was identified as the Europeanist fraction, or more generally by that part of European capital that (for one reason or another) was under particularly heavy pressure from global competition, and was at the same time very dependent upon the European market as a base from which to defend itself against that competition. This Europeanist fraction, however, only became dominant within the ERT after the early walk-out of the British bosses of Shell, Unilever and ICI, which, as noted in the previous chapter, took place shortly after the ERT's founding. As can be seen from table 4.1, these firms were among the most globalised of the ERT's original membership. They moreover were from very internationally oriented and competitive sectors (oil, foods and chemicals), and they were 'represented' within the Roundtable by British CEOs. These three factors together, I would suggest, help to account for the neo-liberal and globalist orientation on the part of these three British members, and it was this orientation which I claim to be the main reason behind their early departure. It is thus that this particular episode was in fact a first and most significant manifestation of the fractional struggle between 'globalists' and 'Europeanists' within the ERT.

According to Davignon, the three British industrialists disagreed with the ERT's focus on concrete industrial projects like creating trans-European infrastructure networks (ICI and Shell having no particular interest in infrastructure), and were also worried by its 'pro-active' and 'political' orientation vis-à-vis the integration process and vis-à-vis the Commission.[1] Harvey-Jones, the most outspoken member of the British trio, is himself quoted to have said that he had drawn 'an important distinction between projects and industrial policy'.[2] Thus the concern with the

Table 4.1 Regionalisation versus globalisation among original ERT membership (around 1983)*

Company	*Sales*[a] (%)			*Assets* (%)			*Employment* (%)			*Regionalisation index*[b]	*Globalisation index*[c]
	Domestic	*ROE*[d]	*ROW*[e]	*Domestic*	*ROE*	*ROW*	*Domestic*	*ROE*	*ROW*		
Asea[f]	48.1	51.9		84.3	15.7		75.4	24.6		–	–
Bosch	76.0		24.0	–	–	–	72.7[f]	37.3[f]		–	–
BSN[g]	73.0	18.0	9.0	75.0	19.0	6.0	72.0	21.3[i]	3.7[i]	18.5	7.5
Ciba-Geigy	2.5	97.5		–	–	–	28.2	71.8		–	–
Fiat	53.0	32.0	15.0	72.0	16.0	12.0	85.0	9.0[i]	6.0[i]	19.0	11.0
ICI[d]	25.0	25.0	50	47.5	13.7	38.8	51.0	11.0	38.0	16.6	42.3
Lafarge Coppée[g]	37.0	11.0	52.0	–	–	–	52.0	11.0	38.0	11.0	45.0
Nestlé[g]	2.0	38.0	60.0	–	–	–	2.0	43.0	55.0	40.5	57.5
Olivetti	54.0	26.0	20.0	59.0	29.0	12.0	54.0	26.0	20.0	27.0	17.3
Philips	6.0	45.0	49.0	20.0	46.0	34.0	20.0	46.0	34.0	45.7	39.0
Renault[g]	71.1	25.7	3.2[f]	–	–	–	75.6	24.4[f]		–	–
Siemens	44.0	56.0		–	–	–	67.0	33.0		–	–
Shell[g]	42.0		58.0	29.0		71.0	48.0		52.0	–	60.3
St Gobain[f]	54.8	45.2		61.0	39.0		47.0	53.0		–	–
Thyssen[f]	57.1	42.9		–	–	–	76.2	15.8		–	–
Unilever[h]	61.0		39.0	52.0		48.0	46.0		54.0	–	47.0
Volvo	24.0	38.0	38.0	69.0	14.0	17.0	76.0	15.0	9.0	22.3	21.3

Table 4.1 Continued

Sources: Stafford and Purkins (1989); United Nations (1983); *The Economist*, 5 January 1985, p. 61; Nunnenkamp, Gundlach, and Agarwal (1994).

Notes: The regionalisation and globalisation indices are in principle calculated on the basis of the geographical breakdown between the rest of Europe and the rest of the world of sales, assets, and employment. However, in two cases – those of Lafarge Coppée and Nesté – the geographical breakdown for assets is missing, in which case the given indices only refer to the averages for sales and employment. This follows the practice applied by the United Nations Conference on Trade and Development in its annual *World Investment Reports*. Due to different accounting practices between companies the data given for each company are only roughly comparable.

* Data are for 1983 unless indicated otherwise;
a sales are by final market unless otherwise stated;
b average of ROE percentages for sales, assets, and employment (or at least two of these three, see note above);
c average of ROW percentages for sales, assets, and employment (or at least two of these three, see note above);
d ROE is an abbreviation for 'rest of Europe' (that is, within Europe and excluding the home country);
e ROW is an abbreviation for 'rest of world';
f data for 1980;
g sales by production area;
h data for 1984;
i breakdown between ROE and ROW not available but estimated on the basis of the ratios (ROE/ROW) for the two indicators for which the geographical breakdown is known;
– = data unavailable (not disclosed by company).

promotion of infrastructure and other concrete pan-European projects was probably interpreted by the British as leading to the creation – with all its *dirigiste* connotations – of a European industrial policy, something that did not fit the ideology of the British (neo-)liberal model. Instead, Harvey-Jones preferred the ERT to become an 'Anglo-Saxon style' business lobby focusing (exclusively) on market liberalisation rather than on big infrastructure projects (Merrit 1986: 24). Although the completion of the internal market was in fact an early priority of the Roundtable, the majority of the original ERT members, as led by Gyllenhammar, insisted on the concrete project orientation (Cowles 1994: 216). According to Cowles, Harvey-Jones thought that the project scheme 'appeared to be supported by CEOs who had a vested interest in construction or steel' (Cowles 1994: 218, footnote 36). Finally, Dekker recalled that the British feared the protectionist inclinations of the French, who, as argued in the previous chapter, formed a prominent group within the Roundtable at that time.[3] Together these pieces of evidence suggest that it was above all a disagreement about the fundamental objectives and political course set out by the majority of the founding Roundtable members that led to the resignation of the three British CEOs. It was a clash of ideologies, whereby the British neo-liberal world view turned out to be incompatible with that of the Roundtable's continental capitalists. In 1984, three new British members were recruited, heading companies – the National Coal Board (the national coal mining industry), Plessey (an electronics firm later taken over by General Electric Company and Siemens) and Pilkington (a glass producer heavily concentrated on the European market) – with a significantly less globalist outlook than that of their predecessors.

In describing the overall strategic orientation of the remaining 14 members of the Roundtable, the term 'neo-mercantilism' is perhaps too strong as not all 'globalists'/free-traders left. Most notable among the representatives of the globalist fraction remaining within the ERT was Helmut Maucher, the CEO of Nestlé, later to become ERT chairman. But most of the other remaining ERT members were heading companies that were either solidly *European* rather than global TNCs, or were so much concentrated on the domestic market that the notion of a European champion was still more of a strategic ambition than an accomplished reality. In fact, for many ERT companies the creation of a European home market was seen as the most important way through which such a strategy could be realised. Thus, in table 4.1 we see that six companies of the remaining 14 (BSN, Fiat, Olivetti, Renault, St Gobain and Thyssen) in the early 1980s still made more than half of their sales in their own domestic market.[4] The Roundtable's membership was henceforth (and at least until 1988) dominated by companies from the Europeanist fraction. If we examine the geographical breakdown of activities between Europe and the rest of the world, we see that most companies are much more European than global, i.e., show a much higher degree of regionalisation as compared to globalisation. Of the seven companies for which these figures are available, we see that only Nestlé and Lafarge Coppée show a globalisation index higher than their regionalisation index. With the same two exceptions (and possibly also Ciba-Geigy) all remaining companies also made more than half and in most cases more than two-thirds of their sales within Europe (thus including domestic sales), with the European concentration of assets and employment usually lying at an even higher level.

With regard to sectors, about half of the ERT companies were now within the two sectors suffering most from Japanese import-competition, the automobile and electronics sectors. Internationally competitive sectors such as oil and chemicals for a long time were hardly represented within the ERT. With respect to nationality we should recall from the previous chapter the qualitative dominance of the French in these years as well as the initial (after the walk-out) lack of British participation. The Europeanists thus having become the dominant fraction within the Roundtable, the strategic project of the ERT in the 1980s was formed around a rather defensive strategy which I will denote as 'protective regionalism'. Let us now examine the constituent elements of this strategy.

The ERT's protective regionalism and its strategy for Europe's relaunching

Three constituent elements of the strategy of protective regionalism may be identified. The first concerns the promotion of the completion of the internal market, which by a majority of the ERT members was rendered in its neo-mercantilist interpretation. The other elements were the promotion of a (French-style) European industrial policy oriented towards the nurturing of European champions – first of all through Community-sponsored infrastructure projects and collaboration programmes in new technologies – and the growing plea of at least an important section of the Roundtable members for some form of Europrotectionism.

A European home market as a bulwark against global competition

As early as June 1983, shortly after its founding, the ERT made an explicit plea for the creation of a unified market as the first priority for the European Community. It did so in a memorandum to Commissioner Davignon drafted at its second meeting in Amsterdam, which significantly was not attended by two of the three British members, who at that time had already left the organisation (if not yet formally) (Cowles 1994: 218). In a language similar to that of the memorandum of the French government that came out a few months later, the ERT stated that:

> Europe remains a group of separated national markets with separated national policies and separated industrial structures. This prevents many firms from reaching the scale necessary to *resist pressure from non-European competitors*. The European market must serve as a unified 'home' base necessary to allow European firms to develop as powerful competitors in world markets. (ERT 1983, my emphasis)

The argument expounded by many early members of the Roundtable ran as follows (see, e.g., Overkleeft and Groosman 1987). In this era of new global competition, European industry needs the basis of a single European market, in order to get sufficient economies of scale, reduce its production costs, and hence become competitive again. As Dekker put it in an interview: 'It [the Single European Market] will give European industry an opportunity to organise on a scale big enough to compete with its main rivals in Japan and in the United States' (Dekker quoted in Stone 1989: 91). In the strategy of the ERT, then, the completion of the internal market was necessary to give a home base to prospective European champions, who would then use the 'world's biggest home market' to conquer the rest of the global market: that is, the internal market was, as former Philips president Van der Klugt put it, 'intended as a springboard [to the world market] for European industry' (Van der Klugt 1988: 2).

Although its most ambitious project, the ERT's strategy went beyond the promotion of the internal market. The 'European scale' had to be introduced in other areas as well. A halt to the existing fragmentation of the European economy was called for on every front. The ERT in particular focused its efforts on the development of new technologies through collaborative European research programmes, and the creation of trans-European infrastructure networks. Therefore, the ERT pleaded for much more than mere market integration and transnational deregulation. The project initiated and promoted by the ERT went beyond mere *negative* integration, as the removal of barriers to trade was to be complemented by a set of *positive* supportive measures, implying an enhanced role for Europe's supranational institutions, and hence ultimately the kind of institutional deepening that more globalist or neo-liberal forces were firmly opposed to.

Industrial policy and 'Europrotectionism'

Going beyond neo-liberalism, the ERT has always stressed that business could not do the job alone, that it needed the state (both at the national and at supranational level) to create the unified market, to support business by co-ordinating co-operation efforts, and to guard their interests against the dangers of the new global competition. What was needed first was the internal market to serve as a 'launching pad for entering the world market' (Dekker quoted in Stone 1989), and, second, a supportive role by the 'European government' in, particularly, the fields of technological co-operation and trans-European infrastructure. For some, this supportive role was also to include protectionist measures in order to defend particular sectors of European industry against outside competition.

The ERT's plea for pan-European (and EC-sponsored) infrastructure and technology projects formed in fact an implicit plea for a European industrial policy. The kind of industrial policy that many ERT members advocated came, moreover, very close to the neo-mercantilist French model, and as such went much beyond the mere provision of framework conditions. Indeed, as noted before, some important similarities can be detected between the French 1983 proposals and the ideas put forward by the ERT in its earlier memorandum on the future of

European industry. Cowles argues that, given the close links between the ERT and the French government, it was of 'little coincidence [that] the French government's industrial initiative reflected the ideas discussed in the original ERT memorandum, and forwarded in private meetings by the ERT' (Cowles 1994: 233).

Both the ERT's favouring of a French-style industrial policy and the calls of some of its members for selective protectionism can again only be understood in the context of structural trends in the world economy, in particular the restructuring race centred around new technologies and the rise of Japan. With regard to the former, European industry was very preoccupied with closing the perceived 'technology gap' between Europe on the one hand, and Japan and the USA on the other (see Grahl and Teague 1990: 168–75; Sharp 1990). As a 1986 Roundtable report put it:

> Europe's industry cannot remain competitive if it fails to compete on technological advance. Without that, industry will have neither a cost-competitive production base nor the means to develop and penetrate new markets with new products. High technology European industry can create the wealth to finance the creation of jobs in sectors which are not vulnerable to low-cost foreign competition. [High technology] is enabling European producers to counter competition from the far East. (ERT 1986: 23)

Again, as with the Roundtable's concern with a secure European home market, the dominant theme here is that of the need for Europe to catch up with the global competition, which is threatening European industry because of its low-cost advantage and scale advantages in the development of new technologies. Therefore, industry as well as government needs to organise itself on a European scale. In the field of research and technology, the ERT thus became a staunch supporter of the Community collaboration programmes in high technology such as ESPRIT, RACE and EUREKA. Moreover, in its early reports, the ERT also showed its enthusiasm for state-sponsored developments of new European industries such as Airbus and Ariane (ERT 1985, 1986).

Perhaps an even more dominant theme than the technology gap was the perceived threat from the Far East, and in particular from Japan. One former ERT associate, who had been with the Roundtable from its founding, recalled that the pressure from Japan was a recurrent theme in ERT discussions throughout its early years: 'that was a very important motive, the pressure of Japan was experienced as very strong . . ., it was almost a persecution complex . . . One felt totally enclosed by . . . the force of the Japanese expansion.'[5] Japanese competition was not only perceived to be strong, it was also seen to be based on unfair advantages because of the support given by the Japanese government and the protection of the Japanese home market. Moreover, the Japanese were seen as violating the principles and spirit of free (or rather 'fair') trade through their alleged dumping practices and 'killer tactics' aimed at dominating the world markets (Stone 1989). Wisse Dekker, ERT chairman from 1988 to 1992, and probably the most outspoken critic of Japanese 'expansionism', in this context declared that 'it is most important that the Japanese understand that world dominance is not the answer to a thriving world economy' (Dekker quoted in Johnson 1989: 51). Dekker later admitted that if it 'had not been for the Japanese threat and the influence it had on industry' the concept of the internal market, and the Roundtable's promotion of it 'would have come at a much slower pace. The Japanese threat injected a sense of urgency' (Dekker 1990: 18).

It was the 'persecution complex' with regard to Japan that was thus also an important motivating force behind the Europrotectionism that became manifest within the ranks of the ERT during the 1980s. The call for protectionism was made not so much in the ERT's reports (for this the opposition of the few remaining 'free-traders' such as Maucher was probably too strong) but rather by individual ERT members vis-à-vis the Commission. Here, the electronics and car sectors were particularly active in lobbying the Commission for protectionist measures like tariffs and import quotas (see Hanson 1998: 58). Often, the industries threatened by Japanese competition made an explicit link between the internal liberalisation resulting from the internal market and the need for external protection, implying that the latter was necessary to compensate for the former.[6] Thus as the increasing intra-European competition resulting from the internal market became more tangible in the second half of the 1980s, some of these firms in fact intensified their efforts to press for EC-level protectionism (Hanson 1998). For a limited time, and only in restricted areas, they were rather successful (ibid.). At the same time, exploiting the opportunities offered by the European home market in the making, this section of European capital clearly pursued a regionalisation strategy inasmuch as their focus upon and dependency on the European market in fact only increased.

Within the internal ERT debate, it was also 'representatives' of the electronics and car industries who took the most explicit protectionist stance.[7] Dekker was again the most public (but by far not the only) campaigner for European protectionism, even if he also declared that he believed in the principles of free trade. His argument (and that of many of his fellow industrialists operating in import-competing sectors) was that, since in particular the Japanese did not play the game by the rules (of free and fair trade), European industry was justified in defending its interests through temporary violations of the free-trade regime. Dekker's case for Europrotectionism also rested upon the notion that both Japan and the USA were not competing on an equal basis with European industry. Whereas America's industry had the Department of Defense to support it by lowering the initial costs of R&D and by guaranteeing a market, and whereas Japan had MITI, playing a similar supportive, cost-reducing role, European industry only had a fragmented market from which it had to compete without any support against this outside competition (for Dekker's argument along these lines see Overkleeft and Groosman 1987: 161–69). Interestingly, Dekker has also linked the issue of the welfare state to the case for protectionism. In line with the neo-liberal view, Dekker saw the welfare state as having made Europe less competitive: 'so if on the one hand you want to keep the welfare state, yet you also want completely free trade, then sooner or later you are going to do things that create tension and conflict' (Dekker quoted in Johnson 1989: 52). However, Dekker's way out of this dilemma was not to plead for a dismantling of the welfare state but rather to advocate a selective protectionism for particular sectors such as his own electronics industry. I would suggest that Dekker's position in fact reflected the general orientation of most members of the ERT at the time. Although it was acknowledged that the so-called 'European model', with its high social security costs and its labour market inflexibility, was in need of reform, a radical restructuring of this model was not envisaged (and indeed does not show up in the ERT's discourse until the 1990s).

The role of the ERT in Europe 1992

The role of the ERT, and more broadly that of transnational business, with regard to the internal market programme has been one of the contentious issues between the intergovernmentalist and supranationalist schools as discussed in chapter 1. Thus as representatives of the latter camp, Sandholtz and Zysman (1989) have claimed a significant role for transnational business and the ERT in particular (although, as I argued, conceptualising this role as functional to the integration logic and serving the needs of the supranational agency of the Commission rather than playing a much more autonomous role). This claim has later been backed up by more detailed empirical studies of scholars not directly intervening in this theoretical debate (see especially Cowles 1994, 1995a; Fielder 1997, 2000). In the other camp we find most notably Moravcsik who maintains that 'structural economic conditions translated [only] into *diffuse* business support' (Moravcsik 1998: 319, my emphasis), and that 'business did not take a pro-active role' (ibid.: 344) as it, 'while providing essential support, *reacted* to initiatives from the Commission, and the Parliament, as well as member governments' (ibid.: 356). Moravcsik explicitly denies that the ERT played any initiating role (ibid.: 355), although he does admit (changing his earlier position, see Moravcsik 1991) that (unlike in his other historical episodes of intergovernmental bargains) transnational actors like the ERT, as well as the Commission as a supranational policy entrepreneur, did play a role in sustaining the momentum behind Europe 1992 once governments had agreed on it (ibid.: 372–73).

I submit that the evidence presented here as well as that gathered by others (Cowles 1994; Fielder 1997) makes Moravcsik's claims untenable. However, my main point below concerns not so much the fact that the ERT played a significant role in the launching of the 1992 programme (as I consider this fact already sufficiently established by previous works) but rather *how* it played this role. I argue that this role should be above all understood at the level of *ideas*, and the translation of these ideas into a concrete programme for the creation of a European home market. It was among the leaders of European TNCs (such as Philips, Olivetti and Volvo) that the *idea* of a unified European market as *the solution* to Europe's alleged economic decline first took a concrete shape and was as such propagated among Europe's political elite. I hence argue that the change from a series of national responses to what can be seen as a European solution to the crisis of Eurosclerosis and Europessimism was to a significant degree helped by the pro-active role of the early members of the Roundtable and the wider business community in shaping a collective *pro-European consciousness* at the elite level. It is in this sense that we can speak of the *initiating* role of the Roundtable.

In fact, as noted in chapter 3, European big business was frustrated by the lack of initiative of most EC-level (with the important exception of Davignon) and national policy-makers with regard to any concrete steps that could drag Europe out of its economic and political quagmire. Indeed, ERT members such as Gyllenhammar and Dekker were among the first within Europe's elite to publicly propose a *European* solution – in contrast to the then dominant *national* (champion) industrial strategies – to Europe's perceived economic and competitive decline. Whereas up to 1985 Europessimism was still the prevailing mood in Europe, the early Roundtable warned in a 1985 report against the danger of the idea of Europe's decline 'being etched permanently into a new European consciousness' (ERT 1985: 3) and concluded that 'Europe does not lack projects, proposals, vision, ambition and success. Europe is not locked into decline – the exit doors are wide open. It remains only to go through them' (ibid.: 15). The early ERT thus mobilised against the then dominant national strategies (see chapter 2), being convinced of the necessity to make a change to the 'European scale'. In the Roundtable's *Changing Scales* report from 1985 (ERT 1985) we still find this to be one of the dominant themes, complaining that Europe is still 'a continent of economic nationalists' (ibid.: 5) and that 'governments continue to behave nationalistically' (ibid.: 7). However, as we have seen, in 1985 the tide was already turning against this economic nationalism. According to Davignon around the mid-1980s, the failure of the national champion strategy was apparent to everyone; it was now to be taken to the European level.[8]

And indeed it was in June 1985 that the 1992 project was launched in the form of the Commission's White Paper, containing 279 detailed proposals aimed at the completion of the internal market – an area without internal frontiers in which the free movement of goods, services, capital and persons would be guaranteed. These proposals were later incorporated into the treaty revision of the Single European Act (SEA) of 1986, which also introduced some important institutional reforms, in particular the extension of qualified majority voting to issues linked to the realisation of the internal market programme (for overviews of the history of the SEA see Moravcsik 1998: ch. 5; Cameron 1992; Sandholtz and Zysman 1989). The SEA also formally recognised the principle of 'mutual recognition' as the 'new approach' to deal with the long-standing problem of non-tariff barriers (NTBs), i.e. (apart from quantitative restrictions), the barriers to trade resulting from divergent standards and regulations in different member states. No longer would these be harmonised (with some exceptions) at the supranational level. NTBs would just be removed by a single stroke by having states recognising each other's national regulations.

It is important to emphasise that, contrary to what intergovernmentalists like Moravcsik (Moravcsik 1991: 62; 1998: 355) have asserted, the Roundtable's plea for a unified European home market has been central to its strategy from the very beginning.[9] It was not a theme which was only later picked up by industrialists after the initiative had already been launched by the Council of Ministers, but it was a theme which, as Cowles (1995a) convincingly shows, was in fact put on the EC agenda by leading industrialists like Dekker and Gyllenhammar, either as members of the ERT or in their individual capacity.[10] The call for internal market liberalisation not only took up a central place in the earlier quoted report from 1985, but as we saw before already figured prominently in the ERT's 1983 memorandum in which the Roundtable asked the Commission for 'supporting political action' necessary to create a 'European market [which] must serve as the unified "home" base necessary to allow European firms to develop as powerful competitors in world markets' (ERT 1983: 2). The call for this European market was later worked out in detail by strategists of Philips in a plan presented by the then Philips CEO Dekker in the autumn of 1984 and again in January 1985. This plan called for the creation of a 'European Community Home Market' by eliminating obstacles in the areas of trade, VAT, standardisation and government procurement, and setting a clear and specific timetable for all of the measures to be taken, with 1990 as the final date for the completion of the internal market (Dekker 1985). Dekker's 'agenda for action' – which was quickly adopted by the whole Roundtable – was also much more concrete and better tailored to the needs of European big business than the earlier document of the Commission on the internal market, which was not well received by big business as it lacked transparency and a specific timetable (Green 1993: 31). In fact, the idea of setting a final date was also used by incoming Commission president Jacques Delors when he, three days after Dekker presented his plan, delivered his first major speech to the European Parliament, setting 1992 (rather than 1990) as the magical year in which the miracle of the internal market would be realised. The similarity between Delors' plan and the Dekker speech made three days earlier does not seem to rest on mere coincidence (see Krause 1991: 72). More importantly, the Dekker plan directly inspired the White Paper of Lord Cockfield (see Cowles 1994; Fielder 1997).

Once the White Paper was endorsed by the Council of Ministers and later promoted to an amendment of the Treaty of Rome by way of the SEA, the role of the ERT in the 1992 project remained critical. At the end of 1986, the ERT, under the initiative of Dekker, created the Internal Market Support Committee (IMSC) which came to consist of some ten prominent Roundtable members, and which was to function as a kind of 'watchdog group', seeing to it that the White Paper would indeed be implemented, that the Commission would propose the right directives in time, and above all, that these directives would be implemented at the national level. With this goal in mind, the members of the IMSC had many private consultations with both the Commission and national government leaders. There were also plenary meetings (of the ERT as a whole) with Delors and with different prime ministers discussing the topic of Europe 1992, meetings that were supported by 'thousands of contacts on an ad hoc basis' between ERT associates and Community officials.[11] Confirming the nature of the power of transnational capital as discussed in chapter 1, these lobbying efforts were also backed up at several times by the threat of exit. Already in 1985 Dekker had publicly suggested that

Philips might well leave the Netherlands if Europe would not get its act together: 'If Europe is neither able nor willing to develop its economic structure then the consequences of that must be drawn.'[12] In the implementation stage, similar threats (of locating investments) were made on several occasions, for instance in a 1987 meeting of an ERT delegation with the Belgian EC presidency and with Delors.[13] These efforts of the ERT in securing the 1992 project were important because, as has been ignored by some scholars (e.g., Moravcsik 1991), the whole process was still in doubt until the June 1988 EC summit in Hanover (Green 1993: 42).

The significant role that the ERT played in this process of 'relaunching Europe' has been recognised by many, not only by scholars but certainly also by many of the actors involved. Former Commissioner Peter Sutherland (who served in the first Delors' Commission from 1985 to 1989), for instance, fully confirmed that the Roundtable did (in his view) play an important role in setting the agenda for the 1992 project, as well as in helping to implement it.

> I believe that it did play a significant role in the development of the 1992 programme. In fact one can argue that the whole completion of the internal market project was initiated not by governments but by the Roundtable, and by members of it, Dekker in particular, and Philips playing a significant role and some others . . . And I think it played a fairly consistent role subsequently in dialoguing with the Commission on practical steps to implement market liberalisation.[14]

Delors himself has also recognised the important role of transnational business, and especially the Roundtable, in supporting the whole 1992 project: 'I must admit the business actors mattered; they made a lot of it happen' (Delors quoted in Krause 1991: 86).

The failure of the neo-mercantilist project

We can interpret the first five years or so of the ERT's existence as a first phase in its evolution. This phase is characterised by two different although interrelated aspects. In the first place, it was a phase in which the Roundtable pursued a bold 'Europeanisation' campaign, an offensive of ideas against the 'industrial nationalism' dominant at the time. The second aspect was formed by the ERT's protective regionalism. In fact, these two aspects are related to the extent that together they constitute a strategic orientation which can be interpreted as a defensive move on the part of large sections of European industry against the pressures emanating from the global restructuring race.

This neo-mercantilist project in the end failed to materialise. The internal market was a big success, and a success for which the ERT could take much of the credit, but in many ways it did not turn out to be the kind of home market that many of the early Roundtable members (of the Europeanist fraction) had envisaged: that is, a relatively protected home market in which Euro-champions could prosper in order to confront the global competition. The internal market did favour the creation of further economies of scale, and did make the European market a more real home market comparable to that of the USA and Japan. But in the end, the internal market programme was not, or was only minimally, supported by the kind of 'flanking' policies that the neo-mercantilists had hoped would nurture the growth of European champions and protect them against global competition. Responding to the demands that were made by among others (members of) the Roundtable, the Commission did launch intra-European co-operation programmes in R&D such as ESPRIT (see Sandholtz 1992), and also started to promote the development of Trans-European infrastructure Networks (so-called TENs), with Delors in 1986 explicitly acknowledging the input of the ERT.[15] Such policies, however, fell far short of the kind of neo-mercantilist industrial *relance* of Europe that had been envisaged by some sections of European business, and, at the inter-state level, had been promoted by the French Government.

The fears of a 'Fortress Europe' (as for instance voiced across the Atlantic) also turned out to be unfounded. Although there was in the 1980s some protectionism (directed mainly against Japan) for the cars and electronics industries, even these limited protectionist policies were gradually dismantled in the course of the 1990s (Hanson 1998). Both within the ranks of Europe's transnational business elite and at the inter-state level – where pro-free trade member states such as the UK, Germany and the Netherlands blocked the more outright protectionist proposals of for instance France and Italy – the neo-mercantilists were losing the political battle. It was thus that, as the internal barriers came down, no external barriers were erected and the internal market provided as much an opportunity for US and Japanese, as for European firms (see Hanson 1998; Wyatt-Walker 1998). The internal market programme – by giving the same opportunities to outside competitors – hence only led to a further opening up of Europe's national economies to the global economy.

Of course, the internal market programme, in its internal dimension, was already a largely neo-liberal project through the deregulatory effects of mutual recognition (Grahl and Teague 1990). The liberalisation of capital flows (which had not been part of the original Common Market project in which – as part of the Bretton Woods regime – capital controls were still firmly in place) moreover added to the liberalisation thrust of Europe 1992, in particular as here too the relevant directives were applied *erga omnes*: that is to say, the principle of non-discrimination based on nationality applied not only to member states but also to third countries (Story and Walter 1997: 256), further integrating the European economy within the globalising world economy. It was thus that, as Tsoukalis (1993: 99, 335) notes, with Europe 1992 the process of European integration entered a qualitatively new phase in which for the first time the integration process came to intervene directly in the existing socio-economic order in the different member states. As it turned out, this intervention became bound up with an intensifying process of neo-liberal restructuring.

The neo-liberal interpretation of the internal market programme in the end thus prevailed. This may to an extent also be attributed to the very ambivalence of some

'Europeanist' firms and their CEOs with regard to their own strategy of protective regionalism. After all, it was clearly the ambition of most would-be 'European champions' to become 'global players' themselves. Thus, for instance, some ERT firms that were at the same time calling for Europrotectionism were also hedging their bets by concluding deals (such as joint-ventures) with American and Japanese counterparts,[16] although, as noted before, some firms also became temporarily more concentrated on the European market in the context of the internal market programme. If the neo-mercantilist project had been more successful, this orientation might have been even further reinforced. The way things turned out, however, pressures for further globalisation in fact increased.

Globalisation and the neo-liberal transformation of the ERT's strategic project

At the end of the 1980s and into the early 1990s we witness a gradual shift in the ERT's strategic and ideological orientation from a neo-mercantilist regionalism towards a neo-liberal globalism. Integrating a structural analysis with one emphasising agency, I argue that this transformation can be explained in terms of the following three elements, constituting different but interrelated aspects of this transformation process. The first one has already been discussed in the previous section and concerns the changing political (and ideological) context within the European political economy as neo-mercantilist forces were losing the political battle against more (neo-)liberal-oriented forces in defining the content of the internal market programme. Faced by these political realities, suggesting a waning influence of the Europeanist fraction of European transnational capital, the neo-mercantilists within the European capitalist elite had to reconsider their options. The struggle between these two contending projects for European integration thus took on a new prominence in the implementation phase of Europe 1992. It was a struggle that, as I will argue, partly took place within the ERT from 1988 onwards, but before 1988 largely unfolded outside its ranks, and in this sense also preceded the shift in the ERT's orientation. One should hence stress that the early Roundtable – being mainly a club 'representing' the Europeanist fraction of European industrial capital and excluding more globalist firms – was not yet a forum in which a comprehensive concept of control uniting Europe's emergent transnational capitalist class could be articulated. That transnational neo-liberal social forces did take an interest in the socio-economic content of the integration process and that they actually sought to shape this content is in fact evidenced by the story of the ERT from the late 1980s onwards, when its membership was reinforced by capitalists from this neo-liberal fraction and its course also subsequently shifted further away from neo-mercantilism.

The second element, then, in my explanation refers to the changing composition of membership of the Roundtable, in particular the re-joining of the globalist fraction from 1988 onwards, and the general rise of this fraction within the ranks of the ERT and the European transnational capitalist class more widely. Although I thus focus here on a *structural* analysis, this structural change itself cannot be explained in purely structuralist terms. Although on the one hand globalisation and increasing global competition, reinforced by the relaunched integration process in the absence of European-level protectionism, presented large transnational firms with new constraints, it also presented them with new opportunities which some of these firms deliberately seized. As argued in chapter 1, structures are both constraining and enabling, as well as both constituting and constituted. Thus globalisation can on the one hand be conceptualised as a set of changing structural conditions impinging upon the agency of socio-economic actors, in this case TNCs, but it must at the same time also be seen as a process constituted by the agency of these same actors. Thus to the extent that European TNCs shifted their corporate strategies more to globalisation than to mere regionalisation they also contributed to the subsequent deepening of the globalisation process. Moreover, they have done so not only through their changing economic behaviour but also through their – or rather those of their owners and managers – changing political agency, opposing protectionism and advocating a much more open form of regionalism.

With regard to globalisation changing agency I here refer not only to changing behaviour but also to the kind of constitutive effects of structure discussed in chapter 1, i.e., the transformation of the identity and interests of actors. On the one hand, and in the first instance, globalisation must be viewed as changing the *strategic* behaviour of firms, as well as changing the strategic outlook of a club like the ERT. On the other hand, and at a deeper level, I argue that ultimately globalisation changes actors in terms of changing the politico-ideological content of their agency. Some fractions of transnational industrial capital are more globalised than others, and I hypothesised in chapter 1 that this would make a difference in terms of the tendentional ideological outlook of these fractions as crystallising in the process of class formation. This is not to say that as their firms become more global, the CEOs of these firms simply turned into neo-liberal ideologues. This process of ideological change must be understood at the collective level of a changing class strategy rather than at the level of individuals (where in our case some top managers may also have been succeeded by ones with a more globalist and neo-liberal outlook). It is within the Roundtable that this collective ideological shift took place in the course of the 1990s (as documented in detail in the final chapter). And in a structural sense, this shift was enabled by the changing structural conditions analysed below. Enabled but not determined, as ultimately this shift was only effectuated through concrete ideological struggles between the two rival fractions within and outside the ERT. These struggles, then, form the third element of my argument, and the focus of the final section of this chapter and of the final chapter. But I will now first turn to the changing structure of the ERT's membership.

The ERT's changing composition of membership: the re-entry of the globalist fraction

Over the years, the Roundtable has witnessed significant changes in its membership along all three dimensions identified in chapter 1, i.e., relative degree of globalisation, sectoral composition and national composition. First, and most importantly, the number of companies that show a relatively high level of globalisation (as opposed to 'mere' regionalisation) has steadily risen. Thus, among its present ranks the ERT finds firms like Shell, Unilever, ICI (which rejoined after its earlier walkout), BP, Roche and Bayer, all companies with a very significant global presence and similar strategic outlook. Second, it was already noted in chapter 3 that two highly competitive and globally oriented sectors – i.e., oil and chemicals (including pharmaceuticals) – that in the first years were virtually absent from the ERT's roster are now among its largest sectoral groups. Finally, regarding national representation, as indicated in chapter 3, since the end of the 1980s the French presence and influence has been in relative decline whereas the participation of 'liberal' British and German industrialists has significantly increased. These changes together, I claim, indicate a significant shift in the composition of membership towards what we have denoted as the globalist or neo-liberal fraction. This is also reflected in the changing leadership of the ERT, in particular the chairmanship (from 1996 to 2000) of Maucher, head of one of Europe's most globalised companies (Nestlé), and now of Morris Tabaksblat, formerly the head of an equally global food company (Unilever), and now of the Anglo-Dutch publisher Reed Elsevier (which makes a large part of its turnover in the USA).

The 'merger' with the Groupe des Présidents

A crucial episode in the ERT's changing composition of membership is the 1988 merger with the *Groupe des Présidents* (GdP), already briefly discussed in chapter 3. As was indicated, the GdP counted relatively more representatives of the globalist fraction than the ERT did at that time. This difference in the composition of membership between the two groups also made the GdP more (neo-) liberal in its outlook. As Floris Maljers of Unilever, former member of the *Groupe des Présidents* and later to become vice-chairman of the ERT, pointed out, the GdP had in comparison with the ERT more 'liberals than protectionists'.[17]

Table 4.2 presents a list of the new members and their companies that joined the ERT through the incorporation of the GdP. Of the 12 new members there were two heads of British, and two of Anglo-Dutch companies, the latter two being the very global firms Unilever and Shell, returning to the ERT's fold. The British contingent – with its traditional internationalist outlook – within the ERT was thus reinforced. With the oil companies Total and Shell, and the chemical companies Roche and Hoechst, the 'representation' of these sectors was also reinforced, a trend that was to continue into the 1990s. Finally, and critically, most of the companies of the new members had already attained a degree of globalisation that was considerably higher than most of the older ERT companies. In sum, the merger with the GdP constituted a re-entry of the globalist fraction into the Roundtable's membership, a re-entry enabling a subsequent ideological shift of the ERT. Maljers for instance noted that with the entry of the GdP, members of the Roundtable became more 'liberal'.[18]

According to Roundtable members and associates who were with the ERT at the time of the merger, the decision to merge the GdP into the ERT was in the first place one of simple rationalisation.[19] Still, there were other reasons as well. First, it is likely that as the ERT had proved itself to be an influential player in the European policy process, developing close links with the Commission and national governments, and being credited with much of the success of the Europe 1992 project, the members of the GdP came to perceive the Roundtable as playing a potentially useful role in articulating the interests of European transnational capital.

Second, we should also place the merger with the GdP in the context of, on the one hand, the relative decline of the Europeanist fraction as it faced the unfolding political failure of its neo-mercantilist project, and the rise of the globalist fraction on the other, worried by still lingering protectionist and interventionist tendencies. With regard to the latter, it must be noted that some sections of European industry, including companies of ERT members, until at least the end of the 1980s continued to perceive the rising global competition (and in particular that of Japan) as a threat that called for Europrotectionism. It has been suggested that one reason why Shell, Unilever and other firms wanted to join the ERT was that they wanted to steer the Roundtable further away from the remaining protectionist inclinations and push it into a more liberal direction.[20] As we shall see, they have indeed. On the other hand, though, at the end of the 1980s it had already become apparent that the neo-liberal interpretation of the internal market had prevailed over its neo-mercantilist rival, and it was in this context that the strategy of protective regionalism was

Table 4.2 New ERT members after the 1988 merger with the *Groupe des Présidents* (1987 data)

Name	*Company*	*Sector/Country*	*ROW*[a] *share of (%)*		
			Sales	*Assets*	*Employment*
Yves Boel	Sofina	financial holding/Bel.	–	–	–
Nigel Broackes	Trafalgar House	property development and construction/UK	–	–	–
Fritz Gerber	Roche	chemicals/Swi.	56	–	50
Klaus Götte	MAN	mech. eng./Ger.	–	–	–
Wolfgang Hilger	Hoechst	chemicals/Ger.	40	–	28
André Leysen[b]	Geveart	financial holding/Bel.	–	–	–
Floris Maljers	Unilever	foods/Neth.	40[a]	50	62
François-Xavier Ortoli	Total	oil/France	36	–	35
Tony Ryan	GPA Group	global aircraft leasing/Ireland	–	–	–
Robert Scholey	British Steel	steel/UK	–	–	–
Jacques Solvay	Solvay	chemicals/Bel.	25	–	24
Lo van Wachem	Shell	oil/Neth.	51	62	54

Sources: ERT membership lists; own research; figures on ROW share from Stafford and Purkins (1989).

Notes

a ROW is an abbreviation for 'rest of world'

b André Leysen heads the financial holding company Geveart but is also chairman of Agfa-Geveart, a Belgian subsidiary of German chemicals giant Bayer.

also gradually losing its appeal as a (potential) concept of control for the European capitalist class. It can be argued that 'representatives' of the globalist fraction would not have been willing to join the ERT in 1988 if this reorientation was not already to an extent taking place; indeed, as we saw, they had left the organisation in 1983 as at that time the gap between their vision of a 'new Europe' and that shared by a majority of members of the early Roundtable was still too large.

Third, then, several companies that were formerly still oriented towards the European market were now also setting on a course of global expansion. Although this process, as we shall see below, only fully materialised into the 1990s, we may hypothesise that at least in some cases this globalisation strategy was already anticipated at the end of the 1980s, gradually shifting the strategic orientation of these firms away from the neo-mercantilist project. It is to this globalisation of European industry that I will now turn.

The globalisation of European industry and the contradictions of Europrotectionism

Given that, at least by the beginning of the 1990s, the option of protective regionalism was no longer on the cards, the choices for European big business were increasingly narrowed down, increasing the structural pressure to comply with the apparent logic of the globalisation process, i.e., by 'going global' as well. As noted before, this had in fact been the ambition of many of Europe's still rather regionally oriented TNCs all along. Still, the ERT's original project had constituted a *defensive* strategy in which the preferred course was first to build up a strong position within the newly created and protected European home market. As, on the contrary, external barriers were only further lowered, and costs in Europe remained relatively high, the pressure to join the globalisation game – i.e., to shift production outside Europe – quite logically increased.

Table 4.3 presents data on the degree of transnationalisation, and the relative degrees of globalisation versus regionalisation of selected ERT companies for various years. The companies selected are all from the ERT 1999 membership roster, and include only those companies (30 in total) for which more or less comparable data were available. Although it has not been possible to gather all the relevant data (as these are not disclosed by many companies), a number of trends do emerge from this table.

Looking at the overall degree of transnationalisation, we see that for the 27 companies for which these data are available, total foreign sales average 78.4 per cent in 2000 (in two cases the figures are for 1999). Looking at the development over time, 19 companies for which we have these data show a rise in foreign sales from an average of 67.2 per cent around 1987 (in a few cases the data are from 1986 or 1988) to 81.4 per cent in 2000. As a large majority of those companies have been members of the ERT since the end of the 1980s, this shows a continuing rise of transnationality in the ERT's membership throughout the 1990s. The figures for assets and employment (where the data are more sparse) present a less complete picture but generally show a similar upward trend. Thus, to give a few examples,

Table 4.3 Degrees of regionalisation and globalisation of selected ERT companies for selected years (1983–2000)

Company[a]	*Year*	*ROE*[b] *share (%) of*			*ROW*[c] *share (%) of*			*Total foreign (%)*		
		Sales	*Assets*	*Empl.*	*Sales*	*Assets*	*Empl.*	*Sales*	*Assets*	*Empl.*
Air Liquide	'97	28	28	26	46	56	44	74	84	70
	'00	28	31	–	50	55	–	78	86	
Akzo Nobel	'00	47	–	40	47	–	41	94	–	81
Bayer	'87	39	–	–	39	23[d]	–	78	–	–
	'90	38	–	–	40	23[d]	30	78	–	–
	'97	–	–	20	–	–	36	84	62	56
	'00	–	–	–	55	48	45	–	–	–
Bertelsmann	'88	34	–	–	33	–	24[e]	67	–	57
	'91	36	–	–	27	–	22 [e]	63	–	50
	'97	32	–	–	35	–	–	68	–	–
	'00	29	–	–	40	–	22[e]	69	–	59
BP	'87	25	–	–	29	–	–	54	–	–
	'90	28	–	–	38	–	–	66	–	–
	'00	13	–	20	59	–	60	73	74[f]	80[f]
Daimler-Benz	'86	23	–	–	34	–	–	57	–	20
	'90	28	–	–	29	–	–	57	–	19
	'97	32	–	10	35	–	15	67	39	25
(Daimler-Chrysler)	'00	14	–	–	67	–	–	81	–	56
Danone										
(BSN)	'83[g]	18	19	–	9	6	–	27	25	28
(BSN)	'87[g]	22	22	–	10	4	–	32	26	39
	'90[g]	29	32	–	8	4	–	37	36	44
	'97	39	–	–	23	–	–	62	–	–
	'99	37	41[h]	24[h]	30	29[i]	56[i]	67	70	80
Ericsson	'87	48	–	27	29	–	20	77	–	47
	'90	47	–	30	41	–	23	88	–	53
	'97	46	–	–	50	–	–	96	–	–
	'00	52	–	–	44	–	29	96	–	–
Fiat	'83	32	16	9	15	12	6	47	28	15
	'87	35	16	–	11	6	–	46	22	–
	'90	35	–	–	9	–	–	44	–	–
	'98	38	–	21	25	19	19	59	43	40
	'00	40	–	26	27	–	24	67	–	50
Fried.Krupp	'87	23	–	–	20	–	–	43	–	16
	'90	31	–	–	20	–	–	51	–	19
	'97	32	–	–	33	–	–	65	–	43
(ThyssenKrupp)	'00	24	11	–	39	33	–	63	44	45
ICI	'84	25	14	11	50	38	38	75	52	49
	'87	25	18	–	50	40	–	75	58	–
	'90	26	17	–	51	39	–	77	56	–

Table 4.3 Continued

Company[a]	*Year*	*ROE*[b] *share (%) of*			*ROW*[c] *share (%) of*			*Total foreign (%)*		
		Sales	*Assets*	*Empl.*	*Sales*	*Assets*	*Empl.*	*Sales*	*Assets*	*Empl.*
	'97	25	20	11	44	56	63	69	76	74
	'00	20	16	–	65	59	–	85	75	–
GKN	'00	28	31	–	37	55	–	65	86	–
J. Smurfit[g]	'84	15	–	–	72	–	–	87	–	–
	'87	10	–	22	77	–	60	87	–	82
	'91	47	41	37	37	47	49	84	88	86
	'97	69	40	46	26	46	30	92	86	76
	'00	59	–	–	33	49	36	92	–	–
Lafarge	'83[g]	11	–	11	52	–	38	63	–	49
	'87[g]	10	–	6	48	–	46	58	–	52
	'90[g]	19	–	–	40	–	39	59	–	–
	'97	33[h]	–	51	44	–	29	77	–	80
	'00	32	38	–	49	51	–	81	89	–
Nestlé[g]	'83	38	–	–	60	–	55	98	–	–
	'87	41	–	–	57	–	56	98	–	–
	'97	40	–	38	58	–	59	98	84	97
	'00	30	21	–	68	66	–	98	87	97
Philips	'83	45	46	46	49	34	34	94	80	80
	'87	55	–	–	40	–	–	95	–	–
	'97	43	34	32	52	47[j]	51	95	81	83
	'00	40	–	–	55	46[j]	–	95	–	–
Pilkington	'96	42	55	–	42	31	–	84	86	–
	'00	–	–	–	42	37	–	–	–	–
Pirelli	'87	40	–	38	35	–	30	75	–	68
	'90	42	–	40	34	–	32	76	–	72
	'97	38	–	–	49	–	–	87	–	–
	'00	44	–	–	45	–	–	89	–	–
Reed Elsevier	'00	13	–	10	67	–	60	80	–	70
Renault	'85	26	–	–	3	–	–	29	–	–
	'87	35	27	–	17	9	–	52	36	32
	'90	38	26	21	10	5	6	48	31	27
	'97	45	41	23	16	9	11	61	50	34
	'00	45	–	–	20	–	–	65	–	–
Repsol	'97	4	5	3	13	34	17	17	39	20
(Repsol YPF)	'99	4	1	2	31	68	44	35	69	46
Rhône Poulenc	'97	29	–	17	51	–	41	80	–	58.0
(Aventis)	'00	15	10	–	41	50	–	66	60	–
Roche	'87	41	–	28	56	–	50	97	–	78
	'90	38	–	25	58	–	54	96	–	79

Table 4.3 Continued

Company[a]	Year	ROE[b] share (%) of			ROW[c] share (%) of			Total foreign (%)		
		Sales	Assets	Empl.	Sales	Assets	Empl.	Sales	Assets	Empl.
	'96	35	–	28	63	–	52	98	–	80
	'00	36	–	–	62	–	50	98	–	–
Royal Dutch Shell	'84	–	–	–	58	71	54	–	–	–
	'87	–	–	–	51	62	54	–	–	–
	'97	–	–	–	54	63	62	–	–	–
	'00	–	–	22	54	68	57	–	–	79
Siemens	'83	–	–	–	–	–	–	56	–	33
	'87	27	–	–	24	–	–	51	–	36
	'90	30	–	–	25	–	–	55	–	38
	'97	29	24	23	37	23	27	66	47	50
	'00	31	–	26	45	–	34	76	–	60
St Gobain	'83	–	–	–	–	–	–	45	–	53
	'87	28	26	35	15	9	15	43	35	50
	'90	39	36	38	20	20	29	59	56	67
	'97	29	–	–	33	–	–	62	–	–
	'00	39	38	42	31	41	31	70	79	73
Solvay	'87	65	–	57[h]	25	–	24[i]	90	–	81
	'90	71	–	–	23	–	–	94	–	–
	'97	56	–	68	37	–	21	93	–	89
	'00	53	–	–	41	–	–	94	–	–
Suez L. des Eaux	'97	46	–	–	13	–	–	59	–	57
	'00	51	42	44	24	47	24	75	89	68
Total (TotalFina-Elf)	'98	–	–	31.5	–	–	30	–	–	–
	'00	31	40	31	47	47	24	78	87	75
Unilever	'84	–	–	–	39	52	54	–	–	–
	'87	43	–	–	37	43	60	80	–	–
	'90	–	–	–	39	–	62	–	–	–
	'97	–	20	30	52	63	68	–	83	98
	'00	30	–	–	58	64	71	88	–	–

Sources: For 1997 and above: company annual reports. For earlier years: Stafford and Purkins (1989); Stopford (1992).

Notes: The data are only roughly comparable across companies due to differences in accounting practices. Sales figures are by final market unless otherwise indicated.

a company names from 1997: where necessary to avoid confusions older and newer names (for instance of possible successor companies due to a merger) are given in parentheses for the relevant years;
b the abbreviation ROE stands for 'Rest of Europe;
c the abbreviation ROW stands for 'Rest of World';
d capital expenditure;
e USA only;
f 1998 data (from UNCTAD 2000b);
g sales figures are by production area;
h EU only;
i outside the EU;
j USA and China only;
– Data unavailable (not disclosed by company).

total foreign assets of Danone (formerly BSN) amounted to only 25 per cent in 1983, increasing to 70 per cent in 1999; Fiat saw its total foreign employment increase from 15 per cent in 1983 to 50 per cent in 2000; Friedrich Krupp (now ThyssenKrupp) employed only 16 per cent of its workforce outside Germany in 1987 whereas by 2000 this figure had increased to 45 per cent; and Siemens saw its foreign workforce grow from 33 per cent in 1983 to 60 per cent in 2000. Only in those cases where a high degree of transnationality had already been attained in the 1980s did foreign production increase less dramatically, or remain more or less stable. In short, the deepening of transnationalisation discussed in chapter 2 has also affected most ERT companies.

Central to my argument, however, is not so much the overall degree of transnationality but rather the degree of globalisation, i.e., the share of foreign activities outside the European region. Looking at the sales figures of the same 19 companies as above, we in fact see a strong trend towards globalisation, both absolutely and relative to regionalisation. Thus, the average of sales outside Europe goes up from 34.0 per cent in 1987 to 46.2 per cent in 2000, whereas the figure for sales outside the home country but inside Europe increases only from 33.2 per cent in 1987 to 35.2 per cent in 2000. The largest part of the increase in total foreign sales noted above has thus been due to an increase in sales outside the European region.

As the 19 companies to which the above figures refer include many companies that were already rather global in the mid-1980s (such as BP, Lafarge, Nestlé, Roche and Unilever) these figures in fact do not reveal the true extent to which many ERT companies that used to be much more oriented to and dependent upon the European market – and that dominated the ERT in the first five years – have become more transnational and more global from the late 1980s onwards.

This applies in particular to the French companies, which were with the exception of Lafarge among the least globalised (and even least Europeanised) companies in the original 1983 membership. Thus, for instance, the globalisation index of a company like Saint-Gobain increased from 13 per cent in 1987 to 34.6 per cent in 2000. If we compare (for 2000) the top three (by sales outside Europe) French companies in table 4.3 with the top three from Germany and Britain, we get the following picture. The German top three (Bayer, Siemens and Bertelsmann) have average sales outside Europe of 46. 7 per cent,[21] the French (Air Liquide, Lafarge and Total) average 48.7 per cent, while the British (Reed Elsevier, ICI and BP) are still the most globalised with average sales outside Europe of 63.7 per cent. With regard to the degree of globalisation, then, differences between countries have tended to become less pronounced as the globalisation process has affected European industry in all major countries.

The rising globalisation of those companies that were formerly clearly within the Europeanist camp made the protectionist and mercantilist policies that the leaders of several of these companies had been advocating in the 1980s increasingly counter-productive into the 1990s. The growing importance of 'out-sourcing' meant that protectionism could easily backfire. At the same time, in the course of the 1990s, the Japanese threat was also receding. As the then ERT vice-chairman Maljers, who later became chairman of the supervisory board of Philips after he retired from Unilever, explained: 'The "Dekkerian" [after Wisse Dekker] reasons for controversy [with regard to the free trade versus protectionism debate] have now been faded out.'[22]

The end of the 'European champion' strategy

The thus emerging contradictions of Europrotectionism, and of the neo-mercantilist project, are well illustrated by the parallel failure of some elements of the Commission, most notably Delors himself, to set up a European industrial policy that was still largely predicated upon the French mercantilist model (see Ross 1993, 1995). Indeed, the 'Euro-champion' concept was not only a formula that appealed to and was promoted by some sections of the emerging European transnational capitalist class, but was also developed by European policy-makers searching for a way to strengthen the competitiveness of European industry as part of their strategy to sustain the relaunching of the integration process. However, as George Ross (1993) relates, at the time when the industrial policy initiatives developed by Delors and his supporters within the Commission started to gain enough momentum to at least partly overcome the resistance of the 'liberal camp' within the Commission, the strategy ultimately foundered on the unwillingness of the European companies concerned.

Ross (who has been an observer inside the Delors cabinet) describes how in the early 1990s the crisis in the European electronics industry (involving ERT firms such as Philips, Siemens, Olivetti and Thomson) formed the pretext for promoting 'European solutions' to the global competition faced by the micro-electronics industry, which the Commission regarded as the strategic sector of the 1990s. One plan the Commission had lying on the table, when a (secretive) meeting between Delors (with his advisers) and the CEOs of the electronics companies was finally convened in the spring of 1991, was – following the successful Airbus model – to form a European consortium on semiconductor research and production (Ross, 1993: 37). In the end, however, Ross notes:

> [only] three companies were willing to talk about cooperation . . . but each was simultaneously pursuing plans for strategic alliances with non-European firms, whether American or Japanese. Ultimately their choice was to 'go global' by dealing either with a Japanese or American giant. In the minds of the company CEOs there was really no European option. (ibid.: 40)

Here, we thus see the abandonment of the initial strategy of protective regionalism because of a changing strategic orientation (from 'going European' to 'going global') on the part of the former neo-mercantilists themselves. This strategic shift is also illustrated by the growing number of mergers and acquisitions of European firms across the Atlantic as well as (to a lesser extent) with other parts of the world. Two recent transatlantic mega-mergers that both involved an ERT company (those of Daimler with Chrysler and BP with Amoco) are a case in point.

The new ERT

With the inclusion of many representatives of the globalist fraction from the 1988 merger onwards, the ERT substantially broadened its basis and became much more of an elite forum for the whole of the emergent European transnational capitalist class, or at least its industrial fraction (even if – *inter alia* through interlocking directorships – the Roundtable's members are also part of a wider corporate elite network in which the interests of industry and finance are also linked). The ERT was hereafter no longer predominantly a club of leaders of regional TNCs pursuing a strategy of protective regionalism that was rejected not just by liberal national governments but also by many fellow transnational capitalists outside the ERT (and partially gathered within the *Groupe des Présidents*). The broadening of the ERT's base has also enhanced its legitimacy, and arguably its influence, vis-à-vis the Commission and the national governments. The transformation of the ERT also transpires from its deepening links with capitalist elites outside Europe (in particular the USA) and thus its deepening integration into emerging global capitalist elite networks as noted in the previous chapter. The structural changes within the ERT's membership base thus also point to the continuing deepening of the *global* process of transnational class formation, even if for the business leaders gathered in the ERT there continues to be a rationale to organise themselves politically within the European arena as long as in Europe we find an independent level of policy making that directly affects their interests.

The changing composition of the ERT's membership thus constituted a significant moment in the gradual development of the ERT as an elite forum of, and a platform for, Europe's emergent transnational capitalist class. As its membership was reinforced by leading figures of the globalist fraction, the ERT became a forum – indeed, at least at the transnational level, *the* forum – in which the opposition between Europeanism and globalism could be transcended, and a new *comprehensive concept of control* could be developed. In order to explain the emergence of this new concept of control we now have to move beyond the structural explanation offered in this section, and again take the role of agency into account.

The ERT's changing strategic project and the transnational struggle over Maastricht

Now that I have analysed the structural changes underlying the changing outlook of the ERT, I will continue the analysis of the ERT's changing project, set within the context of the transnational struggle over European order. In the remainder of this chapter I will in particular examine the ERT's activities and strategy as they evolved in the period from 1988 to the Maastricht treaty signed in 1992. Here, we will see that although on the one hand the ERT continued to focus on typical 'Europeanist' projects such as the development of trans-European infrastructure networks, it also began to pay increasing attention to labour market issues, and it was here that as early as the end of the 1980s its discourse became increasingly premised on a neo-liberal ideology. What became a neo-liberal offensive against labour market 'rigidity' was partly a response to the Delors project of constructing a 'Social Europe', as the forces bound up with the social-democratic project temporarily gained strength at the end of the 1980s. Delors' attempts to create a framework of supranational labour market regulation set the Commission on a straight collision course with transnational capital. This struggle between transnational social democracy and neo-liberalism was thus one of the struggles, I would argue, through which the transnational debate on European socio-economic governance was shaped in these years. At the same time, this debate was also structured by the ongoing ideological struggle between Europeanism and globalism within the ranks of Europe's transnational capitalist class.

The ERT in transition: strategy and policy shaping

Next to the internal market, (transport) infrastructure remained another main focal point of the ERT. Within the period 1988–92 the ERT published four more reports on infrastructure – more than on any other specific topic (ERT 1988, 1989b, 1991a, 1992a). After 1992 transport infrastructure stopped being a central focus of the ERT's agenda, although in the 1990s the focus partly shifted towards telecommunications infrastructure and the theme of the 'information society', with the ERT calling for a speeding up of liberalisation and deregulation in this new area of telecommunications technology (ERT 1994b), preferably at the global level within the multilateral framework of the World Trade Organisation (WTO). The reason for this is simply that the ERT by this time had achieved its principal objective of putting infrastructure on the top of the EU's agenda, with many of its concrete proposals entering the stage of implementation. With the Treaty of Maastricht, the goal of creating Trans-European [infrastructure] Networks (TENs) became a formal priority objective of the EU (see below). With its ideas put firmly on the policy track, the Roundtable decided that it could best delegate the implementation phase to a new 'independent' body that would work in close alliance with both industry and the Commission. The ERT first proposed to set up such a body in a 1989 report, with more detailed blueprints presented in following publications (ERT 1989b, 1991a, 1992a). With encouragement from the Commission and member states' governments, the European Centre for Infrastructure Studies (ECIS) was set up in 1993 (the members being selected by ERT member Umberto Agnelli (CEO 1997: 24)) and since then has been very active in producing reports on how to implement the TEN programme, and as such has also been used by the Commission to muster public support for this programme (CEO 1997: 24–25). Infrastructure is thus a good example of an area in which the ERT's agenda setting has been so successful that it can now leave 'the details' (as the ERT is only concerned with the broad picture) to another body. The ERT's then secretary-general, Richardson, refers to this strategy in terms of having '*transferred our interests* [to this new organisation]' (Richardson, quoted in CEO 1997: 23).

A new area in which the ERT became increasingly active is that of labour market, social and employment policies, and it is in this area that we for the first time witness the rise of a rather explicitly neo-liberal discourse.

Labour market and employment policies: the ERT's emerging neo-liberal discourse

Labour market and employment issues are a crucial area in understanding how the Roundtable capitalists position themselves vis-à-vis labour and its interests. It is here that we can most clearly identify the ERT's discourse as emanating from a *class* ideology, and as part of a strategy to maintain capitalist class hegemony in the face of potential labour opposition. This class strategy is formulated from the vantage point of transnational industrial capital, which as was argued in chapter 1, on the one hand has an interest in a highly skilled, disciplined and acquiescent labour force, and thus also in the maintenance of consensual labour relations (hegemony over labour), but is, on the other hand, in such a strong position (making use of its threat of exit) that it can afford to advocate relatively radical policies of deregulation and flexibilisation of the labour market that aim to strengthen the freedom of management. This strategy must also be understood against the background of the rising pressures of global competition, making – in the perception of management – the reduction of the cost of labour imperative for the maintenance of competitive profit levels. Of course, this imperative grows only stronger when protectionism is no longer available as a weapon against global competition. Thus whereas, as we have seen, Dekker (and the ERT) previously chose (whether out of ideological conviction or because of a certain realism about the resilience of post-war institutions) Europrotectionism over a dismantling of the welfare state, the transnational capitalists of the Roundtable have from the end of the 1980s onwards increasingly opted for the latter strategy, or at least have advocated a much more fundamental restructuring of the so-called European social model. It is thus that the ERT's increasingly neo-liberal perspective with regard to labour market issues fits with the transformation of its strategic project.

The ERT for the first time explicitly dealt with the issue of unemployment in one of its first reports, *Making Europe Work* (ERT 1986), which appeared at the time when the European unemployment rate had been reaching record post-war levels. The report identified labour market rigidity as one of the causes underlying European unemployment, but its tone was nevertheless still moderate, with the largest part being devoted to an analysis of the impact of demographic and technological change on the employment structure. In particular, it advocated more investment in (allegedly employment-creating) new technologies, including appropriate (partly publicly financed) programmes at the European level. Since then, the language of the ERT in this policy area has become much more radical, with the theme of labour market flexibility moreover occupying a much more central place within the ERT's strategy as it abandoned its earlier strategic orientation of protective regionalism, in which the threat to European industry was first of all perceived to stem from (unfair) outside competition.

In a report on *European Labour Markets* published four years later (ERT 1990), the ERT's ideas were already shaped by a much stronger neo-liberal discourse. Here it has to be noted that this report was written by a working group led by the later ERT chairman and major representative of the 'globalist' fraction, Nestlé CEO

Maucher. We may assume that it was in particular the globalist fraction of the ERT (strengthened after the merger with the GdP) that at this time adopted the most explicit neo-liberal perspective in this area. As such this report anticipates the consolidation of the ERT's neo-liberal turn a few years later. The core thesis of this and later reports (ERT 1993a, 1997a, 1998) is that 'institutional rigidities' of the European economy lie at the heart of Europe's unemployment problem (ERT 1990: 3 and *passim*). These rigidities, including 'social protection' and 'too high and downward rigid wages' (ibid.: 18), make it difficult for the labour force to adapt swiftly to the exigencies of 'accelerated technical development' (ibid.: 3). In addition to these 'structural causes' of unemployment, the report also emphasises 'individual reasons' for unemployment, pointing to 'the attitudes and behaviour of the employed and unemployed', 'the degree of actual willingness to work', 'excessive wage aspirations, [and] unrealistic expectations concerning job quality' (ibid.: 3, 14). Thus, in formulating an 'agenda for action' to combat European unemployment, the Roundtable suggests increasing 'the awareness of, where necessary, *individual responsibility* for unemployment' as an integral part of national employment policies, countering 'the present degradation of work ethics' by '[t]he development of motivation and positive attitudes [with regard to work]' through education at school and in TV and advertisements (ERT 1990: 41). This discourse clearly reflects the ideology of what Bob Jessop has denoted as the *Schumpeterian Workfare State* in which the social *right* to welfare in case of unemployment is replaced by the social *duty* to work under the conditions and against the price set by the market (Jessop 1992). The transition to the 'workfare state' implies the hollowing out of the welfare state inasmuch as the social security provided by the latter creates a problem of 'moral hazard' (ERT 1990: 4).

Focusing on the *supply side* of (un)employment – i.e., the conditions under which labour as a commodity is offered on the market – the ERT also pays considerable attention to improving education and training. Here, the ERT has in fact in the past decade been very active in promoting ideas like 'lifelong learning' and the 'learning society', concepts that since have also entered into the policy discourse of the EU (see ERT 1989a, 1992b, 1995a, 1995b; European Commission 1995). The new approach in the field of training that the Roundtable advocates – an approach in which flexibility is again one of the 'keywords' (ERT 1990: 38) and emphasis is put on the continuous learning of general, 'multi-purpose' skills – fits the requirements of the new flexible accumulation paradigm and its need for a core workforce that can add functional flexibility to the numerical flexibility provided by the peripheral workers.

The most neo-liberal part of the report is, however, to be found in the ERT's recommendations with regard to what it calls bridging labour supply and demand. Deregulation is seen as 'the key instrument' and 'job security' must ultimately be sacrificed for 'necessary labour market flexibility' (ibid.: 43). In the view of the Roundtable this need for greater flexibility may now be seriously undermined by 'new, centralised and overly harmonised regulations [that] will add to the large number of labour market rigidities already existing in EC countries' (ibid.: 3):

> There is the risk that European policy makers and pressure groups will lose sight of the key issue of unemployment in an unhealthy mixture of interests and power games – attempts of central institutions to assume power on lower institutional levels, attempts to form counterweights to the dreaded power of internationalized industry, attempts to build up European management–trade union coalitions in order to defuse foreign competition or to use the social dumping argument to protect inefficient structures against competition from within the Community. (ibid.: 32)

This statement clearly has to be understood against the background of the 'Social Europe' threat building up around that time. Indeed, much of the radical tone of this report can be explained in the context of transnational capital's fear of a second drive for supranational social regulation, after the defeat of the first 'social action programme' of the 1970s (see Streeck 1993; Van der Pijl 1993). At least in the field of social policies, the Roundtable feared the drive for supranational deepening on the part of the Delors Commission, and advocated a strict application of the subsidiarity principle (ERT 1990: 36). Let us therefore now turn to this part of the Delors project, which in fact drove a wedge between Delors and his associates on the one hand, and the ERT on the other: that is, between the sides of what otherwise had grown into a rather successful partnership.

The social-democratic project versus neo-liberalism

It was around the end of the 1980s that supranational social democracy or the Delorist project for a social dimension to the economic integration process (ultimately to be guaranteed by a federal political structure) temporarily gained momentum as well. In fact, it is claimed here that Maastricht can be partly interpreted as an attempt by social-democratic political forces (under the leadership of Delors) to push for both a social and a federal Europe to re-embed the newly created big European free market and thus protect and consolidate the 'European model of society'. Concomitant, then, with the relaunching of the European integration process, social democracy – as part of a modernisation process that had already started before in most west European countries – manifested itself as a transnational political and social force (albeit one lacking a strong transnational social power base) that entered into the struggle over the relaunched European integration process in opposition to a neo-liberalism that had hitherto been dominating the agenda. To be sure, this struggle between neo-liberalism and supranational social democracy was not always and in every respect a simple confrontation between fully opposing world views, but was in fact strongly mediated by social democracy's (and Delors') basic acceptance of the primacy of market integration (the completion of the internal market), at least to the extent that any state-building projects could, in the words of Delors, only be built on the successes of market building (Ross 1995). Out of the conviction that on the one hand 'the European social model' could only have a future in a stronger, i.e., more supranational Europe, whilst on the other hand Europe could only be relaunched if big business was taken on board, Delors and his supporters had in fact accepted much of the neo-liberal agenda. Nevertheless, as was indicated, it had always been Delors' belief that once the process of market liberalisation had been set in motion, this would create the momentum to allow for a gradual shift from negative to positive integration. It would give the Commission the confidence to push for a social dimension to complement market integration, and in the climate of optimism that would then prevail politicians would also be more likely to implement such a programme at the intergovernmental level. This, then, is precisely the scenario that seemed to unfold at the end of the 1980s.

What Delors had probably not counted on was the extremely hostile reaction this agenda provoked not only on the part of the British government (which was to be expected) but also on the part of (transnational) capital, which, as it had done before at the end of the 1970s, immediately mobilised all its resources to lobby against what came to be called 'Social Europe'. This mobilisation of big business took place in spite of the wave of Europhoria generated by the success of Europe 1992 and the concomitant economic boom, which may be taken to indicate that capital at that time was well aware of the depth of the structural crisis of capitalism (and hence of the temporary character of the economic upswing), and the need for a continuing rationalisation and restructuring. Partly for historical reasons (given the experience of the 1970s and the TNC-unfriendly climate that then prevailed), transnational capital was and still is particularly allergic to any form of *supranational* regulation, also because in principle such regulation can strike at the heart of transnational capital's structural power.

The Delorist agenda and its failure

The European Trade Union Confederation (ETUC) had already been making calls for a social dimension to the internal market right after the adoption of the White Paper.[23] At the member state level, the French government under Mitterrand (of which Delors was a cabinet member) had already in a 1981 memorandum called for the creation of a 'European social area' (Ziltener 2000: 154). Later supported by other member states (in particular Denmark), as well as by the Delors Commission, the social policy issue also figured in the negotiations of the intergoverrnmental conference that led to the adoption of the SEA of 1986. The social content of this treaty amendment was, however, disappointing. The major social policy innovation was contained in Article 118a and related to health and safety issues, but the call for a European social dialogue (Article 118b) remained at the level of symbolic politics and was acceptable to UNICE because of its 'voluntariness' (Ziltener 2000: 163). The programme for a Social Europe had to await the more active policy entrepreneurship of the Commission before it really gained momentum.

The construction of 'Social Europe' was relaunched by Delors in 1988 when, at an ETUC conference, he announced that the internal market programme had to be complemented with a social dimension, first of all in the form of guaranteeing at the European level basic workers' rights and freedoms. Social Europe for Delors and his supporters was first of all about supranational labour market regulation and, concomitant to that, the creation of a European system of industrial relations, including supranational collective bargaining (see Delors 1989). The first step on this road was made with the adoption of the Social Charter of 1989, although this only constituted a mere declaration of broad principles and carried no legal obligations. Indeed, the Charter was a 'highly diluted compromise' (Rhodes 1991: 263), even though the British government still refused to sign it. The Charter was followed by a Social Action Programme in the framework of which the Commission drafted several legislative proposals aiming at the supranational regulation of the European labour market. Most of these directives, however, never went beyond the drafting stage as they were blocked in the Council of Ministers. Some of them have now been revived within the framework of the European Social Dialogue, another initiative of Delors, within which the European 'social partners' can now negotiate agreements – which can then be transposed into directives – within the framework of the so-called 'social chapter' of the 1991 Maastricht treaty. So far, however, only three directives have come out of this process, on parental leave, on part-time work and on fixed-term work, directives that moreover have been criticised for setting very general standards that are below those already in place in most EU countries.[24]

Generally, European 'social partnership' not only remains restricted to a very limited area but in practice seems more a mechanism through which neo-liberal flexibility is implemented, *with* the support of *both* 'social partners' (i.e., in a way that ensures the maintenance of social consensus), than an instrument for the creation of an organised space for European industrial relations as envisaged by Delors. In retrospect, the Maastricht 'social chapter' was in fact the high-point of the efforts of the Commission to create a 'social dimension', and the very weakness of that text (see, e.g., Vogel-Polski and Vogel 1991) can be taken as a measure of the defeat of Delors and 'his' social-democratic project in the ongoing struggle over European socio-economic order (see also Ziltener 2000; Streeck 1995).

As indicated, the failure of the social dimension must be attributed not only to the intransigence of British opposition (behind which other member states were also often hiding), but also to the strong resistance put up by the transnational business lobby (see also Streeck 1993; Rhodes 1991). This lobby was pursued by UNICE, by AmCham, and, not least, also by the ERT. The ERT has also been active in lobbying against for instance the renewed plans for a 'European Company Statute', and in particular its proposed clause on workers' information and consultation rights. Dekker himself, as the chairman of the Roundtable, sent a letter to Delors and all 12 EC ambassadors, in which he argued that industrial relations should remain at the national level (Rhodes 1991: 260).

Although 'Social Europe' was probably the centrepiece of the social-democratic strategy, and certainly its most visible aspect, Economic and Monetary Union (EMU) was in fact also an important part of the Delorist project. EMU had already been on the agenda of the then EEC in 1969, and it now made its comeback in the wake of the 1992 programme, supported by the functionalist argument that a single market with free capital movements had to be supplemented by a monetary union in order to be durable (Padoa-Schioppa 1985). This argument was later seized upon by Delors and others in the Commission in order to extend the relaunching of European integration initiated by the SEA, and in 1988 the Delors Committee on Monetary Union was formed. In the social-democratic interpretation of EMU – which was as such supported by Delors, as well as by parts of ETUC, the socialist fraction of the European Parliament, etc. – monetary union serves the double function of regaining some democratic control over the global financial markets, as well as paving the way to a political union that in turn could even further strengthen 'politics against markets'. The first is based on the argument that only a single European currency can protect the EU countries against the destabilising effects of foreign exchange speculation and thus 'would strengthen democracy in the Union by restoring decision-making to elected representatives rather than unelected speculators' (Holland 1995: 12). During the Maastricht negotiations Delors in vain pleaded for a 'political roof' for EMU which would consist not only of a common foreign and security policy but also of a Community fiscal and social policy carried out by a reinforced 'European government' that could counter-balance the new European central bank (Grant 1994).

In order to gain a more complete picture of the social forces struggle leading up to Maastricht, we should now return to the struggle between the Europeanists and globalist fractions within the ERT and how it sought to overcome these conflicts.

The ERT's post-1988 internal struggle and the search for a new consensus

The expansion of membership that had swelled the ranks of the neo-liberal globalists rekindled the ideological struggle within the ERT inasmuch as it brought about a renewed opposition between globalists and Europeanists. It is true that the outlook of the Europeanist Roundtable members was already gradually shifting towards a more globalist orientation, but it was certainly not shifting fast enough in the perception of the new Roundtable neo-liberals.

Conflicts about trade policy were at the heart of the renewed struggle. One representative of the ERT's globalist fraction at that time, the (then) chairman of Unilever, Maljers, in fact indicated that the 'struggle between liberals and protectionists' became a constant feature of the internal policy debates at the end of the 1980s and beginning of the 1990s.[25] Ever since the neo-liberals re-entered the Roundtable, they vehemently opposed the remaining protectionism within the ERT, attempting to convince their colleagues of the inherent dangers of such a strategy, arguing that it would backfire against them.[26] As argued, partly because of their own re-orientation to the global market in the context of a deepening globalisation process, and partly in the context of a dominant neo-liberal ideology, many (but not all) former protectionists within the Roundtable did indeed gradually become convinced of the virtues of global free trade (see also the next chapter). But it was a slow and painful process.

This internal conflict, however, did not lead to a break-up of the ERT but in fact was a (probably necessary) phase that preceded the emergence of a new consensus.

There was still a clear need for a platform like the ERT, particularly as the relaunched integration process now seemed to move into a critical next phase. At the same time, the pressures of global competition did not abate. To respond to these pressures, a coherent political strategy on the part of European transnational industrial capital as a whole was still as urgent a requirement as ever. Moreover, only a year after the ERT's 1988 expansion of membership, the old world order experienced a major upheaval with the collapse of 'real-existing socialism'. After neo-liberal restructuring had already set in – first and foremost in the USA and the UK – to roll back some of the institutional and ideological legacies of the post-war mixed economy, this momentous historical transformation in which capitalism was seemingly left without any competition (cf. Albert 1993) logically also signified an important ideological victory of neo-liberal social forces over forces that challenged its emerging hegemony within the capitalist heartland. In an alleged 'end of history', neo-liberal restructuring was now set to become a truly global process (Cox 1992a).

Thus, the dissolution of the Soviet Union and the transformation of eastern Europe had the effect of politically and ideologically strengthening the neo-liberal project, something which probably also did not leave the ideological debate within the ERT untouched. The transformation of the 'other Europe' also changed the environment for European big business in another respect: it opened up huge new markets for Europe's TNCs to explore and exploit. This new economic hinterland was seen as offering major opportunities for European industry, giving it a potential advantage over Japanese and American competitors (Hildebrand 1992). If European industry was not to lose out even further in the global restructuring race, Europe had better respond to this challenge – and seize the opportunities quickly and in a concerted manner, ensuring the integration of this new huge potential market into the capitalist system, to the benefit of European transnational capital. At the same time, the success of the Europe 1992 programme, the economic boom of the second half of the 1980s and the end of Europessimism also gave the business elites of Europe a sense that Europe could and should move forward, that now was the time to build upon the success of the first phase of Europe's relaunching. It was these elements together, then, that provided the incentives to seek to transcend the divide between the globalist and Europeanist orientations and to reach a new consensus, and a concomitant programme for a 'New Europe' to be constructed out of the next phase of Europe's relaunching.

'Reshaping Europe': the ERT's agenda for Europe's 'extended relaunch'

It was against this background, then, that the ERT in September 1991 published what is still one of the ERT's most ambitious reports, *Reshaping Europe* (ERT 1991b) in which it offered a blueprint and an action plan for Europe in the 1990s, based on what Holman (1992) has called a 'catch-all strategy', reflecting a comprehensive compromise, but not yet a synthesis, between the two competing perspectives of protective regionalism and neo-liberal globalism:

> Europe stands on the brink of a great opportunity. It is a rare event in history when a whole continent has so clear a chance to reshape itself and build its own future. The recent pace of events in Europe has created this opportunity. Time will not wait for us. This unique opportunity must be grasped with great determination and a clear sense of direction. (ERT 1991b: 11)

The report states four priorities for the future of European integration: 'the completion of the Single Market, an effective industrial policy . . ., a single currency before the end of the decade and firm steps to strengthen the links between the Community and the rest of Europe' (ibid.: 41), i.e., a strategy of both deepening and widening European integration (ibid.: 40). The plea for an EMU is now for the first time prominently present: 'Japan has one currency. The US has one currency. How can the Community live with twelve?' (ibid.: 46).

With regard to monetary union it has to be pointed out that there was in fact not as yet such a strong consensus in favour of it as the report suggests. The major business rationale behind monetary union is that it reduces transaction costs for transnational business. As with a single currency, the risk of currency fluctuations will be much less, which will cut costs and promote economic growth. Both transnational banks and transnational corporations would thus strongly favour EMU (as hypothesised by Frieden 1991). This was therefore, then, also certainly the case for a section of the ERT; however, support was especially strong among those still heavily focused on the European market and less among those companies much more oriented to the world market. There were moreover, as I shall discuss in the next chapter, also other more political and specifically national reasons why support for EMU was not as yet unequivocal across the whole of the ERT's membership.

Those who did strongly favour the single currency, mostly within the Europeanist camp then, often did so in a language that still had some neo-mercantilist undertones. Thus, next to the transaction cost argument, another often heard argument (especially among the French) was that Europe also needed a single currency because this would strengthen Europe vis-à-vis the USA, whose dollar dominated the world economy.[27] Europe needed its own strong currency in order to remain strong and independent as a trading bloc in a volatile global economy. Thus, in 1988 (at a time when the US dollar stood relatively low, making it cheap for US business to invest in Europe), the then president of the Association for Monetary Union (see below) and ERT member, Cor Van der Klugt of Philips, made his case for monetary union as follows:

> if the monetary balance [vis-à-vis the dollar] is not restored fairly soon there is a very real danger that the internal market, which was intended as a springboard for European industry, could turn in a diving-pool into which our dollar-related foreign competitors can plunge. (Van der Klugt 1988: 2)

Although the importance of the convergence criteria was also emphasised by the ERT (ERT 1991b: 46), this neo-liberal argument only became more central to the

Roundtable capitalists in the 1990s when the ERT's neo-liberal shift was further consolidated.

Reshaping Europe can in retrospect be interpreted as a first step in the direction of an emerging synthesis of embedded neo-liberalism. It was, however, only a first step as the distance between the Europeanist and the globalist camps was still too great to be fully bridged. *Reshaping Europe* must therefore still be located within (but also towards the end of) the transition phase in which the strategy of the Roundtable shifted from protective regionalism towards (embedded) neo-liberal globalism. It must be pointed out that the report was written by the then present and the two former chairmen of the ERT, Monod, Dekker and Gyllenhammar, three leaders (and particularly the latter two) who – certainly from the perspective of today – can be seen as representing the 'old guard' of the Roundtable. This, then, may partly explain the strongly Europeanist discourse we still find in the report in several instances. The fact, however, that the report as such was approved by the ERT Plenary shows that the (by and large) Europeanist leadership of the ERT in 1991 still had not made way for the new globalist leadership of today's Roundtable.

With regard to the institutional mode of European integration, the authors of *Reshaping Europe* take a pragmatic viewpoint, stating that 'As businessmen we take no ideological position for or against "pooling" or "merging" sovereignty' (ibid.: 60), but one that is nevertheless (still) biased in favour of institutional deepening. Indeed, the language of the report is often strongly supranationalist, presenting an agenda for the future in which the integration process is to move forward in several different areas: from industrial policy and monetary union to foreign and security policy. A central theme is still that of the continuing need for a sustained Europeanisation – strengthening the 'European dimension' (ibid.: 16) – as the way to enable European industry to compete on a world-wide basis and to allow the European economy to develop its full potential. This includes the construction of a political union with strong institutions 'based on the firm principles of democratic control, majority voting [hence: supranationality] and subsidiarity' (ibid.: 58–59), and with common policies in the areas of foreign affairs, security and even immigration (ibid.: 67). Of course, not all of this integrationist rhetoric can be taken at face value. The Roundtable wants Europe to have both a single market and a single currency, emphasising that this implies the need for strong and effective (central) institutions. In addition, the Community should also pursue a set of *positive* policies (in the area of infrastructure, technology and industrial policy) in order to support European industry in its competition race with the rest of the world. But the Roundtable capitalists are at the same time vehemently opposed to positive policies (or the creation of harmonised standards) in the area of labour market and social policies: 'An over-centralised, over-regulated, and over-harmonised Europe is the last thing we want' (ibid.: 16).

It is within the socio-economic policy fields that we can see evidence of both a stronger neo-liberal orientation *and* traces of the neo-mercantilist orientation contradicting this trend, thus reflecting the (unstable) *compromise* between the Europeanist and globalist camps. With regard to trade policy, the report strongly stresses the need for an open world economy, declaring that 'the objectives of the Uruguay [GATT] Round are vital to world prosperity' (ibid.: 52). In this context, it also remarks that industry no longer wishes 'to be held hostage' to the interests of European agriculture' (ibid.). But at the same time it acknowledges that the 'problems are too deep-seated to be solved overnight'. This must be interpreted as first of all a concession to French interests, as it was the French government that – under pressure from its large agricultural lobby – proved the least willing to make concessions with respect to reforming Europe's common agricultural policy, a reform that the USA demanded as part of the GATT deal. Probably reflecting their closeness to the French state, and generally the more protectionist orientation of French capitalism, the French members of the ERT too were wary of giving in too quickly to US demands on this point (see also the next chapter). Moreover, echoing earlier arguments in favour of Europrotectionism by those members who dominated the ERT in the 1980s, the report also warns – with explicit reference to Japan – that 'predatory behaviour is the enemy of free trade' (ibid.: 55). In 1991, then, the final round of the battle between the liberals and the protectionists within the Roundtable still had to be fought.

In the field of industrial policy, broadly defined, most of the attention still goes to the issue of infrastructure. Here, 'top priority' should be given to the Trans-European Infrastructure Networks (ibid.: 7). With regard to industrial policy more narrowly defined, some contradictions clearly appear in the report's discourse. Thus, at the same time that the report stresses that a 'competitive environment' for industry must mean 'an open market, based on free and vigorous competition, with a minimum of government interference' (ibid.: 42), it also asks the rhetorical question 'how strong . . . Europe [would have been] today . . . without past government intervention? [in specific sectors]', and continues 'we have not yet reached a society in which such decisions could be taken solely by unaided "market forces"' (ibid.: 45). It is here that the report reveals its strongest scepticism towards free markets. Thus governments are asked to keep in mind the following realities:

- Markets have their own imperfections, distorted by taxation and by sudden shifts in sentiment. Their judgement can go into reverse more quickly than industrialists can build new factories, train new workers or develop new products.
- Markets can even work against the forces of competition, when a company which represents a major competitive force is eliminated or withdraws overnight and it takes ten or twenty years for a new competitor to grow or take its place.
- However well one's own market functions, the operation of outsiders who read the rule differently can make nonsense of all the benefits of free and open competition. (ibid.: 44)

The first two points clearly imply a strong rejection of the Anglo-Saxon model of capitalism dominated by the short-termism of financial capital and a concomitant mode of corporate governance. The continental system in which management has a relatively strong autonomy, in which long-term growth is fostered, and in which companies are well protected against hostile take-overs is clearly preferred over the shareholder capitalism of the UK and the USA, in which return on equity is the most important measurement of corporate performance. This of course in the first place reflects the long-term *productivist* perspective of industrial capital and the managers who control it. As I shall note in the next chapter, however, the views of the ERT in this area shifted later in the 1990s as well.

The last point in the quotation echoes the language of neo-mercantilism, as 'outsiders' probably refers to non-European competitors. It is on the basis of this argument that the report pleads for an industrial policy that is on balance as much premised on the interventionist French model as on the liberal 'framework' model of Germany. The ERT notes that competitiveness 'cannot be achieved by protecting the inefficient', but nor 'by allowing industries of the future [think of the micro-electronics sector represented in the ERT by companies like Philips and Siemens] to slip into an early grave' (ibid.). It can safely be assumed that many of the more globally oriented new members (as well as older members such as Maucher of Nestlé) did not agree with the report's contents on these points, but they apparently were not yet in a sufficiently strong position to determine the ERT's agenda in this area.

The ERT and Maastricht

In contrast to the 1992 project, the ERT's direct involvement in the Maastricht process was limited. Whereas with regard to the internal market programme, the Roundtable clearly played an initiating role, setting the agenda for the politics of European integration where politicians failed to move Europe forward, it now seemed that the politicians had again taken the initiative. The obvious reason that can be given for this apparent difference in the ERT's role is that it was the earlier success of the Single Market, and the new 'Euro-optimism' to which it led, that enabled the politicians to move forward on their own. Unlike the situation in the beginning of the 1980s, Europe's policy-makers no longer needed the businessmen of the Roundtable to regain confidence in the building of Europe's future. The apparent success of the 1992 programme, already leading to a spur of cross-border mergers and new investments (Sandholtz and Zysman 1989: 118–20), together with the economic upswing that had been taking place within Europe since 1985, produced a climate in which Europe's national political leaders found it relatively easy to upgrade their common interest and take another leap forward in the further deepening of European integration. It is in this respect that Maastricht can be partly seen as a kind of non-functionalist 'spillover' effect from the 1992 project (Sandholtz 1993: 19–23). To the extent that the spillover proposition helps us to explain the Maastricht treaty, it must be pointed out that this already implies an indirect but nevertheless significant role for the Roundtable. That is to say, inasmuch as the ERT played an initiating role in the relaunching of Europe, it *ipso facto* also helped to set the stage and create the pre-conditions for the second phase in Europe's 'relaunch'.

Moreover, when we analyse the (socio-economic) *content* of the Maastricht treaty, we encounter several of the ideas that the ERT, or at least part of the ERT membership, had been advocating for years, in particular the idea of monetary union as a necessary complement to the internal market, as well as an enhanced European role in infrastructure and research and technology, the latter finding their way into the treaty as chapters on 'Trans-European [infrastructure] Networks' and 'Research and Technological Development'. Furthermore, other parts of the treaty, most notably the social protocol, were testimony not only to the efforts of social-democratic forces to put this on the agenda, but as much, if not more, to the role of transnational capital – represented *inter alia* by the ERT – in watering it down, and seeing to it that this minimal programme would only be minimally implemented. The ERT also had made quite extensive use of its high-level contacts to promote its agenda. Delors got an advance copy of the *Reshaping Europe* report,[28] and there have been several consultations between the ERT and important Commissioners like Frans Andriessen, Ray MacSharry, Sir Leon Brittan and Delors himself: that is, with people 'to which we [the ERT] could explain our views on the Maastricht process'.[29] At the national level there have been similar consultations between individual members of the Roundtable and key policy-makers of their respective national governments.[30]

With regard to monetary union, the lack of a strong consensus within the ERT meant that it could not push as strongly for EMU as some members would have liked. However, these members did organise themselves in a separate organisation, the aforementioned Association for Monetary Union of Europe (AMUE), founded in 1987. AMUE secretary-general Bertrand de Maigret has explained the relationship between the ERT and AMUE as follows: 'We decided that the ERT would not work on monetary issues, and that we would. We have friendly links, a kind of division of tasks' (quoted in CEO 1997: 30). At the time of the Maastricht treaty, however, this 'division of tasks' must probably also be understood in light of the rather narrow consensus in favour of EMU within the ERT. Among the core membership of AMUE we find many ERT companies such as Fiat, Philips, Siemens and Total, whereas prominent (former) ERT members – such as André Leysen, Giovanni Agnelli and Davignon – are long-serving members of AMUE's governing board.[31] From the start, the industrialists of AMUE had close contacts with the Commission, and in particular with Delors, in their efforts to promote monetary integration. At a joint press conference of a delegation of AMUE (consisting of the CEOs of Fiat, Philips, Solvay and Total) and Delors the latter expressed his appreciation for the 'very important' support of AMUE and stated that 'company managers not only follow us, but often precede us'.[32] As early as April 1988 – two months before the Delors Committee was set up – AMUE presented a detailed blueprint for monetary union, and in the following years it published annual surveys indicating wide business support across Europe (Moravcsik 1998: 393, 434). On the eve of the Hannover summit at which the Delors Committee was created, AMUE sent a communiqué to the government leaders expressing their support for the creation of an independent European Central Bank.[33] Although more research needs to be carried out on the role of

AMUE, it is at least evident that a large section of transnational business had effectively organised itself to help to set the agenda with regard to monetary union. Moreover, the close connections between the ERT and AMUE do suggest that it is by and large the same elite of European transnational capital that has constituted at least one powerful interest pushing for both Europe 1992 and EMU.

The Maastricht compromise and the changing political economy of European integration: between Rhineland capitalism and neo-liberalism

In ideological terms, Maastricht was, more than the 1992 programme, a project not just of big business but also of social-democratic political and social forces. The social-democratic interpretation of Maastricht has, however, failed to materialise. The social chapter has not gone much beyond mere symbolic politics (Rhodes 1992; Vogel-Polski and Vogel 1991; Streeck 1993). Political union still seems far away after the treaties of Amsterdam (1997) and Nice (2000) also failed to deliver on this score. The hope that EMU might restore democratic control over policy making has been contradicted by the institutional set-up of EMU (see below).

Still, the compromise embodied in Maastricht was not a triumph for Thatcherite neo-liberalism either; nor, for that matter, did it reflect the construction of a neo-mercantilist Europe. In fact, Maastricht contained elements of all of our three rival projects, even though it was biased in favour of the neo-liberal project, as the central part of the treaty, monetary union, came to reflect what Gill (1998) has called disciplinary neo-liberalism. The neo-liberal design of EMU is inherent in its convergence criteria and the later Stability Pact (later rebaptised the Stability and Growth Pact on the insistence of the French) of 1997 – stipulating sanctions in case of 'excessive deficits' in the third and final stage of EMU (since 1 January 1999) – but also in the independence of a European Central Bank (ECB) bound by the treaty to maintain price stability at the expense of other goals such as employment and growth (see also Martin and Ross 1999). Indeed, the austerity race produced by countries' efforts to meet the convergence criteria has led in many cases (Italy is probably the best example) to severe cut-backs in social spending and thus a restructuring of the welfare state (see Hall 1998).

At the same time, however, the aforementioned chapters on 'Trans-European Networks' and 'Research and Technological Development' did provide a basis for some form of European industrial policy or *Ordnungspolitik* clearly more in tune with the German model of Rhineland capitalism (Albert 1993) than with the (UK) neo-liberal model. Although these policies did not amount to a neo-mercantilist strategy – from which Europe indeed only further moved away with Maastricht – they did speak to the interests of that part of European industry that in the past had propagated a more mercantilist conception of the European project. Finally, the albeit rather weak 'social chapter' nevertheless constituted an important ideological interpellation of Europe's social-democratic forces and trade union movement, and at the same time (in a longer-term perspective) still offers them an albeit weak legal–institutional base from which to pursue their project further. It was thus that Maastricht can be seen as partly the outcome of the struggle between our three projects, a struggle within which neo-liberalism became increasingly dominant, but was still forced to articulate its ideology with elements of contending projects.

In retrospect, then, although in many respects an awkward comprise between many different parties and interests, Maastricht represented a first reflection of a gradual emergence of what I have denoted the embedded neo-liberal synthesis, to which I will now turn in the final chapter.

5 Transnational class agency, the rise of 'embedded neo-liberalism' and the evolving European order

This chapter will analyse the rise of what I have identified as embedded neo-liberalism as a new concept for European socio-economic order. Embedded neo-liberalism is on the one hand interpreted as the outcome of the transnational struggle over European order, i.e., the struggle between the rival capitalist class strategies of neo-mercantilism and neo-liberalism, as well as between a supranational social-democratic project and a business elite united, in this context, behind a largely neo-liberal concept. It is thus that embedded neo-liberalism can be taken as reflecting a wider structural movement within the political economy of European integration. On the other hand, the concept of embedded neo-liberalism is also interpreted here as the new comprehensive (indeed more comprehensive than before) ideological orientation of the transnational capitalist elite organised in the Roundtable.

The two manifestations of embedded neo-liberalism are linked through structure and agency. That is to say, the embedded neo-liberalism of the ERT can, on the one hand, be interpreted as *reflecting* the outcome of the broader transnational political and ideological struggles, as it is in the context of these struggles that the ERT members define their common interests and articulate their individual viewpoints into a collective strategy. On the other hand, as the Roundtable, or rather the transnational capitalist elite that is organised (*inter alia*) within the ERT, is also a significant actor within those transnational struggles, its agency must also be interpreted as having *shaped* their outcome. Indeed, as we have seen, two of the main tendencies within this struggle were also manifest within the ERT. In the argument advanced here, the Roundtable has played an important role as an elite forum in which the conflict between neo-liberals and neo-mercantilists could eventually be transcended.

The transcendence of the old globalism versus Europeanism divide has helped to establish the unity of the European transnational capitalist class, but it was a gradual process taking place through fractional struggle. Within this struggle, the globalists had now become the dominant group, but it also required leadership on the part of this now reinforced globalist fraction to effectuate and consolidate what came to be the ERT's neo-liberal shift. What was required was a hegemonic articulation of the now dominant neo-liberal perspective with remaining elements of the neo-mercantilist discourse. It is this articulation, then, that I will call embedded neo-liberalism. The embedded neo-liberalism of the ERT is hence also at the same time formulated in response to the agency of other social forces, and in particular those bound up with the social-democratic project.

This chapter thus interprets embedded neo-liberalism as the emerging hegemonic project of Europe's transnational capitalist class. At the same time I will also seek to show that it is this project that increasingly has come to define the socio-economic content of the current European integration process. Here the agency of the ERT is a key organisational expression of the transnational class agency that in my view has been central, within the context of wider transnational struggle of rival social forces, in constructing this social purpose of the new European order. Here I will argue that the embedded neo-liberal project is ideologically underpinned by what I will identify as a *neo-liberal competitiveness* discourse, and I will examine how this discourse has been constructed within the transnational political arena of the EU. Competitiveness, I claim, has become the key concept in EU policy making, constituting a master policy discourse to which other policy discourses are subordinated. The meaning of the word 'competitiveness' is not fixed, however, but has to be actively articulated through the *agency* of groups that perceive themselves to have a particular interest in defining the term in certain ways. Here I claim that the agency of the ERT has played a significant role in giving an increasingly neo-liberal content to the concept of competitiveness.

The limits of the neo-liberal project in Europe

The concept of embedded neo-liberalism at first sight seems to be an oxymoron. The thrust of neo-liberalism is the disembedding of the market economy from the (post-war) non-economic (social and political) institutions. This is certainly also the thrust of the restructuring advocated by the embedded neo-liberal concept, which, ideologically, is neo-liberal at its core. Thus, in no way should the term 'embedded' in embedded neo-liberalism be interpreted as to imply some kind of return to, or continuation of, the *embedded liberalism* of the post-war era. However, I argue that within (continental) Europe, there are so far stronger limits to this process of disembedding than for instance in the Anglo-Saxon countries, and inasmuch as these limits are acknowledged, the neo-liberal project tends to be reformulated by incorporating elements of other ideological orientations into its discourse as well, albeit at a subordinate level. This is not to suggest that embedded neo-liberalism has solved all (potential) contradictions. Rather, the contradiction that seems to be implied in the term is precisely intended to indicate the contradictions from which this emerging hegemonic project may yet suffer in the longer run (I will return to this point towards the end of this chapter).

In order to explain the concept of embedded neo-liberalism, and its rise within the European political economy, we should return to Karl Polanyi (1957) and his notion of a double movement, or the dialectic between the opposing principles of economic liberalism and social protection. A critique of Polanyi might be that his notion of the double movement is too functionalist, and that he moreover tends to ignore the fundamental class dimension of capitalist society. However, if qualified in some respects, Polanyi's ideas can very well be integrated with a Gramscian historical materialist framework. We then see that the double movement, on the one hand, indeed (as in Polanyi) reflects the dialectic of 'class struggle' to the extent that labour and other forces will organise to demand social protection as the disembedded market continues to disrupt their lives. On the other hand, it also reflects the logic of (class) hegemony, and the two are interlinked. Thus, precisely because of the double movement, a class or class fraction that aspires to hegemony must in the longer run articulate its interests both ideologically and materially with those of the 'population' at large: that is, it cannot afford to fully ignore the principle of social protection.

Here, however, we should return to our differentiation of capital fractions. Embedded neo-liberalism, in essence, represents the interests of transnational *industrial* capital, a class fraction of which, as argued in chapter 1, the ideal-typical perspective always tends to be an articulation of the two Polanyian principles. It is from the perspective of this capital fraction, the increasingly global industrial TNCs, that the concept of embedded neo-liberalism has crystallised. Given its relative distance towards any single domestic society, the ideological perspective of the globalist fraction has tended towards neo-liberalism or the principle of economic liberalism. However, pure *laissez-faire* would both hurt its own direct economic interests (as it still needs the state to educate the workforce, to maintain social and political stability, to provide the infrastructure, to pursue macro-economic policies that favour growth and investment, etc.) and, more abstractly, would undermine capitalist class hegemony as it might provoke a counter-hegemonic movement seeking to re-establish political and societal control over capital and the free market. In embedded neo-liberalism, the neo-liberal project stops short of fully disembedding the market economy from its post-war social and political institutions. The emphasis is still on the freedom of capital and the freedom of markets, and therefore on the need to fundamentally restructure the post-war 'European model'. Therefore, the kind of model of capitalism that embedded neo-liberalism promotes does not constitute the kind of embedded market economy Polanyi wrote about. But it is recognised that this restructuring will have to be a gradual process, in which some degree of social consensus is maintained. Within at least continental Europe, the neo-liberal project, I argue, therefore had to be articulated with some elements of opposing projects in order to become hegemonic.

Within continental Europe, in this respect, the neo-liberal project, as a potentially hegemonic project, reached its limits earlier than for instance in the UK and the USA. Here, neo-liberalism could achieve (at least temporarily) some form of social hegemony through an articulation with neo-conservatism: that is, free market economics combined with right-wing rhetoric on the nation-state, law and order and 'family values' (see Overbeek 1990 for the UK case). On the continent the situation was different. First, neo-liberalism needed to be modified in order not to harm the interests of industrial capital. Whereas British capitalism is dominated by the City and is also more service oriented, (manufacturing) industry is still strong in a large part of continental Europe, particularly France, Germany and Italy. This makes an anti-industrial policy as pursued under the past British Conservative governments unthinkable in the eyes of most continental European capitalists (as well as of most politicians). Second, compared to the Anglo-Saxon countries, the position of organised labour, and the traditions of corporatist labour relations and of social consensus (particularly in the Rhineland countries) have proven so strong as to make it impossible for neo-liberal forces to adopt the same antagonistic stance (vis-à-vis labour) as again, for instance, the Thatcher regime did. Thus, neo-liberal policies of deregulation, and flexibilisation, although desirable from the point of view of big business, can only be implemented with the consent of the trade unions. In this respect, we must note that embedded neo-liberalism as a class strategy (vis-à-vis labour) has two components. On the one hand, it fully asserts the control of capital over labour, seeking to restore the freedom of capital and management that the growing power of labour under embedded liberalism threatened to undermine; it seeks to weaken labour (as a political force) and to make its employment more favourable to the employers. On the other hand, it still adheres to the ideology of social partnership in order not to lose the benefits that go with that (such as a high degree of trust or 'internal flexibility') and because it is recognised that only in this way can hegemony be achieved.

In sum, we may also interpret embedded neo-liberalism as a hegemonic project unifying Europe's transnational capitalist class and expressing its collective interests, while at the same time appealing to a wider set of interests and identities. Here, the ideological power of Europe's capitalist elite manifests itself in the extent to which it shapes the discourse in which European socio-economic policy making is embedded.

The ERT's post-Maastricht strategy and discourse: consolidating the neo-liberal shift and the rise of embedded neo-liberalism

In the immediate post-Maastricht period, with the European economies in recession again (in the context of increasing global pressures), and the integration process going through another low, it seemed as though in many respects Europe was back to square one. Thus, at the end of 1993 the ERT writes in its new general report *Beating the Crisis* that:

> Europe has become a high-cost, low-growth economy that is not adapting fast enough and is therefore losing its competitive advantage to more dynamic parts of the world . . . With its financial, economic and political systems still *fragmented* and its leaders *divided*, Europe has failed to organise itself for economic growth as others have done. (ERT 1993c: 5 and 8, my emphasis)

It was, as we have seen, on the basis of a similar analysis that in early 1980s, the Roundtable called for a unified home market that could serve as a bulwark against the forces of globalisation. At that time there was no radical call to overhaul Europe's structures and institutions, no call for a fundamental change in policy (although there was a call for a rather radical Europeanisation). The strategy was basically a defensive one vis-à-vis global competition. Ten years later, the ERT formulates a rather different response to the renewed crisis. As we shall see, much of the programme presented in *Beating the Crisis* is now explicitly neo-liberal, focusing on deregulation, labour market flexibility, downsizing the public sector, etc., while the commitment to global free trade is expressed unequivocally.

The emphasis on the positive role of market forces has never been as strong as in current Roundtable discourse, and marks a significant departure from the ERT's 1991 *Reshaping Europe* (ERT 1991b) report (as discussed in the preceding chapter). Indeed, the industrialists of the Roundtable now seem to give more priority to deregulation and flexibilisation as instruments to enhance competitiveness than to industrial policy proper. In sum, then, as I will show in more detail below, in the post-Maastricht period, we see a continuing shift away from protective regionalism and towards neo-liberal globalism.

Examining the ERT's activities in the post-Maastricht period, we see that the Roundtable remains focused on shaping the (ideological) framework of European socio-economic governance, but that at the same time its attention shifts towards some new issue areas, and away from some older concerns such as infrastructure and technological co-operation. We can observe that the increasingly globalist outlook of the ERT is also reflected in a more outward-looking perspective with regard to the themes and issues addressed by the ERT. Thus, Maucher, the then ERT chairman, singled out the following new important themes for the ERT of the 1990s: 'external relations, the Trans-Atlantic Dialogue, Eastern enlargement and economic relations with developing countries'.[1]

The ERT's long-standing main concern, the completion of Europe's internal market, was officially achieved on 1 January 1993. Since then, the ERT has, however, stressed that some areas are still not fully integrated into the single free market, and has been calling for a rapid liberalisation in the areas of energy, telecommunications, transport (cutting state aids), and public procurement (eliminating discriminatory practices). New areas of attention are the (investment) relations of European industry with the 'developing world' (see, e.g., ERT 1994a), education (as discussed in chapter 4), and (to a lesser extent) environment (ERT 1994d, 1997b).[2] The most important new focal point of the ERT's strategy, however, can be captured by the term 'competitiveness', a word that, as I will suggest later on, is partly due to the efforts of how the ERT increasingly found its way into the policy discourse of the EU. The sustained attention to labour market and social policy issues also fits within this new competitiveness discourse (see below).

Let us now examine in more detail the *substance* of the ERT's post-Maastricht agenda. Examining the ERT's ideas in different policy areas, I will argue that a new consensus has emerged, one that reflects the emerging synthesis of embedded neo-liberalism.

Analysing the ERT's new discourse and strategy in four policy areas

In this section, I will analyse the changing strategic and ideological orientation of the Roundtable in the policy/issue areas of industrial policy, trade policy and other aspects of Europe's external economic relations, the project of monetary union and social and labour market policies. Together, these areas cover most of Europe's currently evolving supranational regime of socio-economic governance. Moreover, as I will contend, the ideas of the Roundtable in these areas can also be seen as the constituent elements of an emerging concept of control on the part of Europe's capitalist elite. The first area is about the role of the state in the economy, and thus defines an important part of the relation between state and capital. The second policy area concerns the external dimension, and hence the relations of European capital with the rest of the global economy. The third issue dealt with here, that of monetary union, in fact falls under the heading of policies that constitute the macro-economic framework but is here dealt with separately because of its present centrality in the process of European integration. The final policy area to be discussed concerns the relation between capital and labour, and again addresses the role of the state with respect to the question of how (if at all) the state should play a role in regulating labour relations.

In all these areas we witness a sustained neo-liberal shift and the emergence of a new embedded neo-liberal consensus. At the same time, within the bounds of this consensus, some differences of opinion persist, differences that are related to continuing, albeit much diminished, structural differences along the dimensions identified in chapter 1 (degree of globalisation, sector and national embeddedness). Therefore, if circumstances change, old or new conflicts might again open up.

Industrial policy

With regard to industrial policy we have seen in the preceding chapter that in the 1980s a majority of the ERT members favoured a strong industrial policy: a European industrial policy premised on the neo-mercantilist notion of promoting the growth of European champions. One could call this model of industrial policy the 'French model', and indeed we have seen that there was considerable convergence between the French government's 1983 plan for a common industrial and research area and the Roundtable's strategy. Although, with the partial exception of the *Reshaping Europe* report, as a collective body the ERT was careful not to plead too explicitly for sectoral interventionism, many members did support the French idea of nurturing new high-tech sectors like micro-electronics. More generally, as we have seen in the preceding chapter, an important part of the Roundtable (including its leadership) continued up to the early 1990s to adhere to a model of capitalism that not only clearly went beyond (neo-liberal) *laissez-faire*, but actually positively valued (when used with discretion) state interventionism as a means to enhance industrial competitiveness. This scepticism vis-à-vis the free market all but disappeared in the discourse of the ERT of the 1990s.

The rival model of industrial policy would be the 'horizontal' German model in which the role of the state is an 'enabling' (Streeck 1997) one. As the ERT moved away from its early neo-mercantilist orientation it came closer to favouring such a German-style *Ordnungspolitik* as the model for a European industrial policy. However, this was a gradual process born out of a continuous struggle around these two rival concepts. Throughout the 1980s, and into the 1990s, the rival French and German conceptions of industrial policy continued to play a role in the often 'intense' internal discussions about this topic.[3] That is to say, although the dominant section of the original ERT membership shared the French approach, the consensus on this was never unanimous. Probably with the 1988 merger with the GdP, this struggle intensified to the extent that those ERT members whose orientation remained basically favourable to a neo-mercantilist industrial policy now met the fierce opposition of the reinforced globalist fraction.

Within a pure neo-liberal model, the only legitimate industrial policy is competition policy policing the free market. Such a perspective may suit the interests of transnational financial capital but industrial capital, even its most globalised fraction, needs the state to go beyond this passive role, actively seeking to secure the 'conditions for competitiveness' as the Roundtable discourse has it (see ERT 1993c). Hence, rather than the British-neo-liberal model, it was the ordo-liberal German alternative – in which the role of the state is restricted to that of providing a 'stable political and economic framework to encourage investment and innovation' (ERT 1993c: 9) – that became the preferred concept around which all fractions could rally.[4] Although the ERT associate for the then ERT chairman, Maucher, complained that in spite of the latter's efforts to promote it, the concept of *Ordnungspolitik* was still little understood by other nationalities within the Roundtable, as it simply does not exist in other countries/languages,[5] we can still argue that the ERT's present ideas on industrial policy do reveal at least an implicit choice for some kind of German model. Thus, the aforementioned associate confirmed that the 'consensus' around the idea that government should provide the 'framework conditions' rather than intervening directly in industrial development has become 'much stronger' compared to the 1980s.[6] It is also a consensus that is for instance shared by the prominent French ERT member, Bertrand Collomb, the CEO of Lafarge, who stated that European industrial policy should not be based on the French model 'of a few years ago' in which 'the public authorities are themselves actors in the process'. Rejecting any 'implication' of the state 'in the industrial choices' (hence rejecting subsidies and other forms of sectoral support), the French business leader emphasised that industrial policy should be – like in the German model – restricted to creating an environment that supports competitiveness.[7]

We have thus witnessed a definite shift towards an industrial policy approach based on the German model, but around the edges of this new consensus we still find different shades of opinion. Thus some Germans may note, as one German ERT associate did, that the German model has often been 'a model of negligence' to the extent that its *Ordnungspolitik* was often not explicitly geared to improve and maintain the competitiveness of business,[8] and hence favour a concept of industrial policy that goes 'beyond the German model' in the sense of being more actively premised on the goal of industrial competitiveness.[9] Some of the British members, in contrast, might still be sceptical of any concept of industrial policy, even though they might subscribe to it in practice. Thus the then ERT vice-chairman, Sir David Simon (BP), emphasises that for him any 'industrial policy' should be limited to 'the macro-economic framework of the economy, which means stability in the value of money, and low inflation, and an encouragement of flexibility in the economy and of growth and innovation. The micro-economic implementation side should be left to business.'[10] The French, on the other hand, are said in some cases still to favour the kind of 'vertical' industrial policy that has served them well in the past at the national level and hence support a more direct involvement of the state, and thus also of public money (and not just in the area of infrastructure), in European industry. Thus, at least in the mid-1990s, 'opinions are [still] split' on the issue of whether the EU should also play a role in not just co-ordinating but also funding prospective technology programmes or infrastructure projects.[11] Nevertheless, as a collective, the Roundtable now unequivocally speaks out in favour of the 'free market line',[12] a line that at the same time goes beyond pure *laissez-faire*. A similar shift can be witnessed in the field of trade policy.

Trade policy

As we have seen, trade policy was at the heart of the struggle between Europeanists and globalists after the latter gradually began to dominate the ERT. The crucial battle probably took place on the conclusion of the Uruguay Round of the GATT trade talks (in December 1993).[13] With respect to the struggle within the ERT, the most negative stance (towards a conclusion of the Round) was taken, as suggested in chapter 4, by the French members who initially followed the line of the French government that had rejected the so-called Blair House agreement (critical to a successful conclusion of the Round) on agriculture (see Devuyst 1995). Other members too were wary that Europe might sell itself short in a quick conclusion of the trade talks. The then ERT vice-chairman Floris Maljers (Unilever) recalled that in the end, however, he and Helmut Maucher (Nestlé) – another staunch free-trader – succeeded in convincing most of their colleagues, including the French, that European industry should no longer let itself be 'dictated' to by the agriculture lobby. Also Jérôme Monod, then ERT chairman, was in the end prepared to 'give priority to his position as industrialist and not to the national position of France on the need to protect agriculture'.[14] After having reached internal unity on this point, the Roundtable subsequently intensified its lobby campaign for a speedy conclusion of the Round, and was probably one of the more important actors instrumental in changing the position of the French government.[15] According to the then director of the GATT, Peter Sutherland, 'the ERT was active and supportive of the Uruguay Round at the later stage when I was at the WTO'.[16]

Thus, in the ERT's December 1993 report *Beating the Crisis*, it was stated that 'the interests of industry at large and the cohesion of the trade system as a whole must not be sacrificed to the special interests of particular sectors' (ERT 1993c: 26). In fact, I would propound that with the benefit of hindsight the struggle over the Uruguay Round ended in the final defeat of Europrotectionism within the Roundtable and the European capitalist class more widely. Since then there seems to be a stronger than ever consensus around an unconditional commitment to global free trade. Indeed, ERT members and associates all stress that the balance has clearly and definitely shifted in favour of the free-traders' camp.[17] Almost three years after the conclusion of the Uruguay Round, David Simon (BP) commented thus upon the whole issue of the struggle between the two camps:

> I think the battle is nearly over. I think the WTO, and the process of international negotiation, has made it pretty obvious that the free traders are in the ascent, I mean, it is quite clear [that] the last WTO battle, . . . which reflected the sort of split [between 'free traders' and 'Europrotectionists'] was actually won by the free traders. I mean, even the French gave ground, so I think the proof of the pudding is there.[18]

Nevertheless, reflecting a persistent distinctiveness of the French in spite of the ongoing globalisation process, it seems doubtful whether all French industrialists within the ERT are now just as supportive of global free trade as their German or UK colleagues. Here nuances do persist. Thus, Collomb, of the very global (even from the early 1980s) French company Lafarge, declared himself a 'realist' in the debate on trade policy, which, according to him, means that although one 'fundamentally believes in free trade' one also acknowledges that if 'others do not play the rules of the same game, Europe should know how to use the same weapons in order to have a "level-playing-field" '.[19] The 'conversion' of the French may in this sense as yet not constitute a complete ideological conversion to free trade, but rather have a more pragmatic background. Still, the dominant line of ERT thinking, and a line that its French members have also accepted, is now definitely very pro-free trade.

Another important dimension of external economic relations is formed by the investment relations with the outside world. As we have seen in chapter 2, next to trade, FDI flows have increasingly come to dominate global economic transaction flows, and have become the driving force behind the globalisation process. As such, the rising interest of the ERT in the topic of investment in emerging markets (as noted above) can also be seen as a reflection of the growing centrality of FDI in the internationalisation strategies of Europe's TNCs (not least those TNCs that are represented in the ERT), and hence, as a reflection of the increasing globalisation of the Roundtable companies. As was noted in chapter 2, an ever more liberal attitude vis-à-vis FDI both in the industrialised world and in the host countries of the developing world has played a crucial enabling role in this process. The ERT thus notes with satisfaction that 'A new and powerful *engine of liberalization* is at work today: since the mid-1980s, host countries are competing for new investments by liberalizing and deregulating their economies (competition on rules)' (ERT 1993a: ii, original emphasis). In its reports the ERT calls upon governments to sustain these trends, and seeks to further 'propagate the role of FDI as a tool for economic development', calling upon European (big) industry to adopt 'global market strategies' and allocate their investment accordingly (ibid.: I, see also ERT 1994a).

Monetary union

Monetary union became of course the heart of the Maastricht Treaty, and its failure or success the linchpin around which the integration process presently revolves. As argued in the preceding chapter, within the ERT it was, however, probably not until after Maastricht that a broad and strong consensus in favour of EMU emerged. Indeed, analysing the internal debate within the ERT, a complex pattern emerges. A first conclusion might be that the strongest support has from the start come from the import-competing producers for the European market, or what we have also more abstractly identified as the Europeanist fraction. However, increasingly support has also come from members with a more global outlook, and indeed some of them, for instance Sheehy of BAT (no longer a member), had promoted EMU from the beginning.[20] This would then confirm Frieden's (Frieden 1991; cf. Sandholtz 1993) hypothesis that support for EMU, because of the interest in lower transaction costs, would be high among transnational capital generally, including export-competing producers for the world market and global financial institutions. But the picture is more complex. Although for instance a global TNC like BAT has indeed a large presence outside Europe (showing a high degree of globalisation), the European market has also always been very important to it (showing also a high degree of regionalisation). Thus, like the more purely European TNCs, BAT and similar companies would equally benefit from the lowering of transaction costs and the exchange rate stability resulting from a single European currency. However, the benefits would be much smaller for those global giants whose presence on the European market (outside the home country) is small compared to that on the non-European market. Companies like Shell, British Petroleum and ICI would for example fall in this category. I would hypothesise that their support for a single currency has been lukewarm at most, and that they might even see costs outweighing benefits. Thus, we still need to distinguish between companies in terms of their presence in and dependence upon the European market. Moreover, we see that with companies like Shell and BP, the sectoral dimension is again also important. As the Brussels representative of BP (and ERT associate) explained, since the oil sector only deals in one currency, namely the US dollar, there are few direct benefits for an international oil company in a single European currency.[21] But significantly, BP, within the ERT and in other forums, nevertheless has expressed its support for monetary union, not because it would so much serve its own narrow material interests, but for 'political reasons'. That is to say, BP (and probably other ERT members whose companies are in the same structural position) became convinced that EMU, now that the Maastricht countdown had begun, was critical to the further success of the integration process and the European single market, and it is this political objective to which BP was also committed.[22]

The country dimension, finally, also played a role in the internal ERT debate on EMU. Whereas the French and Italian members were enthusiastic advocates of the single currency, some of the German members were initially more sceptical. One German ERT associate recalled that when the French and Italians at ERT discussions made their pleas for monetary union, 'we [the Germans] remained simply silent'.[23] According to the same source, the German members were sceptical of the benefits of EMU because, as still many in German society hold, the strong D-Mark would be better not given up. However, they did not express their scepticism for political reasons. One such reason was their own belief in the European project, and their acceptance (given the French and Italian positions) of the centrality of monetary union to this project. Another reason was that their Italian and French colleagues themselves in part made their case on the basis of political arguments, arguments the Germans felt they were in no position to object to.[24] Thus what played a role for the Italians and the French was the idea that the present EMS was very asymmetrical to the extent of being virtually a D-Mark zone with all the power accruing to the Bundesbank. The fear for German regional dominance was then reinforced in the wake of German reunification.[25] Within German big business, support for EMU has, however, in recent years been growing because German companies have increasingly come to perceive substantial economic advantages to a single currency as well. Particularly after the 1993 crises of the EMS (which saw the D-Mark soar against various devalued EMS currencies, in particular the Lira), the realisation dawned that the present D-Mark centred monetary system could no longer guarantee the exchange rate stability crucial to Germany's export-oriented industry, and that therefore they might have to give up their D-Mark in order to ensure such a stability for the future.[26]

Thus, we have seen how, for different reasons, sections of the Roundtable who were initially sceptical about EMU have now also thrown their weight behind the project (even though some might have some private reservations), making for a very large consensus in favour of monetary unification. Since then, the ERT has actively campaigned for the single currency. As the implementation of the final stage of EMU (involving the irrevocable locking of exchange rates and the introduction of a single currency) was in the wake of the collapse of the EMS in 1993 far from certain, the ERT thus for instance sent a letter to the European Council on the eve of its Madrid summit in December 1995, in which it reiterated its full support for monetary union and asked the government leaders to ensure 'monetary stability based on economic convergence and financial discipline'.[27] Although there is no direct evidence of a link between this support of the ERT and the decisions taken by the European Council, the Madrid summit has subsequently proved important in keeping the momentum behind monetary integration, inasmuch as the heads of state and government unequivocally announced that the third and final stage of EMU would begin on 1 January 1999.

The stress put by the ERT on 'convergence' and 'financial discipline' also indicates the importance it attached to the Maastricht criteria. Many Roundtable members now see the value of the treaty on monetary union not just in terms of the stability and efficiency gains it is supposed to bring, but also in terms of the, in their view, salutary disciplinary effects on fiscal policy. As the then ERT vice-chairman, Leysen, noted:

> Maastricht has already exercised its biggest effect. It would never have come to such a convergence if it had not been for the Maastricht criteria. Belgian politics [for instance] is unthinkable without Maastricht; then we would not have any brake on making big deficits.[28]

This emphasis on the disciplinary dimension of EMU contrasts with the view expressed by business advocates of monetary union at the end of the 1980s, when, as we saw in the preceding chapter, a single currency was often seen primarily as one more instrument to defend the interests of European industry against global competition. It is hence also with regard to the issue of monetary union that we find evidence of a neo-liberal shift in the ERT's outlook.

Labour market and social policies

It is with regard to social policy that we see the clearest manifestation of the rising hegemony of neo-liberal ideas within the ERT. Although its discourse has remained articulated with a continued adherence to the ideology of social partnership, the Roundtable, as we have seen in the preceding chapter, did from at least 1990 onwards advocate neo-liberal policies of flexibilisation and deregulation. Moreover, although the ERT's stance was slightly more moderate and consensus-oriented than the position of the orthodox practitioners of the neo-liberal faith, when it came to the proposed construction of a 'Social Europe', the opposition waged by the Roundtable was, as we have seen, as fierce as for instance that of the British government. The ERT's reports on this policy area in the 1990s continued to be defined by a strong neo-liberal content.

Thus, the ERT's 1993 follow-up report on labour markets starts out with the warning – showing that it is well aware of the negative employment effects of the current restructuring pursued by European large firms – that 'a hard core of persistent unemployment will remain into the next century', but adds that this core might yet be reduced if Europe is willing to 'flexibilize and upgrade the supply of labour', as 'Only a readapted labour force and more flexible labour markets can ensure that economic growth will translate into significant job growth' (ERT 1993b: 8, ii). With respect to the measures proposed, the emphasis has shifted even more towards the reduction of costs, and in particular those of labour, the ERT arguing for both wage moderation and wage flexibility (with 'lower wages, where necessary') as one of the preconditions for 'durable employment and European competitiveness' (ibid.: 15–16). In fact, the ERT in its 1993 report bluntly states that 'A very large amount of the effort to adjust European labour markets will rely on labour' (ibid.). In later reports, and in the context of the growing European debate on employment policies (see below), the ERT repeats the point that the 'cancer of over-regulation' is a 'direct factor behind excessive [*sic*] unemployment' (ERT 1997a: 14), and there is thus 'a crying need for greater flexibility in labour laws at [the] national level' (ERT 1998: 26).

If we look more closely at the different groups within the ERT, we can still detect different shades of opinion, but these differences all remain within the limits of the broadly (embedded) neo-liberal consensus. Thus, for instance, the British within the Roundtable might be more outspoken in their criticism of workers' co-determination than the Germans, who have been socialised in this system of *Mitbestimmung*. But the latter would nevertheless not advocate the export of the German model to the European level, and, in fact, increasingly, 'in this era of globalisation', come to perceive disadvantages of the system.[29] For the overwhelming majority of both present and past Roundtable members, the bottom line is that there is 'no room for harmonisation' in the social policy field at EU level.[30] At the same time, however, as a group of primarily industrial capitalists, the ERT also remains keenly aware of the need for social consensus, rejecting the neo-liberal, confrontational, mode of labour relations. Although the ERT opposes supranational labour market regulation, it still emphasises that some degree of basic social harmony is indispensable for European industry to prosper (see ERT 1993b: 9). Thus, whereas, as we have seen in the preceding chapter, the ERT at the time waged opposition to the Maastricht social chapter, it was also recognised by at least part of the ERT that given the balance of social and political forces at the time its inclusion (albeit it as an 'appendix') was inevitable. Moreover, given the generality of the actual chapter, and the lack of activism on the part of the Commission after the departure of Delors when it comes to operationalising the general principles of the chapter into concrete policy making, leading ERT members have expressed that they can very well 'live with it'.[31]

It is in the area of labour market policy that the defeat of the Delorist project (Ziltener 2000) has allowed for a strategy of *hegemonic articulation* vis-à-vis social-democratic social forces, a strategy that I will argue centred around the concept of *competitiveness* as the uniting slogan.

Embedded neo-liberalism and European socio-economic governance: the new competitiveness discourse

It is on the basis of the new embedded neo-liberal orientation as analysed above that the ERT has sought to shape the content of the socio-economic governance regime that has evolved out of the successful relaunching of the European integration process. As noted before, embedded neo-liberalism is neo-liberal at its core – thus reflecting the outlook of the most globalised sections of European capital – while at the same time it seeks to accommodate the orientations of other social forces. This hegemonic project – although preserving some elements of the post-war European model – entails a comprehensive transformation of the European order, a restructuring process that has already been going on for some time and that may yet deepen in the years to come.

In this context, the Roundtable's discourse in the aforementioned report on labour markets (ERT 1993b) makes it clear that what is needed is not merely – to use Peter Hall's terminology – a *second order* policy change, i.e., a change of instruments, but a *third order* change, which is 'marked by the radical changes in the overarching terms of policy discourse associated with a "paradigm shift"' (Hall 1993: 279). The desired 'adaptation' of labour thus necessitates a fundamental restructuring of state–society relations, which will need the consent of different social forces in order to be successful. Again, the ERT is well aware of this, and, speaking the language of hegemony, it appeals for the creation of a 'new social consensus':

> Enabling Europe to return to high employment growth requires more than replacing policy instruments, it calls for a change of our economic and social structures. But governments are only able to change structures when there is a *new social consensus*, i.e. the convergence on principles and, ultimately, agreement on the goals for that change among the social partners, governments, the opinion leaders and ultimately, population . . . We need a consensus on the European level that *only a healthy, efficient and competitive private sector is able to provide sufficient jobs, and that markets should be left to allocate labour efficiently*. (ERT 1993b: 9, original emphasis)

This consensus that the report speaks about has to be created first of all at the elite level of European political and civil society, i.e., between the (European) 'social partners', policy-makers, political leaders (at both the European and national levels), etc. Ultimately, however, this new social consensus also needs to be disseminated further 'down', that is among the population at large: 'Each country and each community needs to reach broad-based agreement on how to re-establish a distorted [*sic*] social balance' (ibid.: ii). As indicated, the key concept in the discourse in which this hegemonic project of Europe's transnational capitalist class is articulated is that of 'competitiveness'. Competitiveness has been able, I submit, to come to function as such a key concept because of its potential to represent the 'general interest', as it appeals equally to neo-liberals, neo-mercantilists and social democrats. But what competitiveness actually means, and how it has to be achieved, is an open question decided in concrete struggles. Below I argue that competitiveness is increasingly being defined in neo-liberal terms and that the ERT has been one important forum promoting such a definition.

Constructing a new social consensus: the neo-liberal competitiveness discourse

Competitiveness is the keyword in the aforementioned Roundtable report *Beating the Crisis* (ERT 1993c) as well as in subsequent reports (see especially ERT 1994c, 1996, 1997a), and is singled out by ERT members and associates as the number one theme. A former senior official of the ERT explains the way in which competitiveness has become the key concept as follows:

> The members of the European Roundtable perceive it as their role to make some input into policy making at European level on those issues which are of crucial importance for the economic strength of Europe, what we are now calling the sort of general term of competitiveness. And competitiveness is now a useful word but it is really like a paper bag into which you put things.[32]

What this quote illustrates is that competitiveness is, although not a neutral term, nevertheless a concept to which a variety of meanings can be attached. Here my argument is that the neo-liberal shift in the ERT's ideological outlook is also reflected in a change in the meaning of 'competitiveness' within its discourse. Although competitiveness as a political catchword has only recently risen to its current heights, competitiveness was already much talked about in the 1980s, not least by the ERT. However, then the meaning of competitiveness was still primarily bound up with the neo-mercantilist ideology that, as we have seen in the preceding chapter, underpinned a significant part of the ERT's strategic project in the 1980s. With reference to the transnational business elite organised in the ERT, we have thus observed a shift from a *neo-mercantilist* competitiveness discourse towards an increasingly *neo-liberal* competitiveness discourse. Within the context of the transnational struggle over Europe's socio-economic order, we may, however, also identify a third, social-democratic competitiveness discourse. I argue that in the course of the 1990s the neo-liberal discourse had become hegemonic, but only by being articulated with elements of the opposing discourses.

In the neo-mercantilist discourse competitiveness means enhancing the global market power of European industry *against* non-European competition through government intervention and protectionism: it means being able to compete in the global market place by first shielding oneself from the forces of globalisation, in order to then enter the fray on the basis of increased strength achieved through *non-market* means. Partly convergent with this is the social-democratic competitiveness discourse that in part came to underpin the Delorist project at the end of the 1980s (cf. Albo 1994). In the much more market-centred vision of the 'new social democracy' (Geyer 1993) promoted by Delors, competitiveness was to be achieved not by negating the market, but by 'organising' it in such a way that its productive capacities are developed. This translates into an employment strategy that does not focus on deregulation but rather on investment in education, training, high technology, infrastructure, etc., as productivity-enhancing policies aimed at improving the capacity of *labour* (rather than just capital) to adapt to the exigencies of the global economy, thus avoiding unemployment and protecting workers' income (see Albo 1994; see also Reich 1992).

In the presently hegemonic neo-liberal discourse – articulated and propagated first and foremost by the ERT – competitiveness is still about not losing out in the global competition race. The means to the end however have changed, thereby transforming the nature of the end as well. Now competitiveness is about survival of the fittest in a fully open environment of a global free market, in which no 'artificial', that is non-market based, means to enhance one's position are allowed. Competitive performance is what the market measures it to be. Competitiveness now means complying with the logic of a globalising world economy. The Roundtable's *new competitiveness discourse* – expressing the ideological core of the embedded neo-liberal project – thus impels all firms, governments and supranational bodies such as the EU to open up to the global economy and let the market forces of globalisation do their beneficial work. The regionalisation process of European integration should be made fully subordinate and instrumental to the globalisation process. As the ERT puts it: 'In today's global market, the policies of each member state must become outward-looking, and sharply focused on competitiveness' (ERT 1994c: 1). In this discourse, globalisation is taken as an inevitable reality against which industry and society cannot and should not protect itself, but a reality that should be faced head on, meeting its challenges first of all by freeing business from the 'burden of regulation', and the 'distortion' generated by too large a public sector (ERT 1993c: 6–7).

The competitiveness discourse promoted by the ERT of today, however, still goes beyond orthodox neo-liberalism. Contradicting the principles of pure *laissez-faire*, the Roundtable stresses that the role of the state should not merely be one of ensuring the 'self-regulation' of the market (guaranteeing private property rights, free contract, the value of money, etc.), but is conceived much more positively as an 'enabling force' (ERT 1993c: 14). It is from this perspective, then, that the ERT for instance does not just ask government to enhance competitiveness through deregulation, the creation of a flexible labour market, and through 'lean government' (ERT 1993c: 7) – although these 'needs of industry' are increasingly emphasised – but also through creating 'conditions of competitiveness'. This includes (European) public policy oriented to 'innovation and new technology', 'education and training' and 'trans-European infrastructure' (ERT 1993c).

Being a central element, then, in all three projects, a goal to which all mainstream European socio-economic and political forces were wedded, we can understand how competitiveness has come to be such a 'useful word' for the ascending neo-liberal forces seeking hegemony. As argued, what the ERT in this context has thus been trying to 'put in the bag' called competitiveness have increasingly become elements of a neo-liberal discourse on labour market reform, a restructuring that the ERT argues to be a precondition for both 'wealth-creation and employment' (ERT 1994c: 1). By articulating competitiveness to these latter goals, the Roundtable effectively appeals to wide sections of society, including the political and social forces bound up with social democracy or organised labour. The concept of competitiveness thus, I argue, has become the linchpin of a process of hegemonic articulation in which an essentially neo-liberal ideology is articulated with elements of contending orientations, such that their 'potential antagonism is neutralised' (Laclau 1977: 161).[33]

The competitiveness ideology and the EU's evolving socio-economic governance regime

The first testimony (at the EU level) of the power of the new competitiveness discourse was the Commission's White Paper *Growth, Competitiveness, Employment* (European Commission 1994), which since then has become one of the main intellectual reference points in the EU socio-economic policy debate. The White Paper, written under the direction of Jacques Delors and often seen as his last political will, was intended as a response to the post-Maastricht recession that had pushed the unemployment rate to again new post-war records. Different pieces of evidence suggest that the ERT had a significant input into the development of this key Commission document. At the press conference after the December 1993 Brussels summit at which Delors had presented his White Paper, the then Commission president recalled his consultation with industry and the support he had received for his proposals from the ERT.[34] The week before, Delors had also participated in the press presentation of ERT's *Beating the Crisis* report,[35] which was in fact explicitly conceived as its contribution to the Commission's future economic strategy.[36] As one former senior official of the ERT commented upon the relation between the two reports:

> It was very parallel, and we saw their drafts and they saw our drafts. And one of my friends, a very senior official in the Commission, said to me, there is basically no difference between them, particularly if you look at the introductory part of the Delors book, which is a bit written I think by Delors himself – very similar: growth, investment, competitiveness, and employment. What we have tried to do is to get these things fixed together in people's minds. *Beating the Crisis* is a very short and a very clear statement. But the message is the same: these things all go together – you won't fight unemployment if you don't fight for competitiveness, you won't get growth if you don't have investment.[37]

Indeed, careful reading of the two reports does reveal some striking similarities. Most importantly, they share the basic premise that higher growth and employment can only be achieved through promoting the competitiveness of European industry. Moreover, the strategy (with regard to these objectives) outlined by the White Paper also echoes that of *Beating the Crisis.* In the Commission document, the road to higher employment follows a strategy based on the three 'inseparable elements' of, one, a 'macro-economic framework which instead of constraining market forces . . . supports them', two, structural adjustment of policies 'aimed at increasing the competitiveness of European industry and at removing the rigidities which are curbing its dynamism', and three, 'active policies and structural changes in the labour market and in the regulations' (European Commission 1994: 61). The paper of the Commission straightforwardly identifies labour market inflexibility – to 'be traced back to specific institutional, legal and contractual circumstances in each country' – as a major cause of Europe's *structural* unemployment (ibid.: 16, ch. 8). Contrary to Keynesian theory, and contrary to some analyses (see Hall 1998) of the effects of the Maastricht criteria, cutting budget deficits is seen as helping to overcome recession by freeing public resources for private investments (European Commission, 1994: 65–67).

Reflecting the renewed Roundtable theme of a Europe falling once more behind the rest of the world, the Commission writes 'The truth is that although we have changed, the rest of the world has changed even faster' (ibid.: 10). Instead of invoking the spectre of non-European countries (read: Japan) engaging in 'economic warfare', however, the paper plainly states that protectionism 'would be suicidal' (ibid.: 9) and that the EU must 'demonstrate [the] recognition of the unavoidable globalization of the economy' (ibid.: 13). The primary goal of industrial policy is defined as 'to create as favourable an environment as possible for company competitiveness' (ibid.: 14). This definition signalled a move away from the kind of French-style industrial policy that Delors, as we saw in chapter 4, had (unsuccessfully) sought to promote in the years before. Moreover, just as the concept of industrial policy is redefined to cast it in a more liberal frame, so the Delorist vision of a 'Social Europe' is further watered down in the paper. Speaking of 'the new model of European society', the paper calls for a 'less passive and more active solidarity', with 'decentralisation' and 'subsidiarity' as central guidelines in implementing what the paper proposes as 'a sort of European social pact' (ibid.: 15). Then ERT vice-chairman Sir David Simon (BP) thus appreciated the White Paper for its 'balance between the social and the industrial vision', making 'an attempt to reconcile the two'.[38] We might also say that what the paper reflects in comparison with the Delorist programme of before was a significant change in this balance in favour of the latter (cf. Ross 1995: 224–25). As another former ERT vice-chairman, André Leysen, pointed out, this new balance between what we might also call the social-democratic vision on the one hand and the (embedded) neo-liberal vision on the other, signified 'quite a swing-over for Delors'.[39] The greatest significance of the White Paper, however, lies in the way it articulates the objectives of growth and employment with that of competitiveness, an articulation that since has become central to the emerging policy consensus around European unemployment.

Notwithstanding this testimony to the ideological power of the Roundtable capitalists, Delors' paper was still largely an attempt at a compromise between neo-liberals and social democrats, agreeing 'with [the] liberals about the need to deregulate labor markets and make the welfare state less rigid, but within a broader context designed to prevent social divisions from themselves rigidifying' (Ross 1995: 225). Next to the emphasis on investment in 'trans-European networks' and in the 'information society' – policies that had also been advocated by the ERT but as part of a different strategy – typical Delorist themes such as the social dialogue also pointed to traces of a social-democratic competitiveness discourse. Since then, however, competitiveness has increasingly been defined in neo-liberal terms within the Commission's policy discourse.

Benchmarking Europe

Another testimony to the ERT's success in promoting the concept of competitiveness in European governance has been the setting-up by the EU of a 'Competitiveness Advisory Group' (CAG) at the beginning of 1995, just over a year after the ERT had first proposed the creation of the group in its *Beating the Crisis* report, where it described the task of such a group as 'keeping competitiveness in the forefront of the policy debates' (ERT 1993c: 27). In line with the Roundtable proposal, the membership of the CAG consists of CEOs, as well as leading trade union representatives and other 'eminent persons' (usually former politicians), but is dominated by the former group.[40] At the time of its founding, three ERT members joined the 13-member council, and at present Marco Tronchetti Provera (of Pirelli) maintains the links between the two groups. It should not surprise us therefore that the 'advice' this group has so far given (in six-monthly reports to the

European Council) closely resembles that of the ERT, with both groups spreading the new competitiveness gospel (see the CAG's first four reports as collected in Jacquemin and Pench (eds) 1997). As a former senior official of the ERT remarked: 'One thing that is quite important in this whole scenario is multiplicity of messages and delivery systems around the whole theme.'[41] From the perspective of the ERT, the CAG plays a very useful complementary role, not only because it has official EU status, but also because it has a few prominent trade union representatives among its members, which can be taken as an indication of the extent to which the (embedded) neo-liberal competitiveness discourse has also incorporated more social-democratic forces.[42]

As an operationalisation of its competitiveness ideology, the ERT has recently, in tandem with the CAG, started to promote the concept of 'benchmarking' vis-à-vis the Commission and the member states (see ERT 1994c; Competitiveness Advisory Group 1995). Benchmarking means measuring the performance of individual firms and sectors, but also of nations, against the performance of the 'best competitors' in the world (ERT 1994c: 4). In its report *Benchmarking for Policy-Makers*, the ERT is very explicit about how policy-makers should 'measure' competitiveness. The country or (macro-) region that is most competitive is the country that is most successful in attracting mobile capital: 'Governments must recognise today that every economic and social system in the world is competing with all the others to attract the footloose businesses' (ERT 1996: 15). That the expected outcome of this competition for transnationally mobile capital will be a deepening of neo-liberal restructuring transpires from the kind of 'benchmarks' that are for instance proposed with regard to the policy goal of employment creation: the level of 'labour costs . . . the flexibility of labour; working and factory hours . . . termination costs' (ibid.: 13). The Maastricht criteria are also mentioned as a successful application of the benchmarking concept (ibid.: 18). Significantly in the context of the current labour-shedding restructuring that is taking place in part under the discipline of Europe's growing capital markets, the ERT sees 'shareholder value' as the principal benchmark for private enterprise itself: 'The overriding measure of competitive performance for any commercial enterprise is the return it is able to provide its shareholders' (ibid.: 9). In sum, although the report also declares that 'Europe's social systems . . . need to be reformed, not eliminated' (ibid.: 2), the limits of the embeddedness of the ERT's neo-liberalism do become apparent here.

At the same time, the ideological potential of a concept like benchmarking, and indeed its capacity to appeal to a wider set of forces within society and to incorporate them into the emergent hegemonic bloc, is also not lost on the Roundtable capitalists, as the report stresses that benchmarking is 'not just an analytical device' but also 'carries a symbolic message':

> At a time when the European model of society is experiencing some difficulties, and change may be perceived as painful (though not nearly so painful as the results of not changing), *the role of symbols* in mobilising human effort may become more important, and benchmarking can be part of this. (ibid.: 17, my emphasis)

Competitiveness and benchmarking have also accordingly become the key concepts within the public (socio-economic) policy discourse of the EU. Analysing the policy documents of the Commission, one also sees how these concepts are mobilised to promote a programme of neo-liberal restructuring aiming to remove, in the words of the Director-General for Industry, the still remaining 'rigidities and distortions . . . that prevent Europe from fully exploiting its potential' (European Commission 1997a: 5). The ERT's promotion of the concept of benchmarking vis-à-vis the Commission has been particularly successful. Thus the ERT has organised several seminars with Commission and government officials to promote the concept.[43] According to the ERT, 'the results' from these discussions had produced a 'large degree of consensus . . . between the business and public policy representatives' (ERT 1996: 1). Indeed, as a testimony to this consensus, in the same month that the ERT published its report on benchmarking the Industry Directorate-General came out with a document entitled *Benchmarking the Competitiveness of European Industry*, in which it suggested that benchmarking should be used as a central policy guideline at all levels of EU governance (European Commission 1996: 16). In a follow-up communication, the Commission explicitly acknowledges the input of the ERT as the first business organisation to draw the Commission's and the Council's attention to the benchmarking concept (European Commission 1997b: 3). In this communication – and at the request of the Council of Ministers[44] – the Commission launched a number of concrete initiatives to put the concept of benchmarking into practice, including the establishment of a 'High Level Group on Benchmarking' – made up of 'experts' from industry – and the initiation of a number of so-called pilot projects in different member states to start identifying Europe's 'weaknesses and inefficiencies' at the enterprise, sectoral and public policy level (European Commission 1997b).

Invoking the inevitability of globalisation and 'hence' the need for adaptation, the Commission defines benchmarking as a tool for improving competitiveness and with that as 'a tool for promoting the convergence towards best practice' (European Commission 1996: 16; 1997b). This involves the global 'comparison of societal behaviour [*sic*], commercial practice, market structure and public institution' (European Commission 1997b: 3). As the High Level Group on Benchmarking – chaired by a board member of the ERT company Investor – makes clear in its first report, the object of all these 'comparisons' is to promote rapid 'structural reforms' that will allow Europe to adapt to the exigencies of globalisation: 'this involves further liberalisation, privatisation . . ., more flexible labour laws, lower government subsidies, etc.' (High Level Group on Benchmarking 1999: 13). Similarly, in a language much more radical than that of the Delors White Paper, the Commission identifies labour market reform as a 'vital factor for the competitiveness of European industry', calling for 'a radical rethink of all relevant labour market systems – employment protection, working time, social protection and health and safety – to adapt them to a world of work which will be organised differently' (European Commission 1996: 11). The report even goes so far as to state that 'evidence suggests' that there is a direct causal (negative) relation between the level of labour market regulation and the level of employment (ibid.; see also European

Commission 1997a). Labour market flexibility, finally, is also at the heart of the formulation in the so-called employment chapter of the 1997 Treaty of Amsterdam. In fact, the objectives of employment and labour market flexibility are mentioned in the same single sentence, the latter being the means to achieve the former: 'Member States and the Community shall . . . work towards a co-ordinated strategy for employment and particularly for promoting a skilled, trained and adaptable workforce and labour markets responsive to economic change' (Article 109n).

The Amsterdam employment chapter has in fact been one step in the development of what the Commission calls a new European employment strategy (European Commission 1999a) developed by the EU in response to the persistent crisis of mass unemployment in the 1990s and the growing concern over this on the part of Europe's political elites, in particular as in the second half of the 1990s social-democratic parties had come to power in most member states. This employment strategy is seen by some as part of a wider 'new social policy' agenda – comprehensively formulated at the Lisbon Summit of March 2000 – that moves away from the 'old' idea of supranational market-correcting regulation, and towards promoting market-enabling strategy 'which [in the words of the European Council] combines competitiveness and social cohesion' (see also Ferrera, Hemerijck and Rhodes 2000; Rhodes and Ferrera 2000).[45] Although this agenda of what former Commissioner for Social Affairs, Flynn, earlier called a process of adapting the 'European social model' in order to preserve it,[46] might thus be given an optimistic interpretation of representing a 'European third way' that is genuinely distinct from neo-liberalism (see Rhodes 2000), I would contend that it in fact fits very well within the framework of embedded neo-liberalism, which, although distinct from Anglo-Saxon neo-liberalism, does have as its primary objective the fundamental restructuring of the European political economy in such a way as to prioritise the principle of economic liberalism over that of social protection.

The new European employment strategy: embedded neo-liberalism in practice

The new European employment strategy had in fact started with the Delors White Paper followed by the European Council employment summit held at Essen, and since has been further institutionalised in the so-called 'Luxembourg Process' of EU-approved and monitored 'National Action Plans'. This *Europeanisation* of employment policy (Cameron 2000) does not represent a new form of *positive* integration beyond the *negative* integration of the market, as in fact no common employment policy is pursued, but rather national policies are co-ordinated within an overall European framework. This framework is first and foremost a normative one, formulating a new *policy paradigm* for employment policy, establishing the *benchmarks* for national policies by formulating 'guidelines' and 'recommendations' (see, e.g., European Commission 2000a). In fact as such, European employment policy is representative of a general shift that we may observe in the area of European social policy from direct 'hard' regulation to 'soft policy co-ordination' (Ferrera, Hemerijck and Rhodes 2000: 65–69).

The fact that employment policies remain primarily the responsibility of the member states (the Amsterdam treaty is very clear on this) already points to the limits of this new European answer to the persistent employment crisis, in particular given the constraints imposed by the internal market (and the regime competition it engenders) and EMU plus the Stability Pact. As Streeck writes: 'as long as the management of unemployment continues to be considered, in the sense of the Essen agreement, as a *Hausaufgabe* of national governments acting under international institutional and market constraints, the privileged means for it is to increase labor market "flexibility"' (Streeck 1998: 21). It is, however, also the European employment 'policy' itself that is oriented towards promoting that latter goal of neo-liberal restructuring.

Based on the 'four pillars' of 'employability', 'entrepreneurship', 'adaptability' and 'equal opportunities', the so-called European employment strategy reflects a shift from the Keynesian paradigm of *market-correcting* and market-steering macroeconomic full employment policies, sometimes complemented by micro-economic interventionism, towards a new *transnational* policy paradigm of *market-making* employment policies. Not redistribution, but creating the opportunity to participate in the market, is the object of these policies. 'Employability' thus stands for *marketability*, thus, again in the words of Streeck, '[defining] the responsibility of public policy, not in terms of *de-commodification* of individuals, but to the contrary of creation of *equal opportunities for commodification*' (Streeck 1999: 6, his emphasis). This is to be further promoted by improving 'adaptability' of workers, i.e., through the flexibilisation of labour. Indeed, the whole employment strategy is clearly based on the premise that labour market flexibility is key to reducing unemployment. It is thus that the Commission in its latest *Joint Employment Report* notes with satisfaction that member states have made substantial 'progress in reforming the labour markets' and claims this to be an important factor behind the recent slight drop in the EU unemployment rate (European Commission 2000b: 2).

In sum, then, although the EU's employment strategy is officially meant to provide the social cohesion part of the new Lisbon agenda – in which the EU has set itself an ambitious 'new strategic goal for the next decade: to become the most competitive and dynamic knowledge-based economy in the world'[47] – it in fact seems above all to promote the further commodification of labour. In any case, this strategy and related 'social' initiatives do not represent a belated move towards the 'Social Europe' that Delors wanted to contruct, but rather in its present form represents the consolidation of the embedded neo-liberal hegemonic project inasmuch as it completes the incorporation of social democracy (which being in power in the large majority of EU governments, of course, had both the opportunity and the electoral motivation to put employment high on the European agenda). The social-democratic project does see elements of its competitiveness discourse return in the European employment strategy, but in such a way that the proclaimed goals of high employment and social cohesion are rendered compatible with the neo-liberal goals of market making and market liberalisation. In this context, then, Bieling speaks of '*communitarian* neo-liberalism' (Bieling 1998).

As long as the policy responses to European unemployment are tied to a neo-liberal competitiveness discourse that serves the interests of the most transnationalised segments of European capital, prospects for any alternative policy response remain bleak. In the past years many of Europe's largest firms have been consistently cutting back their workforces in the ongoing restructuring process. Whereas the success of Fordism was based on expanding aggregate demand through paying high(er) wages to what became a relatively secure work-force, the present accumulation regime is based on cost cutting, including labour-saving 'rationalisation' (Harvey 1989). In this Schumpeterian process, 'the work of modernisation', the ERT writes, inevitably 'leads to creating some jobs but shedding others' (ERT 1997b: 2). The ERT implicitly admits that its companies have been responsible for much of the shedding and that the creation of new jobs will thus have to come from small and medium-sized companies in their 'partnership' with large companies, i.e., through increased sub-contracting, etc. (ibid.). It is unclear how the contracting out of jobs that used to be done within the TNC by workers with relatively secure and full-time jobs, to SMEs employing part-time flex workers, is in itself going to contribute to higher employment. The ERT would answer that if overall competitiveness is improved through deregulation and flexibilisation, market forces will be released that will in themselves generate new jobs. Here, the United States – 'the current best' against which 'Europe needs to benchmark itself' according to present ERT chairman Morris Tabaksblat (Tabaksblat 2000) – is the leading example.

The emerging European model of capitalism

The outcome of embedded neo-liberalism rather than a pure or orthodox neo-liberalism, I have argued, was necessary inasmuch as the latter could never have generated sufficient consent on the part of subordinate social groups. It was particularly within the European context that the neo-liberal offensive had to overcome the resistance of the institutionalised traditions of corporatist class relations, social and industrial protection offered by an often interventionist state, and other elements of 'embeddedness'. It was also in this context that a rival social-democratic project could develop within the European arena, mounting a significant, if in the end unsuccessful, challenge to the neo-liberal project. Moreover, as pointed out, a pure neo-liberal strategy would also undermine the long-term accumulation prospects of the industrial capital that still makes up a dominant section of European capitalism. And it was in this context that the neo-mercantilist strategy emerged.

Embedded neo-liberalism can thus be interpreted as the outcome of the struggle between the three rival projects of neo-liberalism, neo-mercantilism and social democracy. It is the potentially hegemonic articulation – through the new competitiveness discourse – of a predominantly neo-liberal ideology with elements of the alternative ideological discourses of the social-democratic and neo-mercantilist projects. Thus, the 'embedded' component of embedded neo-liberalism addresses the concerns of both the former Europrotectionists and the European labour movement and social-democratic political forces, but this incorporation is done in such a way that these concerns are in the end subordinated to the overriding objective of neo-liberal competitiveness. Indeed, the latter seems to increasingly become the primary goal of European socio-economic governance. This is apparent first of all from the competitiveness discourse that is now underpinning the Commission's strategy with regard to industrial policy and macro-economic management. Second, it transpires from the failure of the social dimension as discussed in the preceding chapter (now only further weakened after the departure of Delors), as well as from the new European employment strategy that focuses on market-making flexibilisation strategies, deepening the commodification of social relations. Third, it is manifested in the openness of Europe's regionalism, as the unequivocal commitment to free trade and freedom of foreign investment (despite occasional flare-ups of trade conflict in limited areas such as agriculture) has allowed the full integration of the European region into the globalising world economy. Finally, it is apparent from the neo-liberal character of EMU.

Let us now, in order to better understand this hegemonic project for European integration, return to the question of the struggle over the emerging EU (supranational) model of capitalism as discussed in chapter 3. What kind of model of capitalism is being constructed with the rise of a European socio-economic order serving an embedded neo-liberal social purpose? Returning to our typology, it is clear that the French statist model – which is itself in the process of being neo-liberalised – is no longer any model for the current EU supranational regime of socio-economic governance. The threat of 'Europrotectionism' was effectively neutralised in the early 1990s, and any French-style interventionist industrial policy is now no longer favoured by either the Commission or the large majority of member states. Indeed, the thrust of EU socio-economic policy making is clearly towards market liberalisation. The principle of mutual recognition as inherent in the internal market programme, and the activism of both the Commission and the European Court of Justice (ECJ) in a process of what Fritz Scharpf calls the 'constitutionalization of competition law' (Scharpf 1999b: 54ff.; cf. Gill 1998), have led to an ever more far-reaching extension of market competition to an increasing number of sectors – from telecommunications to transport and the energy market – hitherto shielded from market discipline. This ongoing commodification process led by the supranational institutions of the EU has thus effectively challenged the mixed economies of the post-war era (Scharpf 1999b: 58ff.). It has also challenged the distinctively French notion (although we witness this phenomenon also in the Rhineland countries) of *service public*: 'no area of *service public* is now beyond European competition law' (ibid.: 61).

In many ways, then, the EU model seems to imply a convergence on the (neo-) liberal British model. Open and free markets, deregulation and labour market flexibility are the key concepts informing the discourse in which much of European socio-economic policy making is embedded. Indeed, within the ERT, the Anglo-Saxon model, and often in particular the US model (see above), seems to be an important source of inspiration. On the other hand, though, as we have seen, the more orthodox neo-liberalism of the Anglo-Saxon model does not entirely fit with the interests of at least an important section of European transnational *industrial* capital. Thus with respect to industrial policy, we have seen how the ERT advocates more an updated German model of *Ordnungspolitik* than the pure *laissez-faire* British model. The same model seems to inspire much of the Commission's line of thinking in this respect (see European Commission 1997b). Indeed, as we have seen, the continuing focus of the EU on Trans-European Infrastructure Networks and the promotion of innovation with regard to new technologies fit with this strategy. With regard to labour market and employment policies, we have seen also that, despite the admiration for the US model, most ERT members are well aware that for now the extremely deregulated labour market – with an increasing number of workers having peripheral 'MacJobs' – of the USA cannot be realised in Europe without fundamentally undermining the social consent that is necessary for any hegemonic project. Although pressures in the direction of an ever more deregulated labour market may well increase under the combined disciplinary effects of EMU (Martin and Ross 1999) and the rise of a new shareholder capitalism in continental Europe (see below), at least for now we still observe some limited elements of embeddedness here both in the ERT's discourse and (even more so) in that of EU policy making.

In those respects, then, the emerging EU model of capitalism thus seems to resemble more the 'Ordo-liberal' German model than the pure Anglo-Saxon neo-liberal model. This may in part reflect the growing dominance of the German members within the ERT, and more widely reflect the weight of German business in the European economy.[48] However, it is a *neo-liberalised German model* (with the national German model itself also currently being transformed under the pressures of neo-liberal globalisation) as, although it does adopt the German concept of *Ordnungspolitik*, it does not embrace the German corporatist traditions to the same extent, nor the particular synthesis of a free market economy with a well-developed welfare state. At the EU level we do not see any adoption of the German model of labour relations in spite of the attempts in this direction made by the Delors Commission. The so-called social dialogue does not represent a belated emergence of Euro-corporatism but is rather, as Streeck argues, an example of the 'neo-voluntarism' that characterises European social policy post-Maastricht (Streeck 1995: 49). As argued, since the defeat of the supranational social-democratic project at the hands of transnational capital, the thrust of EU labour market and social policies has been very much oriented to market-making rather than market-correcting policies.

However, to fully understand the socio-economic content of the emerging European order, we have to take into account that the EU is a multi-level system. Thus much of the embeddedness that is still present in the European political economy must in fact be found at the national level, and indeed groups like the ERT would very much keep it at that level. It is in fact this *national* nature of much of the institutional embeddeness that posits the main problem from a perspective emphasising the principle of social protection. As has been pointed out by many (see, e.g., Streeck 1998; Scharpf 1999b: ch. 3), in the areas of social policy (including the welfare state) and industrial relations, the logic of the internal market – that is, an area without national border control – implies the threat of regulatory or regime competition, putting downward pressures on the levels of social security, workers' rights, etc. In the area of industrial relations, this has already led to a restructuring process in several countries where labour has – under the added pressure of the EMU convergence criteria – concluded several 'social pacts' in order to seek to create new employment through the same market-making strategies advocated by the EU (Ebbinghaus and Hassel 1999). Although some have interpreted these developments positively as the development of a new 'competitive corporatism' (Rhodes 1997, 2000), the fact remains that, as Streeck points out, regime competition, or the location of national systems of industrial relations in international markets (Streeck 1998: 12), means that it may be not so much the form but the *content* of industrial relations that is changing, in the sense that '*material rewards for workers and the institutional influence for labor are more than before tied to a joint commitment with employers to success in competitive markets*' (ibid.: 15, original emphasis). This, then, does not mean that labour becomes excluded from the process but rather that corporatist structures are changing their functions (ibid.; see also Bieling 1998). Indeed, congruent with the concept of embedded neo-liberalism, established corporatist institutions have not been abolished but rather have been maintained and strengthened to implement neo-liberal labour market reform while maintaining social consensus.

The celebrated Dutch model is a case in point here. Indeed, it should not surprise us that this is the model that several ERT members and associates, next to the US model, point to as leading the way for Europe.[49] With the Dutch model as a 'positive example' this implies a vision of the 'European model' in which its 'values' are preserved but its institutions are nevertheless fundamentally restructured.[50] As Roundtable member Collomb puts it in a quotation that nicely illustrates the discourse of embedded neo-liberalism:

> Our common concern is to find what within the European model can be preserved, with the European values, but to change that which seriously harms competitiveness. Hence, the idea is not to reproduce the American model but to find a European way, which passes through a strong flexibilisation of the European traditions and habits . . . I think that one can preserve certain values. I think that Europeans attach an importance to the social dialogue . . . but we should also make, which is necessary, this social dialogue more decentralised.[51]

This image of a reformed European model is of course also invoked by the new discourse on the 'Third Way' (e.g., Chancellor Schröder's *Neue Mitte*), which may be interpreted as a discourse of neo-liberalised social democracy (Ryner 2000). Indeed, there is a strong similarity between what is here interpreted as the discourse of embedded neo-liberalism and that of the 'Third Way', to the extent that we may say that the latter represents the social-democratic variety of the former. The Third Way discourse, of course, puts more emphasis on embeddedness than the discourse practised by the Roundtable, as transnational capital from its vantage point has an interest in emphasising what it sees as the need for market liberalisation and flexibilisation vis-à-vis those forces that might still oppose such a restructuring. On the other hand, it is precisely the adoption of the Third Way ideology, with its emphasis on the goal of competitiveness and, increasingly, on the market–liberal means to achieve it, that has enabled the incorporation of social-democratic forces into the current hegemonic project (see also Ryner 2000).

Finally, we should also say something about the relationship between socio-economic content and institutional form in this emerging EU model of capitalism. On the one hand, we have since the SEA observed a supranational deepening with the extension of qualified majority voting (QMV), and the transfer of new policy areas to the supranational level, e.g., monetary policy. This has led to a further hollowing out of national sovereignty, and to a situation where more than ever before national governments no longer have a monopoly over policy making but have to share this with supranational institutions such as the Commission and the ECJ. As such, the current European project goes much beyond the very limited intergovernmental vision of a pure (Thatcherite) neo-liberalism. It is then also in this respect that we have to distinguish embedded neo-liberalism from the latter. On the other hand, most of this supranational deepening has been put at the service of market liberalisation. Thus QMV was introduced primarily to ensure the implementation of the internal market programme, and apart from the failed attempts to create a 'Social Europe' most of the policy activism of the Commission, and even more so the judicial activism of the ECJ, has served to further the goal of negative at the expense of positive integration (see Scharpf 1999b). The latter remains largely at the intergovernmental level and this institutional bias has made progress in for instance the area of social policy very difficult indeed (ibid.; see also Streeck 1995). The aforementioned institutional set-up of EMU of course also fits with this kind of supranational neo-liberal discipline (Gill 1998).

In sum, the new multi-level European socio-economic order represents a model of capitalism in which the primacy of free markets and free enterprise (negative integration) has been re-established over the primacy of politics. At the same time, limited forms of embeddedness remain in place, at the EU level mostly in the form of 'symbolic politics' (i.e., ideological articulation), with the exception of industrial policy, and at the national level also in the form of concrete social institutions and related practices. However, as these national forms of embeddedness are at the same time under the combined pressures of globalisation and Europeanisation – which is not a deterministic process, but, as has been the core argument of this book, one mediated by the agency of social forces – the overall direction in the EU is towards a consolidation of neo-liberal governance.

The contradictions of embedded neo-liberalism and the future of European order

We can conclude that embedded neo-liberalism is both the emerging hegemonic project of the European transnational capitalist class and the concept that increasingly underpins the social purpose of the new European order. With regard to the first, it should be emphasised that this is really a *class* strategy: that is, a strategy articulated and advocated by a *class-conscious* transnational business elite. This class consciousness for instance clearly transpires from the following quotation from current ERT chairman Morris Tabaksblat (of Reed Elsevier), who in a speech to the European Business Summit celebrated the entrepreunerial values, including those of private material reward, inherent to (neo-)liberal capitalism:

> We have to find ways to let more Europeans change the world. To let individuals with great ideas enjoy commensurate reward – to be frank, acquire great personal wealth. We can generate a more entrepreneurial culture in Europe by facilitating and prizing success. Entrepreneurship seeks success. Creating wealth is all too often seen as being at the expense of someone else in Europe – not in terms of the jobs, opportunities, economic fall out it engenders. Accumulation of wealth is how entrepreneurship has been encouraged and rewarded throughout economic history. From Venetian traders to the Dutch entrepreneurs of the Golden Age, from English mill owners to the German industrial dynasts. There is nothing innately shameful about becoming rich, or emulating others who do, nothing un-European about it! (Tabaksblat 2000)

The question remains, then, to what extent the social purpose of the emergent European order may yet be constructed on a different ideological basis from that contained in the idea that the ultimate 'benchmark' for the 'performance' of a society is its ability to accumulate wealth in private hands. In line with the theoretical framework developed in chapter 1, I would argue that the answer to this question will be decided in the ongoing struggle between rival (transnational) social forces, and in particular will depend on the relationship between labour and capital, as well as upon the relationships between different fractions of the capitalist class. It is within these relationships that the contradictions latent in the embedded neo-liberal synthesis may yet in the longer run become manifest. Here we have to emphasise that the hegemony of embedded neo-liberalism rests, above all, on the active consent of transnational as well as national elites (including political elites and those representing labour), and that this consent becomes much more passive among the European populations in general.

The real 'test' of embedded neo-liberalism will probably come at the next serious economic downturn. Current signs are that this downturn is in fact already under way (this was the case even before the terrorist attacks on the USA that took place at the time of writing this section). There is now fear of a real recession on both sides of the Atlantic. This is not the place to make economic forecasts, but the argument made is that if the current trends continue and might evolve into a real economic crisis, then the embedded neo-liberal project is bound to face serious challenges in terms of its legitimacy among the European populations.

Neo-liberal globalisation is of course already under attack by the growing anti-globalisation movement, a diverse group of activists lacking as yet a coherent political programme but supported by countless NGOs and effectively disturbing the institutionalised summitry of globalising political and business elites. This societal backlash against neo-liberalism – which in fact was preluded by more regionally and nationally contained protests against neo-liberal austerity in countries such as France in 1995 (see Van der Pijl 1997) – is seen by some as revealing the limits of the discipline of neo-liberalism; limits recognised also by part of the globalising elites (see Van der Pijl 1998: 163–65). Within a European context, however, more serious would be a situation in which an economic crisis undermined the still rather passive consent of a large majority of the population as yet trapped in a consumerism enabled by past high growth rates. With regard to the project of European integration, this would add to the already existing legitimacy deficit faced by the EU (Scharpf 1999b).

The looming legitimacy crisis of the EU may in particular become more manifest with regard to the two current central projects of European integration, the enlargement to the East on the one hand, and the project of monetary union in combination with the ongoing liberalisation of the European economy, on the other. Popular support for these projects is already very low (thus in April 2001 support for the single currency in the EU-15 stands at 55 per cent, and support for enlargement at a mere 44 per cent; European Commission 2001: i). Although the past – witness the initial difficulties to get the Maastricht Treaty ratified – may suggest that political elites in the end can safely ignore the lack of popular support, or at least are still able to push through their agenda, the current discussion on institutional reform of the EU (in the wake of the Treaty of Nice) at the highest political level indicates that these elites are in fact no longer placing their bets on past experiences. Let us now look at each of these two central elements of the European agenda in turn, focusing on the project of EMU, which is most central to our concern with European socio-economic governance.

The project of enlargement can in fact be regarded as part of the longer-term process of the gradual extension of what Van der Pijl (1998) calls the Lockean (liberal capitalist) heartland. As such, this project has also been consistently supported by the ERT. Indeed, the ERT already called for a widening of the Community in its *Reshaping Europe* report (ERT 1991b) and subsequently has become increasingly active in this area (see also Holman 2001). The benefits for ERT companies, which have already invested heavily in the countries of central and eastern Europe (CEE), are clear: it will provide them with a continuing guaranteed access to markets – reformed on the basis of the (neo-)liberal principles of the EU – to which they can export and, above all, from which they can export (benefiting *inter alia* from much lower wage levels). In a 1999 report devoted entirely to the role of business with respect to enlargement, the ERT relates the many positive experiences it has with FDI of its companies in the CEE countries, although also pointing to problems such as 'delays in the privatisation process', 'excessive bureaucracy', 'out-dated attitudes to work', and the opposition of some groups to market liberalisation (ERT 1999: 20–23). As the strategy the ERT favours for the CEE countries is fully shared by the Commission (see Holman 2001), it therefore appears that eastern enlargement entails first and foremost the extension of the neo-liberal restructuring going on in the EU since the end of the 1980s to the CEE countries (ibid.: 183). With regard to the consequences of eastern enlargement for the current EU, we can only speculate.

The fact is that even after the Treaty of Nice, many institutional reforms (as well as reforms of the common agricultural policy, and of the structural policies) are still necessary in order to prepare the Union for the absorption of the CEE countries. This combined with the lack of popular support for enlargement – partly because of immigration fears – at least raises the question of what enlargement will mean for the project of deepening integration; the cohesion of the EU; the already weak legitimacy of its institutions; and more broadly, the support for the European project as currently underpinned by a social purpose promoting neo-liberal restructuring.

With regard to European socio-economic governance, it is the disciplinary neo-liberalism (Gill 1998) of EMU in combination with the EU's current drive for further market liberalisation that in the context of an economic crisis would potentially undermine the cohesion of the elite historic bloc underpinning the embedded neo-liberal project. If the ECB continued to adhere to the current monetarist orthodoxy with regard to its interest rate policy, i.e., one that is primarily geared to price stability, EMU may yet have to face the blame for pushing up the unemployment rate even higher in times of economic adversity. As this will also lead to higher social spending and thus put more pressure on the national welfare states, the project of EMU may thus come to be regarded as fundamentally undermining the so-called European social model (Martin and Ross 1999). As at the same time the Stability Pact severely constrains the room for expansionary fiscal policy, the cyclical downturn in the global economy may turn into a deepening recession, which governments can no longer counter through macro-economic policy. Under these circumstances, it is questionable whether the support of trade unions as well as some (sections of) social-democratic parties for EMU in its current monetarist set-up will be sustained. Moreover as the ongoing flexibilisation of European labour markets, reinforced by a monetary union that has taken away other instruments of adaptation, makes it easier not only to hire people in times of economic expansion but also to fire them in an economic downturn, social forces bound up with labour may also start to question this core element of the European project, and demand more social protection again. However, how this exactly will play out remains to be seen as higher unemployment will in the first instance also weaken the power of organised labour.

EMU also has to be understood in the broader context of financial market liberalisation, or the creation of a single European financial area. This project started with the internal market programme, but has been accelerated in the 1990s, fuelled by in part EU-driven privatisation, and will deepen because of the integrative effects of the single currency (OECD 1999: 2; Lannoo 1999: 282). The EU in fact has made the completion of the single financial market into one of its policy priorities (see European Commission 1999b). In the related area of corporate governance, the recent breakthrough on a European Company Statute – after years of blockage because of business opposition to the now removed clause (dealt with in a separate directive) on worker consultation and information rights – and the proposed takeover directive are expected to further contribute to a more (capital) market-driven form of corporate governance (ibid.). These developments – although at present largely supported by the industrialists of the ERT – may in the future lead to a renewed divergence of interests between industrial and financial capital, and especially between money and productive capital perspectives within industry.

Embedded neo-liberalism as articulated by the ERT to an extent reflects the relative weight of industrial capital in continental Europe as opposed to the finance-dominated political economies of the USA and the UK (Albert 1993). It is argued that because of this industrial capital perspective the ERT's neo-liberalism diverges from the orthodox Anglo-Saxon type. At the same time, as we have seen, the ERT is not a club of industrial capitalists only, as many of them are in fact finance capitalists as well. In that sense, then, embedded neo-liberalism may also be taken as representing a synthesis between industrial and financial capital within Europe. Indeed, as argued in chapter 2, in the current context of neo-liberal globalisation these two capital fractions to a large extent share the same perceived interests and the same ideological outlook, at least when it comes to global (financial and industrial) capital. How then, may this convergence of interests between globalising financial and industrial capital yet be undermined?

In neo-liberal capitalist accumulation, profits are increasingly made within, or at least siphoned of to, the sphere of circulation, rather than being made within and re-invested in the sphere of production. This has certainly been the trend within the USA and in the UK where according to Lazonick and O'Sullivan (2000) the rise of a new *shareholder value* ideology has been associated with a shift in corporate strategy from what they call 'retain and re-invest' to 'downsize and distribute' (to the shareholders, that is). Although in the USA this has not led to higher unemployment, it has led, according to this study, to a significant reduction in the number of relatively secure and well-paid jobs (ibid.). As argued in chapter 1, there are indications that this rise of a new shareholder capitalism – driven in part by EU financial liberalisation – can also be observed within continental Europe, and that the money capital perspective (which is the perspective of the shareholder who stands outside the firm and the production process, and is exclusively oriented towards financial return) comes to prevail within industry and within production itself (Van Apeldoorn 2001). The fact that the industrialists of the Roundtable now also invoke 'shareholder value' as the fundamental benchmark for the performance of industry (ERT 1996: 9; see above) does not bode well in this respect, and may also be taken as an indication of the extent to which financial and *rentier* interests increasingly come to dominate Europe's transnational capitalist class. The rise of shareholder capitalism can be expected to further undermine the limited elements of embeddedness still present in the current hegemonic project. We may thus see the rise of social forces calling for a purer form of neo-liberalism (more *laissez-faire*), thus undermining the embedded neo-liberal synthesis.

On the other hand, as argued, there are limits to which productive capital can be subordinated to money capital. Industry needs to continue to produce things, and this requires (re-)investment, innovation, planning, and thus paying attention to long-term concerns that may not be shared by the stock market. To the extent that these limits are acknowledged by some industrialists, this may lead to certain tensions within the transnational capitalist bloc between, on the one hand, an increasing number of owners *and* managers adhering to a money capital perspective (with managers managing in the name of shareholder value and to increase the value of their own stock options), and, on the other hand, still more long-term-oriented industrialists worried about the implications of capital market discipline for their investment strategies. Thus, former Roundtable chairman Maucher, certainly a neo-liberal in many respects, said in an interview with the *Financial Times* that he was worried about the current obsession of managers with short-term results, and complained that it was because of the capital market pressures that his company Nestlé was forced to withdraw its investments from Russia: 'because of the now-fashionable short-term shareholder value thinking that means you get out if you don't get a result within six months'.[52] How these potential tensions will play out it is of course too early to tell. One possible scenario, however, is that here we might see the return of a convergence of interests between (the management of) industrial capital and labour, whose interests are of course directly threatened by shareholder capitalism, the two sides uniting against the rentier fraction of the capitalist class.

Finally, we may note that the current commitment to global free trade on the part of both European transnational capital and the EU is not necessarily irreversible. A strong global recession may see the resurgence of (Euro)protectionism on the part of some sections of European industry that might be particularly hit by a possible global economic crisis. This then might put strains on the incorporation of the former neo-mercantilist project into the hegemonic project of embedded neo-liberalism, though one has to be careful here as the deepening of globalisation of the past decade has made the invested interests in free trade very strong indeed.

The struggle over European order will thus continue. Whether the social purpose of this order may yet be re-organised around the principle of social protection will in the end depend primarily on the extent to which those groups that lose out in the neo-liberal globalisation and Europeanisation process will be able to form a stronger countervailing power at both the national and European levels. From a critical perspective, examining these possibilities, however remote they may seem, should be a necessary complement to the research agenda that has informed this book on the ideological power of Europe's transnational capitalist class. At the moment the prospects appear to look bleak. Globalisation and European regionalisation, through the mediating class agency of transnational capital, have in the end become mutually reinforcing processes, and both have become bound up with a neo-liberal social purpose. It will be a long struggle to change this. It is a struggle that will have to take place at all levels of Europe's multi-level polity, in particular at the European level – which is the level at which one could hope to gain some political-institutional power to at least partially match the larger-than-national scale of the market – and the national level, where we still find the institutions of liberal democracy through which the struggle will also have to be waged. It will above all have to be an ideological struggle, in which social forces rallying around the principle of social protection will have to, if one wants to come to a true counter-hegemony, radically disassociate themselves from the currently hegemonic neo-liberal competitiveness discourse.

Notes

Introduction

1 See for earlier versions of this argument Van Apeldoorn (1996), Van Apeldoorn (1999), Rhodes and Van Apeldoorn (1997). Hooghe and Marks (1999) make a comparable argument about rival projects, although they do not really offer a theoretical framework explaining the rise and relative success of these projects.

2 It is true that not only labour, but also, and in fact even more so, environmental groups, human rights groups, etc. (see, e.g., some of the contributions to Risse-Kappen (ed.) 1995), are to a growing extent active at the transnational level. But I would suggest that this transnationalisation is to a significant extent a response to, or at least enabled by, the transnationalisation of capital and the coming into existence of an ever more globalised world economy.

3 This framework owes much to the work done within the International Political Economy Group of the University of Amsterdam (see, e.g., Overbeek (ed.) 1993; Van der Pijl 1998).

4 This study is based on the analysis of ERT reports, other public documents, and 22 interviews held with 21 (former) associates, members, and senior officials of the ERT.

5 Recently, another variation of the 'second image reversed' *problématique* has been brought on to the research agenda of the IR community, that of how European-level (rather than global) changes, or *Europeanisation*, impacts upon domestic politics and structures (Cowles, Caporaso, and Risse (eds) 2001). Although this study does not focus on the so-called domestic level, its transnational and global political economy perspective maintains that the Europeanisation process itself should rather be taken as an intermediate or intervening variable (in turn conditioned by global dynamics) and that hence, ultimately domestic-level changes also have to be linked to global transformation.

1 Theoretical perspective: social forces and the struggle over European order

1 Within the broad array of neo-Gramscian perspectives (see, e.g., Gill (ed.) 1993), the theoretical perspective adopted in this study in particular builds upon the work of the so-called Amsterdam group within International Political Economy (see especially Van der Pijl 1984, 1998; Overbeek 1990; Overbeek (ed.) 1993; Holman 1996).

2 Within IR, constructivism was first self-consciously used as a label by Nicholas Onuf (Onuf 1989). Later, his example was followed by Alexander Wendt (1992, 1994, 1999) and many others (see, e.g., Adler 1997; Checkel 1998).

3 From *The Eighteenth Brumaire of Louis Bonaparte*. The full quotation reads: 'Men make their own history, but they do not make it just as they please, they do not make it under circumstances chosen by themselves, but under circumstances directly found, given, and transmitted from the past' (in Marx and Engels 1978: 595).

4 The negative conception sees ideology as rooted in a distorted representation of objective (material) reality that serves to defend the interests of the ruling class. As such it is related to the notion of false consciousness. Göran Therborn notes that the concept of ideology as false consciousness – distinguishing between real and false interests – hinges upon a utilitarian definition of interest (i.e., as an objective property of the individual actor), but as Therborn argues:

> 'interests' by themselves do not *explain* anything. 'Interest' is a *normative* concept indicating the most rational course of action in a predefined game, that is, in a situation in which gain and loss have already been defined. The problem to be explained however, is how members of different classes come to define the world and their situation and possibilities in it in a particular way. (Therborn 1980: 10)

It is here that ideological practice must enter into the analysis. For a discussion of the problematic nature of the notion of ideology as false consciousness, see also Eagleton 1991: 10–27.

5 On the one hand, there is no one-way determinism assumed here. The constitution of a class ideology on the basis of a class position is mediated by ideology itself, and therefore necessarily involves a discourse-dependent construction of an intersubjective meaning attached to that class basis (or social position). On the other hand, the difference in ideological outlook between the CEO of Shell and a worker at the bottom of the firm's hierarchy is not coincidental (or the product of a contingent discursive articulation) but *structural* (even though that structure also has an important intersubjective dimension, i.e., in part depends on the actor's ideas about what it means to be a capitalist or a worker). Terry Eagleton makes a very eloquent case for this standpoint through his example of the case of the 'galley slave': 'an objective location within the social formation known as third galley slave from the front of the starboard side' (1991: 206). As Eagleton writes:

> It is certainly true, as post-Marxism properly insists, that the slave's politico-ideological position is not just some 'reflex' of his material conditions. But his ideological views do indeed have an internal relation to that condition – not in the sense that this condition is the automatic *cause* of them, but in the sense that it is the *reason* for them. Sitting for fifteen hours a day in the third row from the front is what his ideological opinions are *about*. What he says is about what he does, and what he does is the reason for what he says. The 'real' here certainly exists prior to and independent of the slave's discourse . . . (Eagleton 1991: 208)

6 Of course we are using the term 'institutions' in a broad (sociological) sense here. In this respect, DiMaggio and Powell see interesting parallels between Gramsci's notion of hegemony and the 'new institutionalism' (DiMaggio and Powell 1991: 38, note 29).

7 This in spite of the fact that Moravcsik uses this term in the subtitle of his impressive historical study of European integration (Moravcsik 1998). Indeed, in the whole introduction and the theoretical chapter of this book, the concept of social purpose is not at all explained and does not seem to be at all central to his argument.

8 Although Moravcsik in his historical study (1998) seeks to refute particular hypotheses derived from neo-functionalist and newer historical institutionalist accounts (Pierson 1998) – both approaches stressing the gradual evolution of an EU *polity* through the agency of supranational institutions (not just with regard to treaty revisions but even more so in the more day-to-day management of the EU) and as a result of the *unintended* consequences of 'rational state actions' – he chooses to do so on the basis of an analysis of five history-making *intergovernmental* bargains (from the Treaty of Rome to the Treaty of Maastricht). As Fritz Scharpf has argued, this tends to make his empirical study rather biased in terms of his case selection: 'In effect, Moravcsik seems to be squandering the wealth of information produced by his supremely well researched case studies on the effort to prove the narrow proposition that, by and large, national

governments are in control of intergovernmental negotiations over treaty revisions' (Scharpf 1999a: 8).

9 This approach thus relates to the so-called Europeanisation literature (see, e.g., Cowles, Caporaso, and Risse (eds) 2001).

10 It is in this sense, then, that the nationality factor partially overlaps with the first factor (degree of globalisation). However, this does not mean that nationality is redundant. In order to understand, for instance, the particular Frenchness of the outlook of French capitalist elites, we have to put this into the context of French state–society relations as they have developed historically, and here the position of French capital within the world economy is one important factor underlying this historical development. But this is a hypothesised link that holds at the level of historical macro-structures, and not necessarily at the micro-level of the ideological outlook of individual capitalists. Thus, a French capitalist controlling a rather global company may still be less globalist than a British counterpart inasmuch as the former's outlook is still also shaped by a nationally dominant discourse that is, say, much less liberal than the one dominant in the British political economy. However, to the extent that a structural change in the position of domestic capital gradually changes state–society relations as well, this may also alter the dominant national discourse.

2 Global restructuring, transnational capitalism and rival projects for European order

1 Thus, Ruigrok and Van Tulder, for instance, referring to UNCTAD's 1994 ranking of the 100 largest TNCs (UNCTAD 1994), suggest that the decline in foreign assets between 1990 and 1992 of 31 companies on this list lends support to their thesis that the internationalisation strategy of many TNCs in the 1990s 'more often constitutes a retreat from globalisation rather than an expansion strategy' (Ruigrok and Van Tulder 1995: 193). However, and apart from the fact that the authors fail to mention that 32 companies still witnessed a growth of more than 10 per cent in this period (see UNCTAD 1994: 11), the growth of foreign activities of large TNCs later in the 1990s indicates that the decline in foreign assets of the companies singled out by these authors was more cyclical than indicative of a structural trend.

2 Thus, although the post-war order of embedded liberalism in principle allowed the national units of the global system some freedom to follow their own path of capitalist development and industrial modernisation (because of the relative autonomy it granted to national welfare states), this era, in fact, paradoxically saw a relative uniformity across countries. This uniformity was induced by the uniform logic of industrial modernisation that the rise of Atlantic Fordism imposed upon the different advanced capitalist states, and generally by the overarching economic, political, and ideological framework of American hegemony. As long as this model of capitalist accumulation and regulation was successful in producing ever higher living standards, thus leaving its hegemony unquestioned, the actual degree of variation was limited (Ryner 1994: 11).

3 Of course, inflation was a problem for other classes as well, particularly given the absence of economic growth. What was not in the general interest, however, was the subsequent (see below) complete reversal of priorities in economic policy on the part of most Western governments, whereby bringing down inflation became the number one priority, even at the cost of considerably higher unemployment. This policy shift, I would sustain, served in particular the interests of the propertied classes.

4 Numerical flexibility expresses the freedom of employers to vary, according to need, the number of workers (hire and fire rules), the hours worked, as well as individual wage levels (hence labour as a flexible input), whereas functional flexibility refers more positively to the functionality of the worker in terms of his or her skills, and his or her adaptability to varying needs in the production process (with a high degree of functional flexibility marking a contrast to that of the traditional Fordist worker). Functional

flexibility, therefore, speaks more to a progressive social-democratic discourse whereas numerical flexibility is clearly the centrepiece of the neo-liberal strategy.

5 For an interesting example of a non-European study making this neo-liberal case, see a US State Department study originally dating from 1984 by Drouin, Ernst, and Wheeler (1987).

6 For the year 1990 (at which time the transnationalisation process had already deepened compared to the early 1980s for which, however, no comparable data are available) the UNCTAD (2000b: 80) has calculated the transnationality index (TI) of the top five (on the basis of foreign assets) TNCs in each of five major sectors. From these figures it appears that motor vehicles and electronics (with TI indices of respectively of 34.7 and 36.1) were still the least transnationalised, whereas pharmaceuticals, chemicals, oil, and food/beverages show much higher indices (respectively 47.1, 51.6, 57.7, and 60.8).

3 The European Roundtable: an elite forum of Europe's emergent transnational capitalist class

1 Letter from Dr Helmut O. Maucher to the author, dated 12 June 1997 (my translation).

2 The importance of both Gyllenhammar and Davignon was emphasised by all interviewees who were with the ERT in the founding years.

3 Pehr Gyllenhammar, 'What Europe Needs is a New "Marshall Plan"', *Financial Times*, 19 January 1983.

4 These reasons were suggested to me by an ERT associate of the time who based his insights on what people of Volvo had told him (interview by author, Düsseldorf, 14 May 1996). *Nota bene*: all interviews cited from now on are by the author, unless specified otherwise. The interviews were all held in the native language of the interviewee: that is, in Dutch, English, French, German, or Italian (all quotations in the text are given in English in an own translation). The functions of the interviewees referred to in footnotes are those held at the time of the interview.

5 Interview with Etienne Davignon by Otto Holman and the author, Brussels, 6 July 1993.

6 Ibid.

7 Ibid.

8 This leading role played by Gyllenhammar was also recognised as such by the media. The Roundtable was usually called the 'G-17' group (or whichever number of members the ERT later had), its members being called the 'G-men'. The actual name at the time was 'Roundtable of European Industrialists', picked by the associates of the Roundtable's early members. Later this changed into 'ERT'.

9 Interview with Etienne Davignon by Otto Holman and the author, Brussels, 6 July 1993.

10 Interview with senior official of the ERT, Brussels, 27 April 1993.

11 Interview with Wisse Dekker by Otto Holman and the author, Eindhoven, 6 September 1993.

12 Interview, Brussels, 24 May 1996.

13 Interview with senior ERT official, Brussels, 27 April 1993.

14 Monod was secretary-general of the RPR at the end of the 1970s, before he was 'Chargé de Mission' for the Prime Minister's Office from 1959 to 1962, and Special Assistant to then Prime Minister Chirac from 1975 to 1976.

15 When Maucher took control of Nestlé in 1981, the company was floundering. In the 16 years that he was CEO profits have, however, steadily grown (to US$2.24 billion in 1996). See William Hall, 'Maucher steps aside at Nestlé', *Financial Times*, 7 May 1997. 'Domestically', Maucher may be seen as an influential figure in both German and Swiss elite circles. In Switzerland, he is one of three members of 'a small clique of Swiss business leaders . . . who are often to be found around the same boardroom table' (William Hall, 'Staying power stands Gerber in good stead', *Financial Times*, 3 April 1997).

16 Andrew Fisher, 'An extremely Anglo-Saxon takeover bid', *Financial Times*, 19 March 1997.
17 See Michael Lindemann, 'Cromme lives up to his reputation', *Financial Times*, 19 March 1997, and Peter Norman, 'Target condemns hostile bid as "asset stripping"', *Financial Times*, 19 March 1997.
18 The phrase 'club of bosses' derives from a Belgian ERT Associate (interview, Brussels, 23 May 1996).
19 Interview with senior ERT official, Brussels, 24 May 1996.
20 As far as I know there is no statute stating the criteria for membership but there is a document containing a list of criteria that was sent out to companies who seek to get their CEO or chairman elected (interview with senior ERT official, Brussels, 24 May 1996). What follows is mainly based on the information given to me by a senior ERT official (ibid.).
21 Interested US companies were IBM Europe, Phillip Morris, Reynolds, and others (interview with senior ERT official, 24 May 1996).
22 Ibid.
23 Interview with ERT vice-chairman André Leysen, Antwerp, 21 May 1996.
24 Interview with senior ERT official, Brussels, 24 May 1996.
25 Ibid.
26 Ibid.
27 See ERT's website: http://www.ert.be/pd/end_frame.htm (accessed 6 August 2001).
28 For a list of ERT's current members see ERT's website: http://www.ert.be/pc/enc_frame.htm (accessed 6 August 2001). For the analysis in this chapter I have chosen to work with this list of May 1999 as most of the narrative of this book ends around that time.
29 *Financial Times'* Europe 500, http://www.ft.com/ftsurveys/ft5_eur.htm (accessed 3 June 1999).
30 *Fortune's* 1998 Global 500, http://cgi.pathfinder.com/fortune/global500 (accessed 3 June 1999).
31 http://www.ert.be/pc/enc_frame.htm (accessed 6 August 2001).
32 See, e.g., Greg McIvor, 'A new king on the board – Barnevik is expected to restructure the Wallenberg empire', *Financial Times*, 23 April 1997. See on Barnevik's success as CEO of ABB for instance, 'The ABB of management', *The Economist*, 6 January 1996.
33 See Paul Betts, 'Italians look to a new prince in Pirelli's Tronchetti Provera', *Financial Times*, 11 March 1997.
34 Interviews with ERT members.
35 Interview by Otto Holman and the author, Eindhoven, 6 September 1993.
36 Of the four original French ERT companies, Lafarge Coppée, with very large activities in North America, forms an exception in this respect.
37 Interview with a former German ERT associate, Düsseldorf, 14 May 1996. According to Cowles, of the three original German Roundtable members, Hans Merkle of Bosch did actively participate in the ERT; the other two, however, Spethmann and Seelig (Siemens), 'had been recruited for the ERT by Commissioner Davignon's office so that there would be "German representation" within the ERT', but were less committed (Cowles 1995b: 14–15).
38 Interviews with German ERT associates (Düsseldorf, 14 May 1996, and Brussels, 30 May 1996).
39 Interview with a senior German ERT associate, Brussels, 30 May 1996.
40 A senior German ERT associate (ibid.) summed up the German position thus:

> German firms were used to, and still are used to, having their interests represented by associations, with little involvement of the top management . . . It doesn't work like that at the European level, where we have above all the French culture in which – and that is also the British culture – the CEOs themselves are intimately

involved in the opinion-making processes. It was hence that for the German culture of interest representation the ERT was something unknown. (interview, Brussels, 30 May 1996)

41 See http://www.ert.be/pc/enc_frame.htm (accessed 6 August 2001).
42 See on Gerber, William Hall, 'Staying power stands Gerber in good stead', *Financial Times*, 3 June 1997.
43 Andrew Bolger, 'Financiers move to support single market', *Financial Times*, 2 March 2001.
44 Interview, Essen, 4 September 1996.
45 Interviews.
46 As one French ERT associate put it: 'effectively because of the direct participation of the big bosses in the Roundtable, the Roundtable can have a *souplesse*, an agility, a rapidity of reaction that big organisations like UNICE often cannot have' (interview, Paris, 24 September 1997).
47 Interview with French ERT member Bertrand Collomb, Paris, 26 September 1997.
48 Interview with a senior German ERT associate, Brussels, 30 May 1996.
49 Ibid.
50 Interview, Antwerp, 21 May 1996.
51 Ibid.
52 Telephone interview, 27 January 1998.
53 Interview, Brussels, 30 May 1996.
54 In the words of one long-serving ERT associate, who drew the comparison with the US Business Roundtable (which has four times as many members as the ERT), the ERT is 'less interested in specific themes . . . *within the life of the firms* [and more] interested . . . in themes of the medium–long term, that is to say, themes that concern the future of Europe', whereas its US counterpart is 'much more *lobbyistic*' (interview, Ivrea, 2 December 1997).
55 Interview, London, 12 September 1996.
56 As I have not been able to determine with certainty all the directorships of each of the listed members, these figures might also be higher.
57 See the WEF's website: http://www.weforum.org/whoweare.nsf/Documents/Who+We+Are+-+Members+and+Partners (accessed 12 August 2001).
58 http://www.weforum.org/whoweare.nsf/Documents/Who+We+Are+-+Governance (accessed 12 August 2001).
59 http://www.weforum.org/whatwedo.nsf/Documents/What+We+Do+-+Regional+Activities+-+European+Economic+Summit+2001#Overview (accessed 12 August 2001).
60 http://www.iccwbo.org/home/intro_icc/leadership.asp (accessed 12 August 2001).
61 Interview with a senior ERT official, Brussels, 24 May 1996. Since its founding, three ERT members have served as European co-chair of this organisation: Jan Timmer (Philips), Jürgen Schrempp (Daimler-Benz), and Jérôme Monod (Suez Lyonnaise des Eaux) (Balanyá *et al.* 2000: 103).
62 Interview with Etienne Davignon, by Otto Holman and author, Brussels, 6 July 1993.
63 Thus in 1991, both trade volume and in- and outflows of FDI were higher with the USA than with Japan (European Commission 1993: 13).
64 This point was also made by a senior German ERT associate who had been closely involved in the TABD but doubted whether such a form of co-operation would ever be possible with the Japanese (interview, Brussels, 30 May 1996).
65 But the ERT does see to it that its position is carefully co-ordinated with that of UNICE when it comes to influencing the Council. Both the chairman of the ERT and the president of UNICE as well as the secretaries-general of both organisations are said to be in regular contact with each other. Although UNICE has official access to the intergovernmental level, the ERT has better access to the national governments (interview with a senior ERT official, Brussels, 24 May 1996).

66 Interviews.
67 Interview with a senior ERT official, 24 May 1996.
68 Telephone interview with Peter Sutherland, 27 January 1998.
69 Interview with a French ERT associate, Paris, 24 September 1997.
70 The third one was François-Xavier Ortoli, just like Davignon Commissioner in the first half of the 1980s.
71 Interview with an Italian ERT associate, Ivrea, 2 December 1997.

4 The Roundtable's changing strategic project and the transnational struggle over European order

1 Interview with Davignon by the author and Otto Holman, Brussels, 6 July 1993.
2 Harvey-Jones quoted in 'Gyllenhammar's vigilantes', *The Economist*, 28 January 1984, p. 67.
3 Interview with Dekker by the author and Otto Holman, Eindhoven, 6 September 1993.
4 For BSN and Renault the figures are by production area (hence where the product is made) rather than by final market (where the product is sold) but also these latter figures were at the time above 50 per cent.
5 Interview with a former German ERT associate, Düsseldorf, 14 May 1996.
6 Thus ERT member Giovanni Agnelli together with other bosses from the car industry asked in a 1987 meeting with the Commission for more European-level protectionism on the basis of the argument that 1992 meant the end of national quotas and other restrictions ('Motor car industry: EEC constructors call for a limit on imports of Japanese cars', *Agence Europe No. 4597*, 25 July 1987).
7 This point was made by several ERT interviewees. Some of the interviewees singled out Philips and Fiat in particular.
8 Interview by the author and Otto Holman, Brussels, 6 July 1993.
9 Moravcsik in fact asserts that the ERT initially opposed the plans for an internal market and that it rather focused on industrial policy and 'projects' such as Trans-European Infrastructure Networks (Moravcsik 1998: 355). Although they, as I argued, also focused on that, there is no evidence (and Moravcsik does not provide any) for the ERT's opposition to the internal market. On the contrary, the record as provided here clearly shows that the Roundtable saw these projects as part of a broader strategy towards the creation of a big European home market. Although some ERT members (from more sheltered sectors) may initially have been sceptical about some (liberalisation) aspects of the idea of a single market, the leadership of the ERT (in particular Gyllenhammar and Dekker) clearly favoured this strategy early on, and before any intergovernmental bargains were concluded. That the ERT and its chairman, Gyllenhammar, called for the creation of a single European market from the very beginning is in fact confirmed by many sources (see, e.g., 'Industry: 17 heads of large enterprises form "club"', *Agence Europe, No. 3584*, 9 April 1983).
10 Dekker for instance was already publicly calling for the creation of a European home market as early as 1982 ('Editorial: the European industrial dimension', *Agence Europe, No. 3491*, 22 November 1982).
11 Interview with Dekker by the author and Otto Holman, Eindhoven, 6 September 1993. Several of these contacts were at the highest level, i.e., with Delors and other Commissioners (see, e.g., 'Industry: the Roundtable of European Industrialists with several Commission members', *Agence Europe, No. 4291*, 1 April 1986).
12 'The multinationals need a European base', *Agence Europe, No. 4887*, 27 April 1985.
13 'Realisation of the Single Market', *Agence Europe, No. 4576*, 25 June 1987.
14 Telephone interview with Peter Sutherland, 27 January 1998.
15 'Consensus of opinion between the European Commission and the Roundtable of Industrialists on support for large-scale infrastructure projects', *Agence Europe, No. 4293*, 4 April 1986.

16 See 'European co-operation: bosses want the common market that Brussels never built', *The Economist*, 26 May 1984, and 'Philips in a new light', *The Economist*, 5 January 1985.
17 Interview by the author and Otto Holman, Rotterdam, 3 September 1993.
18 Interview by the author and Otto Holman, Rotterdam, 3 September, 1993. ERT associate Herbert Oberhänsli also acknowledged that the ERT as a result had become 'more international' and 'more liberal' (interview, Vewey, 14 May 1997).
19 Interviews.
20 This was suggested to me by a former high-ranking official of an important European business association, and former manager of one these companies (Brussels, 21 September 2000).
21 This excludes DaimlerChrysler, which has left the ERT roster in 2000 (otherwise the figure would be 60.7 per cent).
22 Interview by the author and Otto Holman with Floris Maljers, Rotterdam, 3 September 1993.
23 See 'The ETUC is "concerned" by the lack of a social dimension in the conclusions of the summit', *Agence Europe, No. 4123*, 2 July 1985, and 'ETUC reaffirms that the achievement of the large internal market must necessarily be accompanied by social measures', *Agence Europe, No. 4227*, 18 December 1985.
24 The directive on part-time work for instance has been criticised by the European Parliament as setting standards below those of the convention of the ILO (International Labour Organisation), further promoting this flexible form of labour rather than upgrading its regulation.
25 Interview with Floris Maljers by Otto Holman and the author, Rotterdam, 3 September 1993.
26 Ibid.
27 Interview with a French ERT associate, Paris, 24 September 1997.
28 Interview with a senior ERT official, Brussels, 27 April 1993.
29 Interview with Roundtable vice-chairman Maljers by Otto Holman and the author, Rotterdam, 3 September 1993.
30 A senior official of the ERT, for instance, recalls a lengthy meeting between an ERT delegation and the then prime minister Ruud Lubbers at the time of the Dutch presidency, under which Maastricht was concluded (interview, Brussels, 24 May 1996).
31 http://amue.org (accessed 11 September 2001).
32 *Agence Europe, No. 4728*, 22 February 1988.
33 *Agence Europe, No. 4811*, 25 June 1988.

5 Transnational class agency, the rise of 'embedded neo-liberalism' and the evolving European order

1 Letter from Helmut O. Maucher to the author, 12 June 1997.
2 In its contribution to the 'climate change debate' the ERT advocates as the most important principle to respect in the field of environmental policies that 'The competitiveness of European industry should not be damaged', and it has consistently (and so far successfully) lobbied against EU proposals to introduce a European carbon/energy tax aimed at reducing CO_2 emissions.
3 Interview with a former German ERT associate, Düsseldorf, 14 May 1996.
4 Interviews.
5 Interview with Dr Herbert Oberhänsli, Vewey, 14 May 1997.
6 Ibid. Also: interview with a senior German ERT associate, Brussels, 30 May 1996.
7 Interview with Bertrand Collomb, Paris, 26 September 1997.
8 Interview with a senior German ERT associate, Brussels, 30 May 1996.
9 Ibid.
10 Interview with David Simon, London, 11 September 1996.
11 Interview with a senior German ERT associate, Brussels, 30 May 1996.

12 Interview with a senior German ERT associate, Brussels, 30 May 1996.
13 This was for instance the perception of Floris Maljers, then vice-chairman of the ERT (interview by Otto Holman and the author, Rotterdam, 3 September 1993).
14 Ibid.
15 At least according to a senior ERT official, who related that the ERT, then chaired by Frenchman Jérôme Monod, met with French prime minister Balladur to discuss with him how the French government could say yes to the conclusion of the Uruguay Round without angering public opinion, and particularly the farm lobby, too much (interview, Brussels, 24 May 1996).
16 Telephone interview with Peter Sutherland, 27 January 1998.
17 As stressed by several (former) members and associates (interview with ERT vice-chairman Floris Maljers by Otto Holman and the author, Rotterdam, 3 September 1993; interview with ERT vice-chairman André Leysen, Antwerp, 21 May 1996; interview with a former German ERT associate, Düsseldorf, 14 May 1996; and with the associate for Helmut Maucher, Dr Herbert Oberhänsli, Vewey, 14 May 1997).
18 Interview, London, 11 September 1996.
19 Interview, Paris, 26 September 1997.
20 Interview with a senior ERT official, Brussels, 24 May 1996.
21 Interview with Robin Berkeley, Brussels, 29 May 1996.
22 As the aforementioned representative of BP put it: 'We say that the current view of BP is that we believe in the European ideal, that this is something that can help the process along and that therefore in a general sense we support it, but we are not going to get involved [in] sending strong lobby appeals' (interview with Robin Berkeley, Brussels, 29 May 1996).
23 Interview with a former German ERT associate, Düsseldorf, 14 May 1996.
24 Ibid.
25 Ibid.
26 Ibid.; also interview with an ERT associate, Brussels, 30 May 1996. See also Moravcsik 1998: 392.
27 Letter dated 17 October 1995 and signed by Jérôme Monod, then chairman of the ERT. A copy of the letter was also sent to Commission president Santer, and the issue was further discussed with him in a meeting a few weeks later. The ERT also asked the Council specifically to take the decision necessary to keep EMU on track (interview with a senior ERT official, Brussels, 24 May 1996).
28 Interview with André Leysen, Antwerp, 21 May 1996.
29 Interview with a senior German ERT associate, Brussels, 30 May 1996; also interview with a former ERT associate, Düsseldorf, 14 May 1996.
30 Interview, Düsseldorf, 14 May 1996.
31 This was at least the opinion of the British (*nota bene*) ERT vice-chairman, Sir David Simon, who gave as an example the recent directive on European Works Councils, which he saw as a failed attempt to introduce European co-determination; the flexibility of the final directive made it rather harmless (interview, London, 12 September 1996).
32 Interview, Brussels, 24 May 1996.
33 As Ernesto Laclau writes, 'a class is hegemonic not so much to the extent that it is able to impose a uniform conception of the world on the rest of society, but to the extent that it can articulate different visions of the world in such a way that their potential antagonism is neutralised' (Laclau 1977: 161).
34 *Agence Europe, No. 6127*, 12 December 1993.
35 *Agence Europe, No. 6122*, 6 December 1993.
36 Interview with ERT vice-chairman André Leysen (Antwerp, 21 May 1996), who also stated that the ERT made a significant impact upon the White Paper.
37 Interview, Brussels, 24 May 1996.
38 Interview, London, 12 September 1996.

39 Interview, Antwerp, 21 May 1996.
40 For a list of present and former members as well as other information on the CAG, see http://europa.eu.int/comm/cdp/cag/publications/rapport4/index_en.htm (accessed 17 February 2001).
41 Ibid.
42 The ETUC has officially expressed its welcome for the creation of the CAG (*Agence Europe, No. 6422*, 17 February 1995).
43 Interviews (see also *Agence Europe, No. 6859*, 23 November 1996).
44 At the Industry Council of 14 November 1996. The Council recently called again upon the Commission 'to ensure the ongoing development of benchmarking' at all levels (see European Commission, *Bulletin EU*, 4-1999, point 1.3.79).
45 Presidency Conclusions, Lisbon European Council, 23 and 24 March 2000, http://ue.eu.int/en/Info/eurocouncil/index.htm (accessed: 19 September 2001).
46 Flynn quoted in *Agence Europe, No. 6478*, 11 May 1995.
47 Presidency Conclusions, Lisbon European Council, 23 and 24 March 2000, http://ue.eu.int/en/Info/eurocouncil/index.htm (accessed: 19 September 2001).
48 In one report (which was, it has to be admitted, written under the auspices of a German, the ERT's present chairman, Helmut Maucher), the ERT makes a very explicit commitment to such a German conception of socio-economic order when it invokes the concept of *Ordoliberalismus* for describing its preferred principles of 'free market organisation', which include the acknowledgement that government 'does have to shape the economic order by guaranteeing the framework for business through "Ordnungspolitik" [of which ultimately] "liberal interventionism" [may also be a part]' (ERT 1993a: 27).
49 This was done most explicitly by Bertrand Collomb (interview, Paris, 25 September 1997).
50 Ibid.
51 Ibid.
52 Stefan Wagstyl, 'Interview Helmut Maucher: an appetite for Eastern Europe', *Financial Times*, 29 October 1999.

References

Adler, E. (1997) 'Seizing the Middle Ground: Constructivism in World Politics', *European Journal of International Relations*, 3, 3: 319–63.

Albert, M. (1993) *Capitalism vs. Capitalism*, New York: Four Walls Eight Windows.

Albo, Gregory (1994) '"Competitive Austerity" and the Impasse of Capitalist Employment Policy', in: *The Socialist Register 1994*, London: Merlin Press.

Amin, A., and N. Thrift (1994) 'Living in the Global', in: A. Amin and N. Thrift (eds), *Globalisation, Institutions, and Regional Development in Europe*, Oxford: Oxford University Press, pp. 1–22.

Anderson, J., and J. Goodman (1995) 'Regions, States and the European Union: Modernist Reaction or Postmodernist Adaptation?', *Review of International Political Economy*, 2, 4: 600–31.

Andrews, D.M. (1994) 'Capital Mobility and State Autonomy', *International Studies Quarterly*, 38: 193–218.

Armstrong, P., A. Glyn, and J. Harrison (1991) *Capitalism since 1945*, Oxford: Oxford University Press.

Ashley, R. (1986) 'The Poverty of Neo-realism', in: R.O. Keohane (ed.), *Neorealism and its Critics*, New York: Columbia University Press, pp. 255–300.

Baker, A. (2000) 'Globalization and the British "Residual State"', in: R. Stubbs and G.R.D. Underhill (eds), *Political Economy and the Changing Global Order*, Oxford: Oxford University Press, pp. 362–72.

Balanyá, B. *et al.* (2000) *Europe Inc.: Regional and Global Restructuring and the Rise of Corporate Power*, London: Pluto Press.

Bell, D. (1965) [1960] *The End of Ideology: On the Exhaustion of Political Ideas in the Fifties*, New York: The Free Press.

Berle, A.A. and G.C. Means (1991) [1932] *The Modern Corporation and Private Property*, New Brunswick, NJ: Transaction Publishers.

Bhaskar, R. (1979) *The Possibility of Naturalism: A Philosophical Critique of the Contemporary Human Sciences*, Brighton: Harvester Press.

Bieler, A. and A.D. Morton (eds) (2001) *Social Forces in the Making of the New Europe*, Basingstoke: Palgrave.

Bieling, H.-J. (1998) *Neo-Liberalism and Communitarianism: Towards a New Type of Employment Policy in Western Europe?*, Amerdam International Studies Working Paper, No. 54, Amsterdam: University of Amsterdam.

Bieling, H.-J. and J. Steinhilber (eds) (2000) *Die Konfiguration Europas: Dimensionen einer kritischen Integrationstheorie*, Münster: Westfälisches Dampfboot.

Birnbaum, P. (1981) *The Height of Power: An Essay on the Power Elite in France*, Chicago: University of Chicago Press.

Blainpain, R. *et al.* (1983) *The Vredeling Proposal*, Deventer: Kluwer.
Boltho, A. (1982) 'Growth', in: A. Boltho (ed.), *The European Economy: Growth and Crisis*, Oxford: Oxford University Press, pp. 9–37.
Boyer, R. (1997) 'French Statism at the Crossroads', in C. Crouch and W. Streeck (eds), *Political Economy of Modern Capitalism: Mapping Convergence and Diversity*, London/Thousand Oaks/New Dehli: Sage, pp. 71–101.
Burnham, J. (1975) [1941] *The Managerial Revolution*, Westport, Conn.: Greenwood Press.
Cameron, D.R. (1992) 'The 1992 Initiative: Causes and Consequences', in: A.M. Sbragia (ed.), *Euro-Politics: Institutions and Policymaking in the New European Community*, Washington, DC: The Brookings Institution, pp. 23–74.
Cameron, D.R. (2000). *The Europeanization of Employment Policy*, Paper prepared for presentation at the Max Planck Institute for the Study of Societies, Cologne, 30 May.
Caporaso, J.A. (1987) 'Labor in the Global Political Economy', in: J.A. Caporaso (ed.), *A Changing International Division of Labor* (International Political Economy Yearbook, Vol. 2), Boulder, Colo.: Lynne Rienner/London: Frances Pinter, pp. 187–222.
Caporaso, J.A. (1996) 'The European Union and Forms of State: Westphalian, Regulatory or Post-modern?', *Journal of Common Market Studies*, 34, 1: 29–51.
Caporaso, J.A. (1998) 'Regional Integration Theory: Understanding Our Past and Anticipating Our Future', *Journal of European Public Policy*, 5, 1: 1–16.
Cawson, A. (1986) *Corporatism and Political Theory*, Oxford/New York: Basil Blackwell.
Cawson, A. (1992) 'Interests, Groups and Public Policy-making: The Case of the Consumer Electronics Industry', in: J. Greenwood, J. Grote, and K. Ronit (eds), *Organized Interests and the European Community*, Newbury Park, Calif.: Sage, pp. 99–118.
Cawson, A. (1994) 'Sectoral Governance in Consumer Electronics in Britain and France', in: J.R. Hollingsworth, Ph.C. Schmitter, and W. Streeck (eds), *Governing Capitalist Economies: Performance and Control in Economic Sectors*, New York/Oxford: Oxford University Press, pp. 215–43.
CEO (Corporate Europe Observatory) (1997) *Europe Inc.: Dangerous Liaisons Between EU Institutions and Industry*, Amsterdam: CEO.
Cerny, Ph.G. (1994) 'The Infrastructure of the Infrastructure? Toward "Embedded Financial Orthodoxy" in the International Political Economy', in: R.P. Palan and B. Gills (eds), *Transcending the State–Global Divide: A Neostructuralist Agenda in International Relations*, Boulder, Colo./London: Lynne Rienner, pp. 223–50.
Chase-Dunn, C. (1989) *Global Formation: Structures of the World Economy*, Oxford/Cambridge, Mass.: Basil Blackwell.
Checkel, J.T. (1988) 'The Constructivist Turn in International Relations Theory', *World* Politics, 51, 1: 324–48.
Christiansen, T., C. Jørgensen, and A. Wiener (1999) 'The Social Construction of Europe', *Journal of European Public Policy*, 6, 4 (Special Issue 1999): 528–44.
Christiansen, T., C. Jørgensen, and A. Wiener (eds) (1999) 'The Social Construction of Europe', *Journal of European Public Policy*, 6, 4 (Special Issue 1999).
Clegg, S., P. Boreham, and G. Dow (1986) *Class, Politics and the Economy*, London, Boston and Henley: Routledge and Kegan Paul.
Coates, D. (1989) 'Britain', in: T. Bottomore and R.J. Brym (eds), *The Capitalist Class: An International Study*, London: Harvester Wheatsheaf.
Cohen, E. (1995) 'France: National Champions in Search of a Mission', in: J. Hayward (ed.), *Industrial Enterprise and European Integration*, Oxford: Oxford University Press, pp. 23–47.
Colchester, N., and D. Buchan (1990) *Europe Relaunched: Truths and Illusions on the Way to 1992*, London: Random Century (The Economist Books).

Coleman, W.D., and G.R.D. Underhill (eds) (1998) *Regionalism and Global Economic Integration: Europe, Asia and the Americas*, London: Routledge.

Competitiveness Advisory Group (1995) *Enhancing European Competitiveness: First Report to the European Council, June 1995.* Luxembourg: Office for Official Publications of the European Communities.

Cornett, L., and J.A. Caporaso (1992) '"And Still It Moves!" State Interests and Social Forces in the European Community', in: J.N. Rosenau and E.-O. Czempiel (eds), *Governance Without Government: Order and Change in World Politics*, Cambridge: Cambridge University Press, pp. 219–49.

Cowles, M.G. (1994) *The Politics of Big Business in the European Community: Setting the Agenda for a New Europe*, Unpublished Ph.D. Dissertation, Washington: The American University.

Cowles, M.G. (1995a) 'Setting the Agenda for a New Europe: The ERT and EC 1992', *Journal of Common Market Studies*, 33, 4: 501–26.

Cowles, M.G. (1995b) *German Big Business and Brussels: Learning to Play the European Game*, AICGS Seminar Paper No. 15 (November), Washington, DC: American Institute for Contemporary German Studies.

Cowles, M.G. (2001) 'The TABD and Domestic Business–Government Relations: Challenge and Opportunities', in: M.G. Cowles, J. Caporaso, and T. Risse (eds), *Transforming Europe: Europeanization and Domestic Change*, Ithaca, NY: Cornell University Press.

Cowles, M.G., J. Caporaso, and T. Risse (eds) (2001) *Transforming Europe: Europeanization and Domestic Change*, Ithaca, NY: Cornell University Press.

Cox, A. (ed.) (1982) *Politics, Policy and the European Recession*, London and Basingstoke: Macmillan.

Cox, A., and G. Watson (1995) 'The European Community and the Restructuring of Europe's National Champions', in: J. Hayward (ed.), *Industrial Enterprise and European Integration*, Oxford: Oxford University Press.

Cox, R.W. (1983) 'Gramsci, Hegemony and International Relations: An Essay in Method', *Millennium*, 12, 3: 162–75.

Cox, R.W. (1986) 'Social Forces, States and World Orders: Beyond International Relations Theory', in: R.O. Keohane (ed.), *Neorealism and its Critics*, New York: Columbia University Press, pp. 204–53.

Cox, R.W. (1987) *Production, Power, and World Order: Social Forces in the Making of History*, New York: Columbia University Press.

Cox, R.W. (1992a) 'Global Perestroika', in: *The Socialist Register 1992*, London: Merlin Press, pp. 26–43.

Cox, R.W. (1992b) 'Multilateralism and World Order', *Review of International Studies*, 18: 161–80.

Cox, R.W. (1993) 'Structural Issues of Global Governance: Implications for Europe', in: S. Gill (ed.), *Gramsci, Historical Materialism and International Relations*, Cambridge: Cambridge University Press, pp. 259–89.

Cox, R.W. (1995) 'Critical Political Economy', in: B. Hettne (ed.), *International Political Economy: Understanding Global Disorder*, London, etc.: Zed Books, pp. 31–45.

Crompton, R. (1993) *Class and Stratification: An Introduction to Current Debates*, Cambridge: Polity Press.

Crouch, C. (1979) 'The State, Capital, and Liberal Democracy', in: C. Crouch (ed.), *State and Economy in Contemporary Capitalism*, London: Croom Helm.

Crouch, C. (1993a) *Industrial Relations and European State Traditions*, Oxford: Oxford University Press.

Crouch, C. (1993b) 'Co-operation and Competition in an Institutionalised Economy: The

Case of Germany', in C. Crouch and D. Marquand (eds), *Ethics and Markets: Co-operation and Competition Within Capitalist Economies*, Oxford: Blackwell, pp. 80–98.

Crouch, C., and W. Streeck (1997) 'Introduction: The Future of Capitalist Diversity', in: C. Crouch and W. Streeck (eds), *Political Economy of Modern Capitalism: Mapping Convergence and Diversity*, London/Thousand Oaks/New Dehli: Sage, pp. 1–18.

Crouch, C., and W. Streeck (eds) (1997) *Political Economy of Modern Capitalism: Mapping Convergence and Diversity*, London/Thousand Oaks/New Dehli: Sage.

Dahrendorf, R. (1959) *Class and Class Conflict in Industrial Society*, Stanford, Calif.: Stanford University Press.

Dankbaar, B. (1994) 'Sectoral Governance in the Automobile Industries of Germany, Great Britain, and France', in: J.R. Hollingsworth, Ph.C. Schmitter, and W. Streeck (eds), *Governing Capitalist Economies: Performance and Control in Economic Sectors*, New York/Oxford: Oxford University Press, pp. 156–82.

Deeg, R. (1999) *Finance Capitalism Unveiled*, Ann Arbor, MI: University of Michigan Press.

Dekker, W. (1985) *Europe 1990*, Speech by the President of Philips at the Centre for European Policy Studies in Brussels, 11 January.

Dekker, W. (1990) 'Industrialists Drive for a Stronger Europe: Interview with Prof. Dr Wisse Dekker', *Europe 2000*, 2, 2 (March): 17–19.

Delors, J. (1989) 'Europe: Embarking on a New Course', *Contemporary European Affairs*, 1, 1, 2: 15–27.

Delors, J. (1992) [1988] *Our Europe*, London: Verso.

Dessler, D. (1989) 'What's at Stake in the Agent–Structure Debate?', *International Organization*, 43, 3: 440–73.

Devuyst, Y. (1995) 'The European Community and the Conclusion of the Uruguay Round', in: C. Rhodes and S. Mazey (eds), *The State of the European Union, Vol. 3: Building a European Polity?* Boulder, Colo.: Lynne Rienner, pp. 431–49.

DiMaggio, P.J., and W.W. Powell (1991) 'Introduction', in: W.W. Powell and P.J. DiMaggio (eds), *The New Institutionalism in Organizational Analysis*, Chicago and London: Chicago University Press, pp. 1–40.

Domhoff, G.W. (1979) *Processes of Ruling Class Domination in America*, New York: Vintage Books.

Drouin, M., M. Ernst, and J.W. Wheeler (1987) *Western European Adjustment to Structural Economic Problems*, Lanham, Md: University Press of America.

Dumont, A. (1990) 'Technology, Competitiveness and Cooperation in Europe', in M.S. Steinberg (ed.), *The Technical Challenges and Opportunities of a United Europe*, London: Pinter, pp. 68–79.

Dunning, J. (1993a) *Multinational Enterprises and the Global Economy*, Wokingham: Addison-Wesley.

Dunning, J. (1993b) *The Globalisation of Business*, London/New York: Routledge.

Eagleton, T. (1991) *Ideology: An Introduction*, London/New York: Verso.

Ebbinghaus, B., and A. Hassel (1999) *Striking Deals: Concertation in the Reform of Continental European Welfare States*, MPIfG Discussion Paper 99/3, Cologne: Max Planck Institute for the Study of Societies.

Eden, L. (1991) 'Bringing the Firm Back In: Multinationals in International Political Economy', *Millennium*, 20, 2: 197–224.

ERT (1983) *Foundations for the Future of European Industry*, Memorandum to EC Commissioner Davignon, 10 June.

ERT (1985) *Changing Scales*, Paris: European Roundtable of Industrialists.

ERT (1986) *Making Europe Work*, Paris: European Roundtable of Industrialists.

ERT (1988) *Keeping Europe Mobile*, Brussels: European Roundtable of Industrialists.

ERT (1989a) *Education and European Competence*, Brussels: European Roundtable of Industrialists.

ERT (1989b) *Need for Renewing Transport Infrastructure*, Brussels: European Roundtable of Industrialists.

ERT (1990) *European Labour Markets: Employment Policies in Europe for the 1990s*, Brussels: European Roundtable of Industrialists.

ERT (1991a) *Missing Networks: A European Challenge (proposals for the renewal of Europe's infrastructure)*, Brussels: European Roundtable of Industrialists.

ERT (1991b) *Reshaping Europe* (prepared by J. Monod, P. Gyllenhammar, and W. Dekker), Brussels: European Roundtable of Industrialists.

ERT (1992a) *Growing Together: One Infrastructure for Europe*, Brussels: European Roundtable of Industrialists.

ERT (1992b) *Lifelong Learning*, Brussels: European Roundtable of Industrialists.

ERT (1993a) *European Industry: A Partner of the Developing World*, Brussels: European Roundtable of Industrialists.

ERT (1993b) *European Labour Markets: An Update on Perspectives and Requirements for Job Generation in the Second Half of the 1990s*, Brussels: European Roundtable of Industrialists.

ERT (1993c) *Beating the Crisis: A Charter for Europe's Industrial Future*, Brussels: European Roundtable of Industrialists.

ERT (1994a) *European Industry and the Developing World: A Dialogue between Partners*, Brussels: European Roundtable of Industrialists.

ERT (1994b) *Building the Information Highways*, Brussels: European Roundtable of Industrialists.

ERT (1994c) *European Competitiveness: The Way to Growth and Jobs*, Brussels: European Roundtable of Industrialists.

ERT (1994d) *The Climate Change Debate*, Brussels: European Roundtable of Industrialists.

ERT (1995a) *Education for Europeans: Towards the Learning Society*, Brussels: European Roundtable of Industrialists.

ERT (1995b) *Moving Towards a Learning Society*, Brussels: European Roundtable of Industrialists.

ERT (1996) *Benchmarking for Policy-makers: The Way to Competitiveness, Growth and Job Creation*, Brussels: European Roundtable of Industrialists.

ERT (1997a) *A Stimulus to Job Creation*, Brussels: European Roundtable of Industrialists.

ERT (1997b) *Climate Change: ERT Report on Positive Action*, Brussels: European Roundtable of Industrialists.

ERT (1998) *Job Creation and Competitiveness through Innovation*, Brussels: European Roundtable of Industrialists.

ERT (1999) *The East–West Win–Win Business Experience*, Brussels: European Roundtable of Industrialists.

European Commission (1993) *Panorama of EC Industry 1993*, Luxembourg: Office for Official Publications of the European Communities.

European Commission (1994) *Growth, Competitiveness, Employment: The Challenges and Ways Forward into the 21st Century*, White Paper, Luxembourg: Office for Official Publications of the European Communities.

European Commission (1995) *Teaching and Learning: Towards the Learning Society* (White Paper on Education and Training), Brussels, Com (95) 590 final, 29 November.

European Commission (1996) *Benchmarking the Competitiveness of European Industry*, Brussels, Com (96) 436 final, 9 October.

European Commission (1997a) *The Competitiveness of European Industry* (based on the working document of Commission services), Luxembourg: Office for Official Publications of the European Communities.

European Commission (1997b) *Benchmarking: Implementation of an Instrument Available to Economic Actors and Public Authorities*, Brussels, Com (97) 153/2 final, 16 April.

European Commission (1999a) *The European Employment Strategy: Investing in People*, Luxembourg: Office for the Official Publications of the European Communities.

European Commission (1999b) *Implementing the Framework for Financial Markets: Action Plan*, Com (1999) 232, 11 May.

European Commission (2000a) *Recommendation for a Council Recommendation on the Implementation of Member States' Employment Policies*. Brussels, Com (2000) (online: http://www.europa.eu.int/comm/employment_social/empl&esf/news/recommend00_en.htm, accessed: 12 February 2001)

European Commission (2000b) *Joint Employment Report 2000* (online: http://www.europa.eu.int/comm/employment_social/empl&esf/ees_en.htm, accessed 17 September 2001).

European Commission (2001) *Eurobarometer*, *Report No. 54*, Brussels: Directorate-General Press and Communication (April).

Fennema, M. (1982) *International Networks of Banks and Industry*, The Hague/Boston/London: Martinus Nijhoff.

Ferrera, M., A. Hemerijck, and M. Rhodes (2000) *The Future of Social Europe: Recasting Work and Welfare in the New Economy – Report for the Portuguese Presidency of the European Union* (available online: http://www.iue.it/SPS/Staff/Rhodes/Welcome.html, accessed: 17 September 2001)

Fielder, N. (1997) *Western European Integration in the 1980s: The Origins of the Single Market*, Bern/Frankfurt: Peter Lang.

Fielder, N. (2000) 'The Origins of the Single Market', in: V. Bornschier (ed.), *State-Building in Europe: The Revitalization of Western European Integration*, Cambridge: Cambridge University Press, pp. 75–92.

French Memorandum (1983) 'Memorandum on a Common Industrial and Research Area', reproduced in 'Europe Documents', *Agence Europe*, 16 September.

Frieden, J.A. (1991) 'Invested Interests: The Politics of National Economic Policies in a World of Global Finance', *International Organization*, 45, 4: 425–51.

Friedland, R., and R.R. Alford (1991) 'Bringing Society Back In', in: W.W. Powell and P.J. DiMaggio (eds), *The New Institutionalism in Organizational Analysis*, Chicago and London: Chicago University Press, pp. 232–66.

Friedman, M., and R. Friedman (1980) *Free to Choose*, London: Secker and Warburg.

Gardner, J.N. (1991) *Effective Lobbying in the European Community*, Deventer: Kluwer.

Garret, G. (1992) 'International Cooperation and Institutional Choice: The European Community's Market', *International Organization*, 46, 2: 533–60.

Geyer, R. (1993) 'Socialism and the EC After Maastricht: From Classic to New-model European Social Democracy', in: A.W. Cafruny and G.G. Rosenthal (eds), *The State of The European Community*, vol. 2, Boulder, Colo.: Lynne Rienner Publishers, pp. 91–106.

Giddens, A. (1979) *Central Problems in Social Theory: Action, Structure and Contradiction in Social Analysis*, London: Macmillan.

Giddens, A. (1981) *A Contemporary Critique of Historical Materialism*, London: Macmillan.

Giddens, A. (1985) *The Constitution of Society*, Cambridge: Polity Press.

Giddens, A. (1990) *The Consequences of Modernity*, Cambridge: Polity Press.

Gill, S. (1990) *American Hegemony and the Trilateral Commission*, Cambridge: Cambridge University Press.

Gill, S. (1998) 'European Governance and New Constitutionalism: Economic and Monetary Union and Alternatives to Disciplinary Neo-liberalism in Europe', *New Political Economy*, 3, 1: 5–26.

Gill, S. (ed.) (1993) *Gramsci, Historical Materialism and International Relations*, Cambridge: Cambridge University Press.

Gill, S., and D. Law (1993) 'Global Hegemony and the Structural Power of Capital', in: S. Gill (ed.), *Gramsci, Historical Materialism and International Relations*, Cambridge: Cambridge University Press, pp. 93–124.

Gilpin, R. (1987) *The Political Economy of International Relations*, Princeton, NJ: Princeton University Press.

Goldstein, J., and R.O. Keohane (eds) (1993) *Ideas and Foreign Policy: Beliefs, Institutions, and Political Change*, Ithaca, NY/London: Cornell University Press.

Goldstein, W. (1993) 'The EC: Capitalist or *Dirigiste* Regime?', in: A.W. Cafruny and G.G. Rosenthal (eds), *The State of the European Community*, vol. 2, Boulder, Colo.: Lynne Rienner, pp. 303–19.

Goodman, J.B., and L.W. Pauly (1993) 'The Obsolescence of Capital Controls: Economic Management in an Age of Global Markets', *World Politics*, 46, 1: 50–82.

Gordon, D. (1988) 'The Global Economy: New Edifice or Crumbling Foundations?', *New Left Review*, 164: 26–64.

Gourevitch, P.A. (1978) 'The Second Image Reversed: International Sources of Domestic Politics', *International Organization*, 32, 4: 881–911.

Gourevitch, P.A. (1986) *Politics in Hard Times: Comparative Responses to International Economic Crises*, Ithaca, NY: Cornell University Press.

Grahl, J., and P. Teague (1990) *The Big Market: The Future of the European Community*, London: Lawrence and Wishart.

Gramsci, A. (1971) *Selections from the Prison Notebooks of Antonio Gramsci* (translated and edited by Q. Hoare and G. Nowell Smith), London: Lawrence and Wishart.

Grant, C. (1994) *Delors: Inside the House that Jacques Built*, London: Nicholas Brealey Publishing.

Grant, W., A. Martinelli, and W. Paterson (1989) 'Large Firms as Political Actors: A Comparative Analysis of the Chemical Industry in Britain, Italy and West Germany', *West European Politics*, 12, 2: 72–90.

Green, M.L. (1993) *The Politics of Big Business in the Single Market Programme*, Paper presented to the European Community Studies Association, Third Biennial International Conference, Washington, DC, 27 May.

Greenwood, J. (1997) *Representing Interests in the European Union*, London: Macmillan.

Greenwood, J., J. Grote, and K. Ronit (1992) 'Introduction: Organized Interests and the Transnational Dimension', in: J. Greenwood, J. Grote, and K. Ronit (eds), *Organized Interests and the European Community*, Newbury Park, Calif.: Sage, pp. 1–41.

Gyllenhammar, P. (1982) 'Viewpoint', *International Management*, European edition (July).

Haas, E.B. (1968) [1958, with 1968 preface] *The Uniting of Europe: Political, Social and Economic Forces, 1950–1957*, Stanford, Calif.: Stanford University Press.

Haas, E.B. (1975) *The Obsolescence of Regional Integration Theory*, Berkeley, Calif.: Institute of International Studies (University of California).

Hall, P.A. (1986) *Governing the Economy: The Politics of State Intervention in Britain and France*, Cambridge: Polity Press.

Hall, P.A. (1993) 'Policy Paradigms, Social Learning and the State: The Case of Economic Policymaking in Britain', *Comparative Politics*, 25, 3: 275–96.

Hall, P.A. (1998) *Organized Market Economies and Unemployment in Europe: Is it Finally Time to*

Accept Liberal Orthodoxy? Paper presented at the 11th International Conference of Europeanists, Baltimore, 26–28 February.

Hall, P.A., and D. Soskice (eds) (2001) *Varieties of Capitalism*, Oxford: Oxford University Press.

Hanson, B.T. (1998) 'What Happened to Fortress Europe? External Trade Policy Liberalisation in the European Union', *International Organization*, 52, 1: 55–85.

Harvey, D. (1982) *The Limits to Capital*, Oxford: Basil Blackwell.

Harvey, D. (1989) *The Condition of Postmodernity: An Enquiry into the Origins of Cultural Change*, Cambridge, Mass./Oxford: Blackwell Publishers.

Hayward, J. (1995) 'Europe's Endangered Industrial Champions', in: J. Hayward (ed.), *Industrial Enterprise and European Integration*, Oxford: Oxford University Press, pp. 1–20.

Helleiner, E. (1993) 'When Finance was the Servant: International Capital Movements in the Bretton Woods Order', in Ph.G. Cerny (ed.), *Finance and World Politics*, Cheltenham: Edward Elgar.

Hettne, B. (1992) *The Double Movement: Global Market versus Regionalism*, Paper for the UNU Symposium on 'Multilateralism and Images of World Order', Florence, 30 Sept.–13 Oct.

High Level Group on Benchmarking (1999) 'First Report by the High Level Group on Benchmarking', *Benchmarking Papers*, No. 2, Brussels: European Commission, Directorate-General III.

Hildebrand, D. (1992) 'The Restructuring Process in Central and Eastern Europe: Business Strategies for EC Companies', *West European Politics*, 15, 2: 147–59.

Hirst, P., and G. Thompson (1996) *Globalisation in Question*, Cambridge: Polity Press.

Hix, S. (1994) 'The Study of the European Community: The Challenge to Comparative Politics', *West European Politics*, 17, 1: 1–30.

Hix, S. (1998) 'The Study of the European Union II: The "New Governance Agenda" and Its Rival', *Journal of European Public Policy*, 5, 1: 38–65.

Hix, S. (1999) *The Political System of the European Union*, London: Macmillan.

Hodges, M., and S. Woolcock (1993) 'Atlantic Capitalism versus Rhine Capitalism in the European Community', *West European Politics*, 16, 3: 329–44.

Hoffmann, S. (1966) 'Obstinate or Obsolete: The Fate of the Nation-state and the Case of Western Europe', *Daedalus*, 95: 862–915.

Hoffmann, S. (1982) 'Reflections on the Nation-state in Western Europe Today', *Journal of Common Market Studies*, 21: 21–37.

Holland, S. (1995) 'Squaring the Circle', *European Labour Forum (ELF)*, 15 (Summer).

Hollingsworth, J.R., Ph.C. Schmitter, and W. Streeck (1994) 'Capitalism, Sectors, Institutions, and Performance', in: J.R Hollingsworth, Ph.C. Schmitter, and W. Streeck (eds), *Governing Capitalist Economies: Performance and Control in Economic Sectors*, New York/Oxford: Oxford University Press, pp. 3–16.

Hollingsworth, J.R., Ph.C. Schmitter, and W. Streeck (eds) (1994) *Governing Capitalist Economies: Performance and Control in Economic Sectors*, New York/Oxford: Oxford University Press.

Hollis, M., and S. Smith (1991) 'Beware of Gurus. Structure and Action in International Relations', *Review of International Studies*, 17: 393–410.

Holman, O. (1992) 'Transnational Class Strategy and the New Europe', *International Journal of Political Economy*, 22, 1: 3–22.

Holman, O. (1993) *Integrating Southern Europe: EC Expansion and the Transnationalization of Spain*, Unpublished dissertation, University of Amsterdam.

Holman, O. (1996) *Integrating Southern Europe: EC Expansion and the Transnationalization of Spain*, London and New York: Routledge.

Holman, O. (2001) 'The Enlargement of the European Union Towards Central and Eastern Europe: The Role of Supranational and Transnational Actors', in: A. Bieler and A.D. Morton (eds), *Social Forces in the Making of the New Europe*, Basingstoke: Palgrave, pp. 161–84.

Holman, O., and K. van der Pijl (1992) *Restructuring the Ruling Class and European Unification*, Amsterdam International Studies, Working Paper No. 28, Maarssen: CEPS.

Hooghe, L., and G. Marks (1999) 'The Making of a Polity: The Struggle over European Integration', in: H. Kitschelt *et al.* (eds), *Continuity and Change in Contemporary Capitalism*, Cambridge and New York: Cambridge University Press, pp. 70–97.

Hoogvelt, A., and M. Yuasa (1994) 'Going Lean or Going Native? The Social Regulation of "Lean" Production Systems', *Review of International Political Economy*, 1, 2: 281–303.

Jacquemin, A., and L.R. Pench (eds) (1997) *Europe Competing in the Global Economy: Reports of the Competitiveness Advisory Group*, Aldershot: Edward Elgar.

Jessop, B. (1983) 'Accumulation Strategies, State Forms, and Hegemonic Projects', *Kapitalistate*, 10, 11: 89–111.

Jessop, B. (1991) 'Thatcherism and Flexibility: The White Heat of a Post-Fordist Revolution', in: B. Jessop et al. (eds), *The Politics of Flexibility: Restructuring State and Industry in Britain, Germany and Scandinavia*, Aldershot: Edward Elgar, pp. 135–61.

Jessop, B. (1992) *Changing Forms and Functions of the State in an Era of Globalization and Regionalization*, Paper presented at EAPE Conference, Paris, 4–7 November.

Johnson, M. (1989) '"Dutch Cool" Profile of Wisse Dekker', *International Management* (September).

Kalecki, M. (1990) [1943] 'Political Aspects of Full Employment', in: *Collected Works of Michal Kalecki, Volume 1: Capitalism: Business Cycles and Full Employment*, Oxford: Clarendon Press.

Katzenstein, P. (1985) *Small States in World Markets: Industrial Policy in Europe*, Ithaca, NY: Cornell University Press.

Keohane, R.O. (1984a) *After Hegemony: Cooperation and Discord in the World Political Economy*, Princeton, NJ: Princeton University Press.

Keohane, R.O. (1984b) 'The World Political Economy and the Crisis of Embedded Liberalism', in: J.H. Goldthorpe (ed.), *Order and Conflict in Contemporary Capitalism: Studies in the Political Economy of Western European Nations*, New York: Oxford University Press, pp. 15–38.

Keohane, R.O. (1988) 'International Institutions: Two Approaches', *International Studies Quarterly*, 32, 4: 379–96.

Keohane, R.O. (1989) *International Institutions and State Power*, Boulder, Colo.: Westview Press.

Keohane, R.O., and S. Hoffmann (1991) 'Institutional Change in Europe in the 1980s', in: R.O. Keohane and S. Hoffmann (eds), *The New European Community, Decisionmaking and Institutional Change*, Boulder, Colo.: Westview Press, pp. 1–39.

Keohane, R.O., and H.V. Milner (1996) 'Internationalization and Domestic Politics: An Introduction', in R.O. Keohane and H.V. Milner (eds), *Internationalization and Domestic Politics*, Cambridge: Cambridge University Press, pp. 3–24.

Keohane, R.O., and J.S. Nye (eds) (1972) *Transnational Relations and World Politics*, Cambridge, Mass.: Harvard University Press.

Keohane, R.O., and J.S. Nye (1977) *Power and Interdependence*, Boston: Little Brown.

Kozul-Wright, R. (1995) 'Transnational Corporations and the Nation State', in: J. Michie and J. Grieve Smith (eds), *Managing the Global Economy*, Oxford: Oxford University Press, pp. 135–71.

Krasner, S.D. (1995) 'Power Politics, Institutions, and Transnational Relations', in: T. Risse-Kappen (ed.), *Bringing Transnational Relations Back In: Non-state Actors, Domestic Structures, and International Institutions*, Cambridge: Cambridge University Press, pp. 257–79.

Krause, A. (1991) *Inside the New Europe*, New York: HarperCollins.

Krause, A. (1992) 'The People Behind a Unified Europe: Ten Leaders Who Helped Move Europe to 1992', in: *Europe*, EC Commission Office, Washington, DC (January/February): 8–12.

Laclau, E. (1977) *Politics and Ideology in Marxist Theory: Capitalism, Fascism, Populism*, London: New Left Books.

Laclau, E., and C. Mouffe (1985) *Hegemony and Socialist Strategy*, London: Verso.

Lambert, J. (1991) 'Europe: The Nation-state Dies Hard', *Capital & Class*, 43: 9–24.

Lannoo, K. (1999) 'A European Perspective on Corporate Governance', *Journal of Common Market Studies*, 37, 2: pp. 269–94.

Lanzalaco, L. (1992) 'Coping with Heterogeneity: Peak Associations of Business Within and Across Western European Nations', in: J. Greenwood, J. Grote, and K. Ronit (eds), *Organized Interests and the European Community*, Newbury Park, Calif.: Sage, pp. 173–205.

La Porta, R. et al. (1998) *Corporate Ownership Around the World*, Cambridge, Mass.: National Bureau of Economic Research, Working Paper, W6625 (June).

Larrain, J. (1983) *Marxism and Ideology*, London: Macmillan.

Lash, S., and J. Urry (1987) *The End of Organized Capitalism*, Cambridge: Polity Press.

Lazonick, W., and M. O'Sullivan (2000) 'Maximizing Shareholder Value: A New Ideology for Corporate Governance', *Economy and Society*, 29, 1: 13–35.

Lindberg, L.N. (1963) *The Political Dynamics of European Integration*, Stanford, Calif./London: Stanford University Press/Oxford University Press.

Lindblom, C. (1977) *Politics and Markets: The World's Political-economic Systems*, New York: Basic Books.

Lipietz, A. (1982) 'Towards Global Fordism,' *New Left Review*, 132: 33–47.

Lipietz, A. (1987) *Mirages and Miracles: The Crises of Global Fordism*, London: Verso.

McLaughlin, A.M., G. Jordan, and W.A. Maloney (1993) 'Corporate Lobbying in the European Community', *Journal of Common Market Studies*, 31, 2: 191–212.

Madeuf, B., and C. Michalet (1979) 'A New Approach to International Economics', *International Social Science Journal*, 30, 2: 253–83.

Marceau, J. (1989) 'France', in: T. Bottomore and R.J. Brym (eds), *The Capitalist Class: An International Study*, London: Harvester Wheatsheaf.

Marks, G. (1993) 'Structural Policy and Multilevel Governance in the EC', in: A.W. Cafruny and G.G. Rosenthal (eds), *The State of the European Community*, vol. 2, Boulder, Colo.: Lynne Rienner, pp. 391–410.

Marks, G., L. Hooghe, and K. Blank (1996) 'European Integration from the 1980s: State-centric versus Multi-level Governance', *Journal of Common Market Studies*, 34, 3: 341–78.

Marquand, D. (1994) 'Reinventing Federalism: Europe and the Left', *New Left Review*, 203: 17–26.

Marshall, G. (1997) *Repositioning Class: Social Inequality in Industrial Societies*, London/Thousand Oaks/New Dehli: Sage.

Martin, A., and G. Ross (1999) 'Europe's Monetary Union: Creating a Democratic Deficit?', *Current History*, 98, 627 (April): 171–75.

Martinelli, A. (ed.) (1991) *International Markets and Global Firms: A Comparative Study of Organized Business in the Chemical Industry*, London: Sage.

Marx, K., and F. Engels (1978) *The Marx–Engels Reader* (Second Edition), edited by R.C. Tucker, New York/London: Norton.

Mazey, S., and J. Richardson (1993a) 'Introduction: Transference of Power, Decision Rules, and Rules of the Game', in: S. Mazey and J. Richardson (eds), *Lobbying in the European Community*, Oxford: Oxford University Press, pp. 3–26.

Mazey, S., and J. Richardson (1993b) 'Conclusion: A European Policy Style?', in: S. Mazey and J. Richardson (eds), *Lobbying in the European Community*, Oxford: Oxford University Press, pp. 246–58.

Mazier, J. (1982) 'Growth and Crisis: A Marxist Interpretation', in: A. Boltho (ed.), *The European Economy: Growth and Crisis*, Oxford: Oxford University Press, pp. 38–71.

Merrit, G. (1986) 'Knights of the Roundtable: Can they Move Europe Forward Fast Enough?', *International Management* (July).

Miliband, R. (1989) *Divided Societies: Class Struggle in Contemporary Capitalism*, Oxford: Clarendon Press.

Moravcsik, A. (1991) 'Negotiating the Single European Act', in: R.O. Keohane and S. Hoffmann (eds), *The New European Community, Decisionmaking and Institutional Change*, Boulder, Colo.: Westview Press, pp. 41–84.

Moravcsik, A. (1993a) 'Preferences and Power in the European Community: A Liberal Intergovernmentalist Approach', *Journal of Common Market Studies*, 31, 4: 473–524.

Moravcsik, A. (1993b) 'Integrating International and Domestic Theories of International Bargaining', in: P.B. Evans, H.K. Jacobson, and R.D. Putnam (eds), *Double-edged Diplomacy: International Bargaining and Domestic Politics*, Berkeley, Calif.: University of California.

Moravcsik, A. (1998) *The Choice for Europe: Social Purpose and State Power from Messina to Maastricht*, Ithaca, NY: Cornell University Press.

Moravcsik, A. (1999) 'Is Something Rotten in the State of Denmark? Constructivism and European Integration', *Journal of European Public Policy*, 6, 4 (Special Issue): 669–81.

Mouffe, C. (1979) 'Hegemony and Ideology in Gramsci', in: C. Mouffe (ed.), *Gramsci and Marxist Theory*, London: Routledge and Kegan Paul, pp. 168–204.

Nestor, S., and J. Thompson (1999) *Corporate Governance Patterns in OECD Economies: Is Convergence Under Way?* Paper for OECD Conference on 'Corporate Governance in Asia: A Comparative Perspective', Seoul, 3–5 March.

Nollert, M. (2000) 'Lobbying for a Europe of Big Business: The European Roundtable of Industrialists', in: V. Bornschier (ed.), *State-building in Europe: The Revitalization of Western European Integration*, Cambridge: Cambridge University Press, pp. 187–209.

Nunnenkamp, P., E. Gundlach, and J.P. Agarwal (1994) *Globalisation of Production and Markets*, Tübingen: Mohr (Kieler Studien, 262).

OECD (1998) 'Shareholder Value and the Market in Corporate Control in OECD Countries', *Financial Market Trends*, 69 (February): 15–37.

OECD (1999) 'Impact of the Euro on Financial Markets', *Financial Market Trends*, 72 (March): 21–37.

Offe, C., and H. Wiesenthal (1979) 'Two Logics of Collective Action: Theoretical Notes on Social Class and Organizational Form', *Political Power and Social Theory*, 1: 67–115.

Ohmae, K. (1985) *'Triad' De Opkomst van Mondiale Concurrentie*, Utrecht/Antwerp: Veen.

Onuf, N.G. (1989) *World of Our Making: Rules and Rule in Social Theory and International Relations*, Columbia, SC: University of South Carolina Press.

Overbeek, H. (1990) *Global Capitalism and National Decline: The Thatcher Decade in Perspective*, London: Unwin Hyman.

Overbeek, H. (ed.) (1993) *Restructuring Hegemony in the Global Political Economy: The Rise of Transnational Neo-liberalism in the 1980s*, London: Routledge.

Overbeek, H., and K. van der Pijl (1993) 'Restructuring Capital and Restructuring Hegemony: Neo-liberalism and the Unmaking of the Post-war Order', in: H. Overbeek (ed.), *Restructuring Hegemony in the Global Political Economy: The Rise of Transnational Neo-liberalism in the 1980s*, London: Routledge, pp. 1–27.

Overkleeft, D., and L.E. Groosman (1987) *Het Dekker Perspectief*, Deventer/Utrecht: Kluwer/Veen.

Padoa-Schioppa, T. (1985) *Money, Economic Policy and Europe*, Luxembourg: Office for Official Publications of the European Communities.

Pakulski, J., and M. Waters (1996) *The Death of Class*, London: Sage.

Palloix, C. (1977) 'The Self-expansion of Capital on a World Scale', *Review of Radical Political Economics*, 9: 1–28.

Pearce, J., and J. Sutton (1986) *Protection and Industrial Policy in Europe*, London: Routledge and Kegan Paul.

Pierson, P. (1998) 'The Path to European Integration: A Historical–Institutionalist Analysis', in: W. Sandholtz and A. Stone Sweet (eds), *European Integration and Supranational Governance*, Oxford: Oxford University Press, pp. 27–58.

Piore, M.J., and C.F. Sabel (1984) *The Second Industrial Divide: Possibilities for Prosperity*, New York: Basic Books.

Polanyi, K. (1957) *The Great Transformation: The Political and Economic Origins of Our Time*, Boston: Beacon.

Pooley, S. (1991) 'The State Rules, OK? The Continuing Political Economy of Nation-states', *Capital & Class*, 43: 65–82.

Poulantzas, N. (1973) *Political Power and Social Classes*, London: New Left Books.

Poulantzas, N. (1978) [1974] *Classes in Contemporary Capitalism*, London: Verso.

Reich, R. (1992) *The Work of Nations: Preparing Ourselves for 21st-century Capitalism*, New York: Random House.

Rhodes, M. (1991) 'The Social Dimension of the Single European Market: National versus Transnational Regulation', *European Journal of Political Research*, 19, 2/3: 245–80.

Rhodes, M. (1992) 'The Future of the "Social Dimension": Labour Market Regulation in Post-1992 Europe', *Journal of Common Market Studies*, 30, 1: 23–51.

Rhodes, M. (1997) *Globalisation, Labour Markets and Welfare States: A Future of 'Competitive Corporatism'?* Florence: European University Institute, EUI Working Papers: Robert Schuman Centre, 97/36.

Rhodes, M. (2000) 'Globalization, Welfare States and Employment: Is There a European "Third Way"?' (available online: http://www.iue.it/SPS/Staff/Rhodes/Welcome.html, accessed: 17 September 2001), forthcoming in N. Bermeo (ed.), *Unemployment in the New Europe*, Cambridge: Cambridge University Press.

Rhodes, M., and M. Ferrera (2000) 'Recasting European Welfare States: An Introduction', *West European Politics*, 23, 2: 1–10.

Rhodes, M., and B. van Apeldoorn (1997) 'Capitalism versus Capitalism in Western Europe', in M. Rhodes, P. Heywood, and V. Wright (eds), *Developments in West European Politics*, London: Macmillan, pp. 171–89.

Rhodes, M., and B. van Apeldoorn (1998) 'Capital Unbound? The Transformation of European Corporate Governance', *Journal of European Public Policy*, 5, 3: 406–27.

Richardson, K. (1989) 'Europe's Industrialists Help Shape the Single Market', *Europe*, EC Commission Office, Washington, DC (December).

Risse, T., and A. Wiener (1999) ' "Something Rotten" and the Social Construction of Social Constructivism: A Comment on the Comments', *Journal of European Public Policy*, 6, 5: 775–82.

Risse-Kappen, T. (1994) 'Ideas Do Not Float Freely: Transnational Coalitions, Domestic Structures, and the End of the Cold War', *International Organization*, 48, 2: 185–214.

Risse-Kappen, T. (1995) 'Bringing Transnational Relations Back In: Introduction', in: T. Risse-Kappen (ed.), *Bringing Transnational Relations Back In: Non-state Actors, Domestic Structures, and International Institutions*, Cambridge: Cambridge University Press, pp. 3–36.

Risse-Kappen, T. (ed.) (1995) *Bringing Transnational Relations Back In: Non-state Actors, Domestic Structures, and International Institutions*, Cambridge: Cambridge University Press.

Risse-Kappen, T. (1996) 'Exploring the Nature of the Beast: International Relations Theory and Comparative Policy Analysis Meet the European Union', *Journal of Common Market Studies*, 34, 1: 53–80.

Rosamond, B. (1999) 'Discourses of Globalization and the Social Construction of European Identities', *Journal of European Public Policy*, 6, 4 (Special Issue): 652–88.

Ross, G. (1993) 'Sliding into Industrial Policy: Inside the European Commission', *French Politics & Society*, 11, 1: 20–44.

Ross, G. (1995) *Jacques Delors and European Integration*, Cambridge: Polity Press.

Ruggie, J.G. (1982) 'International Regimes, Transactions and Change: Embedded Liberalism in the Postwar Economic Order', *International Organization*, 36, 2: 379–416.

Ruggie, J.G. (1993) 'Territoriality and Beyond: Problematizing Modernity in International Relations', *International Organization*, 47, 1: 139–74.

Ruigrok, W., and R. van Tulder (1995) *The Logic of International Restructuring*, London and New York: Routledge.

Rupert, M. (1993) 'Alienation, Capitalism, and the Inter-state System: Towards a Marxian/Gramscian Critique', in: S. Gill (ed.), *Gramsci, Historical Materialism and International Relations*, Cambridge: Cambridge University Press, pp. 67–92.

Rupert, M. (1995) *Producing Hegemony: The Politics of Mass Production and American Global Power*, Cambridge: Cambridge University Press.

Ryner, M. (1994) *The Political Economy of Globalisation and the Crisis of the Swedish Model*, Paper presented at a conference on 'Labour and Social Policy', Stockholm, Sweden, 16–19 May.

Ryner, M. (2000) 'Der neue Diskurs über den "Dritten Weg": zur Dynamik des sozialdemokratischen Neoliberalismus', in: H.-J. Bieling and J. Steinhilber (eds), *Die Konfiguration Europas: Dimensionen einer kritischen Integrationstheorie*, Münster: Westfälisches Dampfboot, pp. 243–75.

Sally, R. (1994) 'Multinational Enterprises, Political Economy and Institutional Theory: Domestic Embeddedness in the Context of Internationalization', *Review of International Political Economy*, 1, 1: 161–92.

Sandholtz, W. (1992) *High-tech Europe: The Politics of International Integration*, Berkeley, Calif.: California University Press.

Sandholtz, W. (1993) 'Choosing Union: Monetary Politics and Maastricht', *International Organization*, 47, 1: 1–39.

Sandholtz, W., and A. Stone Sweet (eds) (1998) *European Integration and Supranational Governance*, Oxford: Oxford University Press.

Sandholtz, W., and J. Zysman (1989) '1992: Recasting the European Bargain', *World Politics*, 42, 5–128.

Savary, J. (1993) 'European Integration, Globalisation and Industrial Location in Europe', in: H. Cox, J. Clegg and G. Ietto-Gillies (eds), *The Growth of Global Business*, London and New York: Routledge, pp. 150–79.

Scharpf, F.W. (1999a) 'Forum: Approaches to the Study of European Politics', *ECSA Review*, XII, 2 (Spring): 2–9, available online: http://www.eustudies.org/rationalchoice.html (accessed: 8 August 2001).

Scharpf, F.W. (1999b) *Governing in Europe: Effective and Democratic?*, Oxford: Oxford University Press.

Schmidt, V.A. (1996) 'Loosening the Ties that Bind: The Impact of European Integration on French Government and its Relationship to Business', *Journal of Common Market Studies*, 34, 2: 223–51.

Schmitter, Ph.C. (1991) *The European Community as an Emergent and Novel Form of Political Domination*, Estudio/Working Paper 1991/26 (September), Madrid: Centro de Estudios Avanzados en Ciencias Sociales, Fundacion Juan March.

Scott, J. (1997) *Corporate Business and Capitalist Classes*, New York: Oxford University Press.

Servan-Schreiber, J.J. (1967). *Le Défi americain*, Paris: Denouel.

Sharp, M. (1990) 'Technology and the Dynamics of Integration', in: W. Wallace (ed.), *The Dynamics of European Integration*, London and New York: Pinter, pp. 50–68.

Smith, S. (1999) 'Social Constructivism and European Studies: A Reflectivist Critique', *Journal of European Public Policy*, 6, 4 (Special Issue): 682–91.

Soskice, D. (1999) 'Divergent Production Regimes: Coordinated and Uncoordinated Market Economies in the 1980s and 1990s', in: H. Kitschelt et al. (eds), *Continuity and Change in Contemporary Capitalism*, Cambridge and New York: Cambridge University Press, pp. 101–34.

Spohn, W., and Y.M. Bodemann (1989) 'Germany', in: T. Bottomore and R.J. Brym (eds), *The Capitalist Class: An International Study*, London: Harvester Wheatsheaf.

Stafford, D.C., and R.H.A. Purkins (1989) *Macmillan Directory of Multinationals* (2 vols), London: Macmillan.

Steinberg, M.S. (ed.) (1990) *The Technical Challenges and Opportunities of a United Europe*, London: Pinter.

Stern, P. (1997) *The Transatlantic Business Dialogue: New Paradigm for Trade Expansion and Regulatory Harmonisation*, Testimony presented before the House Committee on International Relations, Subcommittee on International Economic Policy and Trade, 10 September, mimeo.

Stone, N. (1989) 'The Globalization of Europe: An Interview with Wisse Dekker', *Harvard Business Review* (May–June).

Stone Sweet, A. and J.A. Caporaso (1998) 'From Free Trade to Supranational Polity: The European Court and Integration', in: W. Sandholtz and A. Stone Sweet (eds), *European Integration and Supranational Governance*, Oxford: Oxford University Press, pp. 92–132.

Stone Sweet, A. and W. Sandholtz (1998) 'Integration, Supranational Governance, and the Institutionalization of the European Polity', in: W. Sandholtz and A. Stone Sweet (eds), *European Integration and Supranational Governance*, Oxford: Oxford University Press, pp. 1–26.

Stopford, J. (1992) *Directory of Multinationals* (2 vols), New York: Stockton Press (Macmillan).

Stopford, J., and S. Strange (1991) *Rival States, Rival Firms: Competition for World Market Shares*, Cambridge: Cambridge University Press.

Story, J., and I. Walter (1997) *Political Economy of Financial Integration in Europe: The Battle of the Systems*, Manchester: Manchester University Press.

Strange, S. (1986) *Casino Capitalism*, Oxford: Basil Blackwell.

Strange, S. (1988) *States and Markets*, London: Pinter.

Strange, S. (1991) 'Big Business and the State', *Millennium*, 20, 2: 245–50.

Strange, S. (1996) *The Retreat of the State: The Diffusion of Power in the World Economy*, Cambridge: Cambridge University Press.

Streeck, W. (1984) 'Neo-corporatist Industrial Relations and the Economic Crisis in West Germany', in: J.H. Goldthorpe (ed.), *Order and Conflict in Contemporary Capitalism: Studies in the Political Economy of Western European Nations*, New York: Oxford University Press, pp. 291–315.

Streeck, W. (1992) *Social Institutions and Economic Performance: Studies in Industrial Relations in Advanced Capitalist Economies*, London and Beverley Hills, Calif.: Sage.

Streeck, W. (1993) *From Market-making to State-building? Reflections on the Political Economy of European Social Policy*, Paper presented at the 89th Annual Meeting of the American Sociological Association, Miami, Florida, 13–17 August.

Streeck, W. (1995) 'Neo-voluntarism: A New European Social Policy Regime?', *European Law Journal*, 1, 1: 31–59.

Streeck, W. (1997) 'German Capitalism: Does it Exist? Can it Survive?', *New Political Economy*, 2, 2: 237–56.

Streeck, W. (1998) *The Internationalization of Industrial Relations in Europe: Prospects and Problems*, MPIfG Discussion Paper 98/2, Cologne: Max Planck Institute for the Study of Societies.

Streeck, W. (1999) *Competitive Solidarity: Rethinking the 'European Social Model'*, MPIfG Working Paper 99/8, Cologne: Max Planck Institute for the Study of Societies.

Streeck, W., and Ph.C. Schmitter (1991) 'From National Corporatism to Transnational Pluralism: Organized Interests in the Single European Market', *Politics and Society*, 19, 2: 133–64.

Swann, D. (1983) *Competition and Industrial Policy in the European Community*, London and New York: Methuen.

Tabaksblat, M. (2000) *How to Achieve What is Set Out in Lisbon*, Speech at the European Business Summit, Brussels, 10 June (online: http://www.ert.be/pd/pdc/endc03thml, accessed: 13 January 2001).

Taylor, P. (1983) *The Limits of European Integration*, London: Croom Helm.

Therborn, G. (1978) *What Does the Ruling Class do When it Rules?*, London: NLB.

Therborn, G. (1980) *The Ideology of Power and the Power of Ideology*, London: Verso.

Thompson, E.P. (1980) [1963] *The Making of the English Working Class*, London: Penguin.

Thompson, J.E., and S.D. Krasner (1989) 'Global Transactions and the Consolidation of Sovereignty', in: E. Czempiel and J.N. Rosenau (eds), *Global Changes and Theoretical Challenges*, Lexington, Mass.: Lexington Books, pp. 195–219.

Tranholm-Mikkelsen, J. (1991) 'Neo-functionalism: Obstinate or Obsolete? A Reappraisal in the Light of the New Dynamism of the EC', *Millennium*, 20, 1: 1–22.

Traxler, F., and Ph.G. Schmitter (1995) 'The Emerging Euro-polity and Organized Interests', *European Journal of International Relations*, 1, 2: 191–218.

Tsoukalis, L. (1993) *The New European Economy*, Oxford: Oxford University Press.

UNCTAD (1988) *Transnational Corporations in World Development: Trends and Prospects*, New York: United Nations.

UNCTAD (1993) *World Investment Report 1993: Transnational Corporations and Integrated International Production*, Geneva: United Nations.

UNCTAD (1994) *World Investment Report 1994: Transnational Corporations, Employment, and the Workplace*, Geneva: United Nations.

UNCTAD (1995) *World Investment Report 1995: Transnational Corporations and Competitiveness*, Geneva: United Nations.

UNCTAD (1996) *World Investment Report 1996: Investment, Trade, and International Policy Arrangements*, Geneva: United Nations.

UNCTAD (2000a) *World Investment Report 2000: Cross-border Mergers and Acquisitions and Development, Executive Summary*, New York and Geneva: United Nations, http://www.unctad.org/wir/contents/wir00content.en.htm (date accessed: 2/08/01).

UNCTAD (2000b) *World Investment Report 2000: Cross-border Mergers and Acquisitions and Development, Executive Summary*, New York and Geneva: United Nations.

United Nations (Centre on Transnational Corporations) (1983) *Transnational Corporations in World Development: Third Survey*, New York: United Nations.

Van Apeldoorn, B. (1996) *The Political Economy of Conflicting Capitalisms in the European Integration Process: A Transnational Perspective*, Research Institute for European Studies (RIES), Athens, Research Paper 31.

Van Apeldoorn, B. (1999) Transnationalisation and the Restructuring of Europe's Socio-economic Order, *International Journal of Political Economy*, Special issue edited by H. Overbeek, M. Ryner, and O. Holman, 28, 1, pp. 12–53.

Van Apeldoorn, B. (2001) *Globalisation, European Integration, and the Transformation of European Corporate Governance: The Rise of a European Shareholder Capitalism*', Paper presented at the Annual Convention of the European Community Studies Association (ECSA), Madison,Wisconsin, 31 May–2 June.

Van Apeldoorn, B., and O. Holman (1994) *Transnational Class Strategy and the Relaunching of European Integration: The Role of the European Roundtable of Industrialists*, Paper presented at the 35th Annual Convention of the International Studies Association, Washington, DC, 28 March–1 April.

Van der Klugt, C.J. (1988) *Why Wait for 1992? Agenda for Immediate Action in Europe*, Speech by the President of Philips, Brussels (June).

Van der Pijl, K. (1984) *The Making of an Atlantic Ruling Class*, London: Verso.

Van der Pijl, K. (1989a) 'Ruling Classes, Hegemony and the State System: Theoretical and Historical Considerations', *International Journal of Political Economy*, 193: 7–35.

Van der Pijl, K. (1989b) 'The International Level', in: T. Bottomore and R.J. Brym (eds), *The Capitalist Class: An International Study*, London: Harvester Wheatsheaf, pp. 237–66.

Van der Pijl, K. (1993) 'The Sovereignty of Capital Impaired: Social Forces, Codes of Conduct and Multinational Corporations', in: H. Overbeek (ed.), *Restructuring Hegemony in the Global Political Economy: The Rise of Transnational Neo-liberalism in the 1980s*, London: Routledge, pp. 28–57.

Van der Pijl, K. (1995) *Transnational Historical Materialism*, unpublished manuscript, Amsterdam: University of Amsterdam.

Van der Pijl, K. (1997) 'The History of Class Struggle: From Original Accumulation to Neoliberalism', *Monthly Review*, 49, 1.

Van der Pijl, K. (1998) *Transnational Classes and International Relations*, London/New York: Routledge.

Van der Wurff, R. (1993) 'Neo-liberalism in Germany? The "Wende" in perspective', in: H. Overbeek (ed.), *Restructuring Hegemony in the Global Political Economy: The Rise of Transnational Neo-liberalism in the 1980s*, London: Routledge, pp. 162–87.

Van Tulder, R., and G. Junne (1988) *European Multinationals in Core Technologies*, New York: Wiley.

Visser, J., and B. Ebbinghaus (1992) 'Making the Most of Diversity? European Integration and the Transnational Organization of Labour', in: J. Greenwood, J. Grote, and K. Ronit (eds), *Organized Interests and the European Community*, Newbury Park, Calif.: Sage, pp. 206–37.

Vogel-Polski, E., and J. Vogel (1991) *L'Europe Social 1993: Illusion, Alibi, ou Realité*, Bruxelles: Editions de l'Université de Bruxelles.

Von Hayek, F.A. (1991a) '1980s Unemployment and the Unions', in: F.A. von Hayek, *Economic Freedom*, Oxford and Cambridge, Mass.: Basil Blackwell, pp. 315–56.

Von Hayek, F.A. (1991b) 'Full Employment at Any Price?', in: F.A. von Hayek, *Economic Freedom*, Oxford and Cambridge, Mass.: Basil Blackwell, pp. 267–99.

Wæver, O. (1994) *The Rise and Fall of the Inter-paradigm Debate*, Copenhagen: Centre for Peace and Conflict Research, Working Paper No. 13.

Wallace, H. (2000) 'Europeanisation and Globalisation: Complementary or Contradictory Trends?', *New Political Economy*, 5, 3: 369–82.

Wallerstein, I. (1974) *The Modern World-system* (part I), New York: Academic Press.

Waltz, K.N. (1979) *Theory of International Politics*, Reading, Mass.: Addison-Wesley.

Wendt, A. (1987) 'The Agent–Structure Problem in International Relations', *International Organization*, 41, 2: 335–70.

Wendt, A. (1992) 'Anarchy Is What States Make of It: The Social Construction of Power Politics', *International Organization*, 46, 2: 391–425.

Wendt, A. (1994) 'Collective Identity Formation and the International State', *American Political Science Review*, 88, 2: 384–96.

Wendt, A. (1999) *Social Theory of International Politics*, Cambridge, Cambridge University Press.

Woods, N. (1995) 'Economic Ideas and International Relations: Beyond Rational Neglect', *International Studies Quarterly*, 39: 161–80.

Wright, E.O. (1989) 'Rethinking, Once Again, the Concept of Class Structure', in: E.O. Wright et al., *The Debate on Classes*, London/New York, pp. 269–348.

Wright, E.O. (1997) *Class Counts: Comparative Studies in Class Analysis*, Cambridge: Cambridge University Press.

Wyatt-Walter, A. (1998) 'Globalization, Corporate Identity and European Union Technology Policy', in: W.D. Coleman and G.R.D. Underhill (eds), *Regionalism and Global Economic Integration: Europe, Asia and the Americas*, London: Routledge, pp. 140–57.

Zeitlin, M. (1974) 'Corporate Ownership and Control: The Large Corporation and the Capitalist Class', *American Journal of Sociology*, 81, 4: 1073–119.

Ziltener, P. (2000) 'EC Social Policy: The Defeat of the Delorist Project', in: V. Bornschier (ed.), *State-building in Europe: The Revitalization of Western European Integration*, Cambridge: Cambridge University Press, pp. 152–84.

Zysman, J. (1983) *Governments, Markets, and Growth: Financial Systems and the Politics of Industrial Change*, Oxford: Oxford University Press.

Index